'In the third of a sequence of magis[...] about early English rural society, Ro[...] Faith forces us [...] problem of how lordship managed to establish itself in Anglo-Saxon England at all. Her profound and radical understanding of how peasant life works on the ground shines through at every point. Everyone who is interested in English society before 1200, or indeed later, must read this book.'

Chris Wickham, Chichele Professor of Medieval History Emeritus, University of Oxford

'Representing the fruit of more than five decades' work on the medieval peasantry, this book takes us closer to the lived world of the Anglo-Saxon peasantry than I would have ever thought possible. It revises traditional wisdom on a host of important subjects, from the origins of feudalism to the impact on the Norman Conquest, and will be *the* go-to book on early English rural society and life for many years to come.'

Levi Roach, Senior Lecturer in Medieval History, University of Exeter

The Moral Economy of the Countryside

Anglo-Saxon to Anglo-Norman England

Rosamond Faith

CAMBRIDGE
UNIVERSITY PRESS

CAMBRIDGE
UNIVERSITY PRESS

University Printing House, Cambridge CB2 8BS, United Kingdom

One Liberty Plaza, 20th Floor, New York, NY 10006, USA

477 Williamstown Road, Port Melbourne, VIC 3207, Australia

314–321, 3rd Floor, Plot 3, Splendor Forum, Jasola District Centre,
New Delhi – 110025, India

79 Anson Road, #06–04/06, Singapore 079906

Cambridge University Press is part of the University of Cambridge.

It furthers the University's mission by disseminating knowledge in the pursuit of
education, learning, and research at the highest international levels of excellence.

www.cambridge.org
Information on this title: www.cambridge.org/9781108487320
DOI: 10.1017/9781108766487

First published 2020

Printed and bound in Great Britain by Clays Ltd, Elcograf S.p.A.

A catalogue record for this publication is available from the British Library.

ISBN 978-1-108-48732-0 Hardback
ISBN 978-1-108-72006-9 Paperback

Contents

Preface

Many conversations are embedded in this book and I am glad to record how much I owe to them. Jean Birrell and I have been discussing medieval peasants and their ideas of 'what behoves' over many years and her work has provided a unique insight into many topics we have both been concerned with. Dan Faith has read and commented thoughtfully on the entire book; Lesley Abrams, Stephen Baxter, Peter and Angela Coss, and Elina Screen have read chapters and made helpful comments; and although each of my four children has approached my interests from a very different perspective, they all have given me perceptive advice. The independent scholar can easily become the isolated one and the fact that the University of Oxford keeps the doors open to its seminars has been the lifeline for me that it is for so many others. The members of the Medieval Archaeology Seminar in particular have over the years shown great tolerance towards the questions of someone with only an historian's training. I am lucky in my academic friends. Over the years I have had the pleasure of many discussions with young historians, most recently Hannah Boston and Richard Purkiss, who have been good enough to share their time and interests with me. Conversations with Ian Forrest have periodically reinforced my sometimes wavering belief that the moral universes of the past are a viable subject for the historian. Working lunches with Tom Lambert and Peter Coss, while both were in the process of writing books of their own, have been as stimulating as they were enjoyable, and hearing Lesley Abrams talking about her own work has over the years been a much-needed lesson in source criticism. On occasions I have shamelessly asked for the expert help one can only get from focussed discussion of one's ideas by a small group and have been generously answered by John Hudson at St Andrews, Roy Flechner at University College, Dublin, and Alice Rio at the Institute of Historical Research. Although this book is about the remote past, I have learned a great deal that is relevant from my village neighbours.

Ever since their prompt response to what must then have seemed a very eccentric project, Cambridge University Press has been consistently supportive and encouraging, and Liz Friend-Smith has steered me cheerfully throughout the various stages of assessment. I should like to thank her and the anonymous readers whose reports, both positive and critical, have made this an infinitely better book than it was when I began writing it, not only in correcting errors and suggesting reading, but in encouraging me to 'raise my game'.

Although James Campbell and I were contemporaries at Oxford, I did not get to know him until quite late in his career, when we were neighbours. Visits to James, as his many friends knew, never failed to result in fascinating conversations. While I have learned a great deal from his writing, as I hope this book will show, it is our talks about the countryside which we both remembered that have informed much of what I have written about what he called the 'curiously orderly world' of early medieval England. This book is dedicated to his memory.

Abbreviations

OE   Old English
ON   Old Norse

1   Introduction: The Moral Economy

This book results from the author's attempts to understand a paradox. The smallest social unit throughout the middle ages was the household, those who were fed from a common hearth. Throughout the six hundred years covered by the book, the households of the powerful were fed by the labour of the households of the less powerful, the peasantry. Yet this appropriation of a precious asset, peasant labour, although clear enough, is surprisingly difficult to explain. It did not result from, and was not sustained by, a shortage of the basis of any peasant economy: land. A countryside that had formerly produced enough foodstuffs to support the Roman elite and feed its army, as well as exporting grain and hides, was well able to feed a population that dropped 'after Rome' and probably did not reach the level of the Roman period until the Norman Conquest, if not later. Appropriation was not economically reciprocal: peasants do not need landowners in the same way that wage workers need employers. Nor, until well after the Conquest, did it depend on legal sanction. Peasants in Anglo-Saxon England, as far as the law was concerned, were free people.

Looking for a chronology of appropriation is one way to approach the problem of explaining it. In the early centuries covered by this book, say the sixth to the ninth, it seems that the powerful people who had hegemony in the English countryside had initially gained their position through successful violence. Sheer plunder, as well as tribute if they were powerful enough to demand it from defeated enemies, could well have gone a good way to put food on their tables. By the time that we have written evidence, however, from early in the eighth century, it reveals something much more systematic. As public figures, kings and lords on the move with their retinues could expect to be quite literally fed by the people of the countryside, who provided them with the wherewithal for meals. The countryside in which these people lived and farmed, for most people were farmers of one kind or another, came to be called 'warland', because as well as feeding itinerant courts, its inhabitants were responsible for, *werian* , 'defended', their land, by fulfilling the important public obligations of army service and defence work which the land itself 'owed'. But kings and lords were not on the move all the time. As private individuals in their domestic space or spaces, they were fed food produced by the labour of a distinctive category of people – some slaves, some peasant smallholders – who cultivated what came to be called their 'inland': the land whose produce was directed to the lord's table. This distinction between the land and people supporting an itinerant elite and the land and people supporting a resident elite came to be fundamental to Anglo-Saxon society.[1] Yet by the late twelfth century, the situation had been transformed: large numbers of the warland peasantry now owed regular labour and rent in cash or kind on the estates of manorial lords.

Establishing a chronology of the appropriation of peasant labour can take us only so far: to record a social and economic situation and the ways in which it changed is not to fully understand it. We may come a little closer to that with an approach deployed in two influential works which both use the idea of a 'moral economy': James C. Scott's book *The Moral Economy of the Peasant: Resistance and Rebellion in Southeast Asia* and Edward Thompson's article 'The Moral Economy of the English Crowd in the Eighteenth Century'. Although both wrote of rural communities threatened by developments beyond their control, they were describing very different cultures and periods and used the term rather differently. The peasants in the modern South East Asian communities described by James Scott were smallholders whose very survival depended on a 'subsistence ethic', the conviction that every individual in the community, irrespective of age and status, had an entitlement to subsistence. This entitlement was a basis of their 'moral economy', the structure of values and obligations which governed whether behaviour was judged right or wrong. Ensuring that all its members survived was part of an individual's obligation to the community as a whole, for as well as being able to support itself 'a household needs a certain level of resources to discharge its necessary ceremonial and social functions.'[2] These were essential principles, which had to be preserved.

E. P. Thompson used the idea of the 'moral economy' to understand a particular situation in a very different society, the corn riots in eighteenth-century rural England. He found that the rioters based their demand for fair dealing and the right price for bread on the standards that had been laid down by the Tudor corn laws enacted nearly two hundred years earlier. That so much emphasis was put on the principle that a fair price and fair dealing should regulate the market led him adopt the term 'moral economy' to contrast with the unregulated market of the 'political economy' of the Utilitarians. It is important to the topic to note that Thompson was not arguing that the rioters had a naïve belief in the 'good old days', but in a particular body of law. Popular movements are sometimes characterised as having been fortified by unrealistic views of a past which never existed. But English resistance movements, though they have often used the language of liberty and rights, have often been notably legalistic and precise in their demand and programmes, very often founding their case not on unrealistic views of an idealised past but on specific legal precedents and procedures and particular documents. That is the case with the resistance described at the end of this book of English peasants to landlord demands. The moral economy is not confined to a single class. Both authors were describing highly unequal societies dominated by powerful individuals, yet both emphasised that there were values which were shared across class and rank. One of Thompson's most striking findings was that the Justices of the Peace, before whom the rioters were brought to trial, on occasion are found to have thought in much the same way about the corn laws as they did. The values of the peasants whom Scott studied were those too of the elites who dominated village communities: they were widely accepted as principles that should govern everyone's dealings with one another.

To insist on the importance of the moral economy is not to say that I believe the 'real' economy to be irrelevant any more than I think it was determinant. 'Intertwined' would be a better term than either. Sometimes the form of appropriation was virtually dictated by the constraints that environmental conditions imposed on peasant production. The different ways in which their produce ended up on the tables of the elite had a great deal to do with the different ways in which peasants farmed their land, where that land was, and how farming changed over time. In spite of considerable advances in the archaeology of crops, techniques, and buildings we are still a long way from understanding the economy of the early medieval farm. One way in which it probably changed less than others was that, while all farms had to provide a living for the farm household, some struggled to do so whereas others were able to produce a surplus. This may have influenced the form in which surplus was appropriated and it certainly influenced the way in which that process was legitimised and the role that played in the moral economy. A few examples may clarify this. That early Anglo-Saxon elites were supported when travelling by supplies collected in the form of produce to be consumed at designated sites was very likely not because peasant farms were producing large surpluses but because they were not. Such a system depended on the capacity of elites to collect small amounts of produce from a large number of small producers over a very wide area. But it could not have been as effective and as long-lived as it was had it not been sustained by the value put on ideas of reciprocity, in which such renders were legitimised as 'hospitality'.

A second example of the connection between economic change and the form in which peasant surplus was appropriated comes from new evidence suggesting that from the mid-Saxon period improved cereal types and cultivation techniques could produce marketable surpluses and support stable groups of consumers. This development is beginning to be referred to as an 'agricultural revolution' and one thing we know about agricultural revolutions is that they have implications for the people who do the work. In this case there may have been a change away from appropriation in the form of direct transfers of produce and towards appropriation in the form of transfers of labour. Two sources of labour were particularly important in improving outputs in medieval cereal production. One was concerted manpower, deployed at the optimal time and in optimal conditions, to get the best results from the sowing, weeding, harvesting, and processing of grain. The other was animal traction power, crucially in England of the plough-team, generally consisting of oxen. These were peasants' own animals in which they had invested time, skill, and resources. Securing a supply of peasants' labour, and their animals' labour, could not have been achieved by simple coercion as was the case with slaves, who had no such resources and depended entirely on their owner for subsistence. From an early century law comes evidence that lords were granting tenancies to families who were, in effect, set up as small-scale peasants in that they were supported from the produce of land they farmed themselves, but whose labour, and rent too in some cases, was required in return on the lords' inlands. In all but one respect, and that an important one, they were serfs. That one respect was that they were personally and legally free.

Not all change, however, can be explained by reference to agrarian development. The moral economy can act as a drag on 'progress'. The labour which a land-lord could extract from most warland peasants before the Conquest seems to have been restricted to 'boons', when at the key points in the faming year, the farmers of an area were accustomed to provide help with the haymaking and harvesting and sometimes the ploughing. Boons were highly specified in terms of the number of days worked and the meals to be provided by the land-lord as *feorm*, a version of the 'hospitality' which had supported elites. In the tenth and eleventh centuries, many very large landholdings were broken down into smaller estates, whose owners did not have the same legitimate access to this traditional supply of peasant labour. In the writings of Archbishop Wulfstan at the turn of the eleventh century, we begin to get hints that they were beginning to look for ways to change this situation. The year

1066 brought a new landowning elite, to whom these traditional constraints were unfamiliar, and who consciously set the relationship between lords and peasants on a new footing. Twelfth- and thirteenth-century writers described the period following the Conquest as one in which there had been a fundamental change in the basis of all rights and obligations connected with land. These were now to be conceived in terms of 'tenure', and 'tenure' deemed to stem from formal contract. Peasants' rights to land were subjected to the same transformation, and the appropriation of peasant produce and labour was now legitimised in the language of this new moral economy.

Newman
m.e. base

Words

Any historian who uses the term 'peasants' will rightly be asked what she means by it. I use it to mean the people of the countryside who largely supported themselves by their own work on the land.[3] The term has become a derogatory one in modern England, where peasants are generally seen as a failed class, confined to the 'developing' world. The situation is quite different in the rest of Europe where the kind of people discussed in this book would be described as, and would describe themselves as, *contadini, paysans, bauer, campesinos*, the 'people of the country-side'. Clearly for a long time England has not been regarded as a 'peasant society' in the sense that most people earn their living working their land. One reason for this cultural difference may be that the English peasantry are often thought to have been eradicated as a class by the economic changes of the eighteenth and nineteenth centuries. Principal among these were enclosure, which deprived them of essential common rights and drove many off the land, the onset of capitalist farming, which eradicated small-scale farms and required a workforce of paid labourers, and industrialisation, which fatally undermined small artisanal production and drove hitherto independent cultivators into the new urban proletariat. I would not dissent from any of this as a 'grand narrative', essentially one whose later stages were proposed by Marx and earlier stages by R. H. Tawney. But like all grand narratives, it can sweep away some important exceptions. A small-scale economy of people who were peasants in all but name survived these changes into the twentieth century. That Scottish crofts do not provide a full livelihood today for anyone who expects a twenty-first-century standard of living is not to say that they are inherently unviable.[4]

An English historian using the term also commonly encounters the assumption that a peasant class necessarily implies the existence of a landlord class. As nearly all our evidence comes from the records made for such a class, this is understandable. No one would deny that early medieval Europe was a world in which 'lords', powerful men, women, and institutions with control over vast areas of land, exercised their power over a population of much less powerful men and women, most of whom were peasant farmers. By far the richest and most detailed accounts of rural Francia in the early middle ages, for instance, belong to a deep-rooted scholarly tradition based on the evidence of the great monastic polyptyques which recorded the fixed and onerous obligations of the serfs and slaves who were tenants of the greatest of medieval landlords: the church. These texts have often been taken as evidence of peasant conditions in general: Eileen Power's Bodo, a serf on the lands of the abbey of St Denis, has retained his iconic place in many depictions of early medieval peasants. More recently, Julia Smith has taken the evidence of similar monastic sources from a corner of north-eastern Europe, an area which she shows to have been one of exceptional commercial vitality, to 'stand as a microcosm of early medieval society as a whole'. Other lines of enquiry have established that a model of society based on the records of great monastic estates is helpful in understanding only particular parts of Europe, at particular periods, in particular political situations, geographically summed up by the pioneer of this approach, H. Verhulst, as being 'between the Loire and the Rhine'.[5] Elsewhere there was a vast variety, magisterially deployed in Chris Wickham's *Framing the Early Middle Ages*: areas where there were peasants without lords, or lords without peasants, or where estates on the model of the polyptyques were 'islands' in a world of largely free peasants. Moreover, envisaging all early medieval English peasants as tenants, working land which belonged to a lord, will stand in the way of understanding them as farmers, heads of families and members of communities and hence of the 'body politic'. To envisage all early medieval English lords as 'landlords', owning land which they leased to their peasant tenants in return for service and rent, will stand in the way of investigating how such power came to be gained. To understand that process is what this book struggles to do. 'Peasants' entails some further pitfalls to be negotiated. One is historiographical. The rich documentation of late medieval English estates has made possible nearly a century and a half of historical studies which have investigated peasants by way of the records of those who exploited them. These have yielded the evidence which are the meat and drink of peasant studies: the land market, social and family relationships, petty commodity production, and legal status, and there is a strong tradition of 'peasant studies' in England, and the debates which this has engendered.[6] Although virtually none of this kind of evidence is available for the period studied here, to approach peasant lives from Anglo-Saxon evidence can be a thankless task, but I hope it is not a worthless one.

Readers who are uncomfortable with 'peasants' may be more comfortable with 'farmers'. Farming is what peasants have always done. The family farm, the basis of the early medieval economy, has survived in many parts of England, and in many more of (mainland) Britain. As in early medieval England the family is still the workforce that keeps these farms going. Great store is still set on keeping the farm in the family. Reciprocal arrangements among neighbours are just as vital now and 'ceremonial and social functions', in James Scott's phrase, still articulate the points at which farm and community meet. And for modern and Anglo-Saxon farmers alike the farm is not simply an economic unit; it has a kind of political identity as well. It is enmeshed in political and economic systems far beyond its borders. For modern farmers some are very remote, like the subsidy systems of the European Union's Common Agricultural Policy, some nearer to hand, like the raft of regulation from the Department of the Environment, Food and Rural Affairs. There are the demands of the Inland Revenue. The demands of the 'state' impinged, increasingly so, on Anglo-Saxon farmers as they too had public obligations and tax liabilities which stemmed from the fact that they cultivated their own land. The networks of local government which form a web over the countryside today have their early counterparts, and sometimes their origins, in the townships, hundreds, and shires of early England. Neighbours still help neighbours with livestock, getting the sheep off the hills in winter, and at peak periods such as harvesting. Off-farm resources are still vital, as are entitlements vis-à-vis other farmers such as the right to put livestock on commons, much diminished nowadays in lowland England but still of great importance in uplands like the Lakeland fells. Powerful landowners still figure in country lives: many of today's farmers are their tenants. I have found that the notion of 'moral economy' proposed by Thompson and Scott has proved to be just as useful in thinking about modern farmers and farm workers as it has for thinking about those of the period the book considers. So, while this book certainly does not make a case for continuity over the centuries between early medieval England and our own times, these similarities have never been far from the author's thoughts.

Freedom and Agency

Perhaps because it is one of the most important, one of the most contentious words in this book is 'free'. It seems to give modern historians more problems than it gave people in the early middle ages, when the existence of slavery made a legal distinction essential. The distinction between slave and free, common across continental Europe 'after Rome', appears too in the early English vernacular law codes. David Pelteret has pointed out that the terminology of slavery in Old English is proof of how central this institution was in Anglo-Saxon society: 'the concepts of servitude and freedom had passed into the thought patterns of the Anglo-Saxons.'[7] Extreme poverty drove many into dependence: some 'traded their bellies for food' to become slaves 'by need', *niððeowetling*. Children of slave parents were *ðeowboren*, slaves 'by birth'. Another cause of poverty, debt, could enslave to slavery too, as could commission of a crime. Captured in war, the better-off could expect to be ransomed, but poor captives were war booty as slaves, *hæft*. There was also an equally precise lexicon of freedom and freeing, which could mark the status of a former slave who had become a free person. These legal distinctions mattered. Throughout the period covered in this part of the book, while economically many peasants were far from free agents, legally they were free people. The concept of 'all free men', however compromised it undoubtedly was by social and economic inequality, retained its identity as a political idea: the institutions of local peace-keeping required the participation of all free adult males. Legal freedom remained an important part of how people regarded themselves, and each other. Had it not been, there would have been no need for lawyers to construct, as we begin to see them doing towards the end of our period, the condition of legal unfreedom that came to be called villeinage. I hope that the use I have made of the vernacular laws, where there is no sign of people who were not slaves having been anything other than free, will have passed scholarly scrutiny. But before I looked at texts I spent a long time looking at farms and farming, the reality for most of the people whose values are discussed here. Working together on *Anglo-Saxon Farms and Farming*, Debby Banham and I followed entirely different lines of approach, and used entirely different evidence, but we came to identify the same characteristic of the rural economy: peasants had agency. It is evident in her contributions to the book on the choices they made about crops, tools, and stock, and in their knowledge of the natural and supernatural worlds. I hope peasant agency is evident in my contributions about their organisation of the landscape to support both pastoralism and agriculture. Both of us think that peasants were capable of co-operation when necessary but neither believes that they lived lives free of conflict: much of the evidence for the values of the moral economy comes from evidence of dispute settlement. Neither of us would think of a peasant farmer except as someone working in a countryside in which most people were like them while there were others, more powerful, very unlike them. But neither would think that lords in the period we were concerned with dominated the rural economy in the way they were to do in the later middle ages. Although farming is not the focus of this book, the extent to which peasant farmers were able to exercise agency most certainly is.

Was England Different?

It has always been difficult to make a case for historical developments in England having taken a different path from those on the Continent without being accused of arguing for 'English exceptionalism'. Such a tension is in the background of the entire book, particularly so in Part I, as the similarities and connections between Anglo-Saxon England and the Carolingian world have played an important part in the historiography of the period. There is no question about the importance of many of these similarities and connections in the culture of a cosmopolitan, literate, Christian elite on both sides of the Channel. Others seem to me to have much deeper social roots, going back to the post-Roman past, or rather, how people perceived that past. Exploring the view of their past on which the Anglo-Saxon elite based their claims to high status helps to explain the resilience of their continuing grip on power. But it also makes a case for this having been part of a more widely shared culture. The values of the barbarian world generally appear in modern scholarship as those of a 'warrior elite', but they were part of the moral economy of the wider society too. 'Germanic' settlement brought England into a post-Roman Europe whose poetry and narratives reflected the 'heroic' values of the barbarian world which fed into the Anglo-Saxon ideas about 'lordship', explored in Chapter 2. An important part of this post-Roman European culture was its narratives of the past: Chapter 3, 'Our Island Story', argues for the importance of Gildas' account of the downfall of the British in forming such a narrative in England. For three major writers, Bede, Alcuin, and Wulfstan, Gildas provided an irresistible argument for England having a military system which was based on the public obligations of those who had land. Common too to post-Roman Europe was the tripartite division of society into nobles, freemen, and slaves: the same division is fundamental to the Old English vernacular laws. Chapter 4 looks at the roots of the importance of notions of rank, honour, and respect in peasant society. English peasant farmers considered themselves the owners of the land they farmed, and the land they farmed was the land which traditionally supported public burdens. It was precisely because they were obliged to take part in local dispute settlements, attend public courts or assemblies, supply the itinerant king and his entourage from their own produce, and contribute to warfare and national defence, that they considered themselves to be free people. That participation in public life was open to, indeed enjoined on, every adult male who had land is a key to understanding the moral economy of pre-Conquest England.

Rank and reciprocity (the focus of Part II) might seem to be incompatible values, but their coexistence is an intriguing aspect of Anglo-Saxon England. Catherine Clarke's work on literary sources of the period portrays them as showing 'strict systems of hierarchical order and the vertical operation of power' while individuals were 'enmeshed in economies of mutual obligation, interdependence and reciprocity.'[8] The value put on reciprocity was not due to any egalitarian notion but to a belief that every action requires its appropriate response. The elaborate compensation tariffs of the *wergeld*, 'man-price', system expressed this principle. Long after violent reprisals had been mediated into financial compensation, injury still demanded its appropriate response. Chapter 5, 'Hospitality', argues that while reciprocity was not an egalitarian idea, and reciprocal relationships in fact legitimised many very one-way transfers of goods from the real economy, the fact that hospitality could be seen as a reciprocal relationship ensured that it retained its place in the moral economy as the legitimation for providing the meals that fed chiefs and kings and lords. Chapter 6, 'Hearth, Household, and Farm', argues that the family farm, the basic economic unit of the rural economy, was in itself a reciprocal system: its viability depended on the labour of all the members of the farm household, who were thus entitled to be supported from the farm's produce. A person's reputation in modern society is constructed in part by people who do not know them personally. In early medieval society it was just the opposite: it was the accumulated personal knowledge by members of the community that gave a person 'worth'.

Part III takes up the notion of 'worth', essential in dispute settlement, described in Chapter 7, 'Neighbours and Strangers', and could earn the essential testimony of a more powerful person who would stand surety for the individual in court. In Chapter 8, 'Markets and Marketing', considering a rural world which was becoming increasingly commercialised, in the sense that many transactions involved money, but was short of currency, worth is interpreted as a form of credit.

Part IV, 'The Wolf Sniffs the Wind', turns to a contemporary witness to the changes that were beginning to undermine the traditional moral economy of Anglo-Saxon England. Archbishop Wulfstan, who died in 1023, wrote at a time when a long period of relative peace had been followed by war: the battle of Maldon in 991 signalling the beginning of Danish raids. Chapters 9 and 10, '*Hwilum Wæs*: Archbishop Wulfstan's

Old Social Order' and 'Land, Law, and Office', suggest that his views of what was happening to society in his own time, which he perceived as caused by a turning away from righteous behaviour, seem to have drawn some key elements, notably reciprocity, from the traditional moral economy of lay society. Even texts of his which have hitherto been regarded as strictly practical can be read as moral works.

Feudalism

Part V considers the impact of the Conquest and the beginning of feudal thinking. 'Feudal' and 'feudalism' are contested terms, and I need to make clear how I use them and what chronology of change this approach has entailed. I use the term 'feudalism' in two very different ways. The first is to describe an economic structure. From a Marxist point of view, *Marxian* societies can be characterised in terms of which class has ownership and/ or control of the means of production. In pre-industrial societies the means of production are land and the labour that made it productive. In these terms, England before the Conquest seems to me to have been a profoundly un-feudal society, and after it to have become a profoundly feudal one. I would like to think that my narrative is compatible with the trajectory Chris Wickham traces in *Framing the Early Middle Ages* in the sense that it ends, as his does, with feudalism. However, the process, in my account, is more sudden than Wickham's steady 'advance of the feudal mode'. It differs in another way too. I have also used the term *Non-Marxian* 'feudalism' in the sense of what Susan Reynolds has called 'non-Marxist feudalism': a set of legal concepts relating to holding land 'in fee' from a superior lord. Under the heading 'The Aftermath of Conquest', two chapters seek to describe how feudal concepts came to provide the values and vocabulary of a new moral economy. Of course there had been throughout Anglo-Saxon England people and institutions with ownership and control of large amounts of land. From the early minsters endowed by royal grants of many hides to the small estates of tenth-century laymen, there were large areas of England which in some real sense were owned by institutions and individuals. These do not seem to me to have gained control over the other element of the means of production, that is to say the labour of the peasantry at large. The means by which they did so is the central enquiry of Parts V and VI of the book, which looks at the situation after 1066. It has seemed to me that the opinions of people who were much closer to that momentous event than we are demand our respectful attention. Of these opinions, two in particular stand out: that the post-Conquest settlement had been a matter of prolonged negotiation, and that all rights to land derived from the Conquest. People came to write and think about these changes in terms of the formal relationships of the 'fee', of hereditable land granted in return for service.[9] Feudal tenure imposed the language of *feodum* , the 'fee' throughout rural society: even peasants had now to become accustomed to 'thinking feudally' and it took the efforts of skilled lawyers to devise ways in which peasant tenures could be differentiated from those of feudal tenures in general. Feudal language served lords well, of course, and much better than it served peasants, but it was not initially simply the language of oppression but a way of thinking about the entire social order.

That change could only take place in the realm of the economy if it did not also take place in the realm of ideas and values is one reason why such attention is paid in this part of the book to words. The new landed elite set their mark on rural England in many ways, but some of its most important effects were ideological and we can trace them through the new terminology in which ideas travelled. Chapter 11, 'New Words in the Countryside', suggests that the vocabulary of Domesday Book itself contributed to the ideological impact of the Norman Conquest. We see how effective were the new ideas, and the new vocabulary, in binding peasants into the new structure of the 'manor' in Chapter 12, 'Narrating the New Social Order'. Legality and the language of contract formed part of the legitimising rhetoric of the new regime. A little-known legal work from early in the twelfth century, the *Leis Willelme*, shows the beginning of new attitudes to peasants' status at law. A very well-known work from the end of the century, the 'Dialogue of the Exchequer', presents an account of the aftermath of the Conquest settlement as a period when agreements negotiated between lords and tenants set their relationship on a new, permanent, and contractual basis. This was to become the accepted view, part of a new moral economy.

Part VI sets the discussion in a new context: 'In the World of the Manor'. Chapter 13, 'Establishing Custom', investigates the agreements which peasants negotiated, setting conditions which would eventually define them in the courts as unfree. In Chapter 14 'feudal thinking' is shown to have influenced the procedures of the new manor courts, and in Chapter 15 the institutions of the manor itself, it is argued, were important in forming peasants' ideas of a shared common interest as a class. The book concludes by arguing that by paying attention to the moral economy of early medieval England, we can better understand why views of the past have played such an important part in rural popular protest.

Dictionaries and Translations

Depending so heavily on particular words and the ideas they conveyed at the time, this book has been written with constant resort to dictionaries and translations. Dictionaries on historical principles contain great riches for this approach. Historians using texts in Old English have since 1898 been able to turn to Bosworth and Toller, *An Anglo-Saxon Dictionary*, and since 1921, the *Supplement*. I have used these rather than the online Toronto Concordance to Old English simply because old habits die hard but I am well aware of the value that digitisation has brought by now taking the searcher directly to a range of sources and interpretations. The *Dictionary of Medieval Latin from British Sources* and the *Anglo-Norman Dictionary*, now both online, have led me to texts and meanings I could never have suspected. The *Oxford English Dictionary*, even the *Concise* which is the one I have to hand, has many times alerted me to the fact that a familiar English term has an Old English root and antiquarian works such as Halliwell's 1848 *Dictionary of Archaic and Provincial Words, Obsolete Phrases, Proverbs and Ancient Customs* provide the added pleasure of finding an ancient word still current in the nineteenth century. The typescript *Agrarian Landscape Terms: a glossary for historical geography* complied by I. H. Adams for the Institute of British Geographers in 1976 passes from hand to hand among local historians for the valuable treasure it is. Much more than a glossary, and a revelation of how much can be gained from assembling the entire terminology of a particular topic, is David Pelteret's *Slavery in Early Medieval England*. The digitised Sources for English Law will, I'm sure, advance the study of Anglo-Saxon law much further: meanwhile I have used Liebermann, *Die Gesetze der Angelsachsen*, and his sources and notes for the legal texts themselves, the translations by Attenborough and Robertson and their excellent notes, and most recently the late Lisi Oliver's edition and translation of the Kentish law codes and her illuminating commentary. I have thus been very fortunate in having had not only the time and leisure in which to write this book but also the tools for the job. However, it being part of the historian's task to be aware of the fact that all historical interpretations are themselves constructs, part of the culture of their time and open to its influences, I have become conscious of the extent to which this is true even of these seemingly neutral works of reference. This is not a new phenomenon: the twelfth-century translator of some Anglo-Saxon laws into Latin provided them with versions and titles which were consonant with his own Romanist learning. The scribes of Domesday Book translated key Norman French terms into the Latin text we use today.

(manor)

One of these was *manerium*. That so many of our ideas about the English peasantry have been formed by the plentiful and much-studied records of the medieval manor has sometimes led to modern translations which may well be anachronistic. The manor, and the search for its origins, was central to the way that some of the greatest medieval historians perceived the middle ages, so it came naturally to A. J. Robertson, translating the late OE laws, to give readers 'lord of the manor' for *land-rica*, 'land-ruler'. The 'manor court' entered Downer's translation of *Leges Henrici Primi* which was written in the twelfth century, long before we have any independent evidence for its existence. Sometimes a word will have shifted its meaning over quite a short period: the *villanus* of Domesday Book was not the 'villein' of the thirteenth century, yet this meaning is attributed to it in the *Dictionary of Medieval Latin from British Sources* as current in the reign of Alfred. 'Villagers' have remained throughout England in the Phillimore edition of Domesday Book, one of the most widely used of medieval texts, although landscape and settlement historians have long since given the English village a much more nuanced chronology and distribution. In view of these problems, at the risk of clogging the text up with annoying interruptions, I have tried to give the reader, who may well be a great deal more proficient linguistically than I am, the chance of making up their own mind about words and passages which are direct quotations by supplying both original and translation: sometimes the published translation(s), occasionally one that I have ventured to propose myself. Other historians will in their turn, detect my own biases and misunderstandings.

The present book revisits some issues raised twenty years ago in *The English Peasantry and the Growth of Lordship* and I have benefitted from this having been a time of much innovative writing by scholars who have illuminated many of the themes touched on here. The process of rebinding Exon Domesday has unbound a wealth of information from which Chris Lewis has now worked out an invaluable and surely authoritative definition of the Domesday manor. Stephen Baxter's analysis of the power base of the Earls of Mercia by showing how commendation worked and why it mattered so much in the construction of a power base has made seeing it 'from below', as I have endeavoured to do, much more possible and the Exon Domesday has been a catalyst for new interpretations of William's motives in ordering the mighty project. Early on in Tom Lambert's reconsideration of the law codes in *Law and Order in Anglo-Saxon England*, which has led him to an important revision of what was becoming an orthodoxy about the legal reach of Anglo-Saxon kingship, he suggests that the laws do not reflect a 'moral order' particular to professionals, but 'ideas which we might suspect had a wider currency' and in the same vein I have taken the laws as exemplifying some basic elements of early medieval culture. George Molyneux's *The Formation of the English Kingdom in the Tenth Century* has made me realise that historians of the landscape will need to pay more attention in future to matters of government policy (and, to be fair, vice versa). George Garnett's *Conquered England* has provided, in my opinion, such a convincing account of some fundamentally new ways of thinking about land which came to England with the Conquest that there seemed no reason not to see if it could have applied to the lower ranks of society too.[10] I was encouraged in taking a 'moral economy' approach by appreciating the extent to which David Bates's *William the Conqueror* is infused with his understanding of the moral universe of the Norman ruler. However, with the exception of an insightful chapter in Hugh Thomas's *The English and the Normans: Ethnic Hostility, Assimilation, and Identity 1066–c.1220*, remarkably little has been written since Maitland on the impact of the Conquest on social relations in the countryside, still less on what might have been thought about it at the time. Peasants are absent from the story of 1066 to the extent that they have even been removed from the picture of them in John of Worcester's Chronicle, used to illustrate Garnett's book on the Conquest. I have tried to put them back in the picture.

Notes

1 Discussions of inland and warland have a considerable historiography. Faith, *English Peasantry*, chapters 1–5, drawing on the work of Vinogradov, Maitland, Stenton, and Douglas, was an attempt to add to the debate in terms of settlement, land use and landlord policy, of which a recent and fundamental critique is Pratt, 'Demesne exemptions'.

2 Thompson, 'The moral economy', Scott, *Moral Economy*, 9.

3 Becket, 'The peasant in England'; Reed, 'Peasantry of nineteenth century England'; Schofield, *Peasants and Historians* has a useful survey of the historiography at 1–32.

4 Dodgshon, From Chiefs to Landlords, chapters 7 and 8.

5 Power, *Medieval Peasants*; Smith, *Europe after Rome*, 170–1; Wickham, *Framing the Early Middle Ages*, 'Rural societies in Carolingian Europe', Devroey, *Études sur le Grand Domaine Carolingien* (Aldershot 1993), *Puissants et Misérables*. Critical appraisals of the polyptyque-based model include Verhulst, 'Étude comparative du régime dominiale'; Devroey and Wilkin, eds., *Autour de Yoshiki Morimoto*.

6 Thus Schofield, *Peasants and Historians* mentions no work done on pre-Domesday sources; Fowler, *Farming in the First Millennium*, Banham and Faith, *Anglo-Saxon Farms and Farming* and McKerracher, *Farming Transformed*

in Anglo-Saxon England are general surveys of agricultural practice which cover none of the preoccupations of peasant studies such as family, gender, community, lordship, and culture.

7 Pelteret, *Slavery*, 44–9, quotation at 48. Rio, *Slavery after Rome*, 167–72 adds valuable examples from saints' lives.
8 Clarke, *Writing Power*, 171.
9 Reynolds, 'Tenure and property'.
10 Lewis, 'Invention of the manor'; Baxter, *Earls of Mercia*; Lambert, *Law and Order*, 15–16; Garnett, *Conquered England*.

Part I

Rank

2   Lordship

> He, eternal Lord, father of glory, started every wonder.
> First he created heaven as a roof, the holy maker for the sons of men
> Then the eternal keeper of mankind
> Furnished the earth below, the land for men,
> Almighty God and everlasting lord.[1]

From the absolute power of the creator God to the control over people and land by powerful men, lordship was one of the most important ideas that structured how people in Anglo-Saxon society thought about their world. Lordship provided a vocabulary of power: it is because the king is *drihten*, 'lord', of all free men that he is entitled to a fine, a *wite*, if a free man is killed. Lordship provided a vocabulary of responsibility: when, in Chapter 7, we consider how people dealt with neighbours and strangers, it becomes apparent that the administration of justice and maintaining social order depended very largely on individuals being 'vouched for' by lords who were legally bound to speak on their behalf. To 'seek' a lord of this kind was an important part of establishing oneself in the networks which were at the base of maintaining 'law and order'. The 'lordless man', armed and accountable to no one, was a threat to order throughout European medieval society: Chapter 9 describes how dangerous he seemed to some of the more reflective members of the Anglo-Saxon establishment. Lordship provided a vocabulary of authority. Anglo-Saxon society was anything but egalitarian. The owner of a large estate and a poor farmer were socially as far apart then as they are today, but the heads of the ordinary peasant households described in Chapter 6 were lords of a kind, too. In short, so much was invested in the idea of lordship that it is not surprising that it was envisaged, and idealised, as a personal relationship as well as an institutional one, and poeticised in the figure of Beowulf, surrounded by his faithful troop of men.

Lordship was thus clearly a form of dominance, yet central to this book is the idea that there was a moral economy that was largely *shared*. This is counter-intuitive. It would be reasonable to suggest that lordship was an idea that would have benefitted lords at the expense of the rest of society.

19

Anglo-Saxon England was certainly a ranked society, in the sense that it had an elite, lords both secular and ecclesiastical, who were recognised as people socially superior to peasants. It was an unequal society: there is no doubt that there were many peasants who were highly exploited by their *land-hlafordas*, the lords of the estates on which they lived. Yet the relationship between lords and peasants was to change profoundly before the creation of the social formation we know of from the later middle ages which centred on the manor, the lord of the manor, and his manorial tenants. In spite of profound social and economic inequalities in early medieval England, political authority was not yet inherent in the owner-ship of land: in that sense, Anglo-Saxon England was not a 'feudal' society. There were other sources of power than control over land and the people on that land. Early medieval lords had authority, but they had the kind of authority which was a product of the violent politics of the time. The men of the highest rank in Anglo-Saxon England before the eleventh century, *ealdormanna*, 'leading men', were of aristocratic birth and were powerful as military leaders or as local rulers. They acted as agents of kings who themselves had gained power through violence: 'the authority of the *ealdorman* is not his own. In the last resort he is another man's man.'[2]

Lordship in the *scir*

If the *ealdorman*'s authority came from the king, the sphere in which he used that authority had been shaped not only by the demands of royal government but also by the working lives of generations. People with power and rank lived, just as peasants lived, in a world of small peoples and small regions which has largely been lost to us, although a few fragments survive of what was once a strong sense of regional identity.[3] The peoples of small regions had a strong sense of what was theirs, and what was theirs was very much bound up with where their working lives were spent, and that in turn had a lot to do with where their livestock went for their seasonal grazing.[4] Medieval peasants are often illustrated in our history books with images drawn from series of 'Labours of the Month', calendars in which arable farming, the cultivation of crops, is very much to the fore: we see peasants out in the fields doing the work of ploughing, sowing, and harvesting which mark the seasons of the year. And of course arable farming was essential if people were to get the staple foods which depended on cereal crops of rye, barley, wheat, and oats, produced near to hand. But they also relied very heavily on their sheep, cattle, pigs, and horses and their products. Their animals' needs encour-aged people to perceive the landscape and its resources on a large scale.

Livestock were turned out to feed in spring and summer, and probably in some places in winter too, on uncultivated land. In some places this meant long-distance transhumance, driving stock to summer pastures; elsewhere it simply meant putting them out in the day and bringing them back at night. But on whatever scale the movement of livestock took place, what lay behind all these infinitely slow journeys, or droves, up the 'sheep way', over the 'ox-ford' or down the 'pig way', up to the sheiling or down to the marshes, was an acknowledged claim by a community to a particular territory. Place-names give us a hint about this, although it is never certain when and how they came to be established: all we know for certain is when they were first recorded. A category of names that were known to Bede in the eighth century, such as the *Cilternsaetan*, did not denote only the inhabitants of those regions, but those who had claims to use the chalk uplands of the Chilterns for their flocks and herds. Susan Oosthuizen has recently given us an insight into the very close connection between claims to territory and the formation of identity.[5] She has untangled the pasture rights on the Fens which belonged to small communities, each of whose names conveys a sense of their having thought of themselves as a group, a small people, with long-standing entitlements. Some of these, who appear in the seventh century list known now as the Tribal Hidage, as the Wisse, the Spalda, and so on, must have been recognisable by contemporaries as distinct 'peoples'.

Oosthuizen's work on the Fenland has shown how the demands of managing a complex ecology might influence social organisation. The very survival of Fenland communities depended on observing agreed arrangements about pasturing, haymaking, managing the water supply, and the arable. The work involved common effort, and to secure this there must be widely acknowledged obligations and well as widely acknowledged entitlements, and respected procedures for the settlement of the inevitable disputes. All the households in the community needed the relevant knowledge and skills, and the preservation of this knowledge needed it to be passed down from generation to generation. Balancing the claims of individuals within a system of common rights and responsibilities, these small Fenland communities were moral economies in miniature, tenacious of their rights, and aware that those rights would be preserved only through common action. They were capable of organisation and cooperation over large areas of country, and lords as powerful as the Fenland abbeys became would have to negotiate with them. At the very end of our period a dispute between Croyland Abbey and the men of Holland came before the royal justices, which had started when 'the men of Holland ... came into the marsh of Croyland as if to war, three thousand men or more, all armed with every sort of arms ... and divided the marsh according to their villages although they were set at some distance ... and they encamped about the abbey like people putting up tents and huts and each setting armed servants to guard their part'.[6]

The Fenland communities have much in common with the small territories known as *sciras* (pronounced 'sheers').[7] In the tenth century the 'shire' would come to mean the counties that we know today which were set up for military organisation and much else and have remained as a unit of local government. The core meaning of the word was 'share', but its uses were manifold. In the sense of a territory with its own common pasture resource, this idea is written into place-names all over England: in the *scir leah* at Shirley, Hampshire with its its '*scir* wood' its '*scir feldi*' or 'open land', its 'Shear Down'. As rivers were important boundaries we have *scir* bourns, Sherburns and Sherbornes, *scir* brooks and fords. The *scir* was the best-articulated small political entity below the level of the kingdom, and one which retained its identity throughout the many changes in what people understood a kingdom to be. Because livestock were so vital to the rural economy, and pasture rights embedded notions of community and entitlement, the *scir* was an element in the moral economy too: that particular peoples had common rights in particular places long preceded the notion of the private ownership of land. As well as these small pasture-based territories, the word *scir* also meant a political territory and a sphere of authority. Under the authority of the *ealdorman*, the *scir* was effectively the political world of peasant farmers and noblemen alike. *Ealdormen* with authority over *scirs* are aristocrats near to the king. They appear in the laws of Ine, King of Wessex, early in the eighth century where they have responsibilities connected with keeping the peace: if an *ealdorman* allows a thief in his custody to escape, he may lose his *scir*, his authority.[8] He has some kind of judicial authority: he may be one of the '*scirmen*' or 'other judges' and he is one of the people with whom another *gesithcund mon*, 'noble', may intercede on behalf of his dependants, presumably in court. In King Alfred's laws he appears as the king's deputy in the *folcgemot*, the public meeting, and he can help a man trying to bring an opponent to justice. The peaceful operation of the court under his supervision is protected by fines and compensation, and his personal authority there by an additional fine.[9]

Although governing a *scir* became a political job entrusted to an *ealdorman*, it took a long time for him to shed his military aspect. This was a society in which warfare depended to a great extent on personal loyalty to lords, and even the largest armies had a flavour of war bands led by chieftains whose troops were bound to them by personal ties. We are not so far from chieftains of the Scottish Lowlands with their clans. What bound such groups together was an invisible network of obligations: of the people of the *scir* to support its head, both materially with food and their armed support in war or out raiding, of the members of the warband to die defending their leader. From another perspective, though, the *ealdorman* looks rather different. He is a lord with personal control over the people of a locality and if 'a man wishes to go from one *boldgetæle*, hamlet, to seek a lord in another he must do it with the knowledge of the *ealdorman* that he formerly *folgode*, followed, in his *scire*'. A fine is due from the man who takes such a man *to men formie*, 'to sustain him', half payable to the king in the *scir* where he formerly followed, half in that to which he comes.[10] Lordship, then, was a very diverse form of authority exercised over land and people, and the area over which it was exercised was both an economic and a political entity. It is sometimes difficult to tell whether a *hlaford*, a 'lord', in charge of a *scir* is an official in charge of a district as a *landrica*, 'land-ruler', or simply a powerful man in a locality. Or both.

Lordship as a Personal Bond

Lordship embedded hierarchy too in a much closer and more personal connection through the relationship known as *mannrædenn*, 'manrent', or commendation. A text called *Swerian* gives the words of an oath of loyalty, sworn on Christian relics: 'I will be loyal and true to N and love all that he loves and hate all that he hates, (however) in accordance with God's rights and secular obligations and never, willingly and intentionally, in word or deed, do anything that is hurtful to him, on condition that he keep me as I deserve, and carry out all that was in our agreement when I subjected myself to him and chose his favour'.[11] Its constituent elements of oath, witness, and reciprocity were so strong that commendation could transmute over the centuries into something very different without losing its place in the moral economy. *Swerian* is one of a group of texts brought together, in Patrick Wormald's view, 'when so much was made of lordship by legislators from Edward the Elder onwards', but its wording may be much older than that, and Dorothy Whitelock saw the reciprocal bonds of loyalty it witnessed as among the fundamental 'bonds of society'. Stephen Baxter's work on the Mercian aristocracy shows how the heart of commendation, the personal connection between two men, could be paired with the economic connection between landholder and tenant while still retaining its distinct identity: the earls granted leases to men who remained 'their men'.[12] None of these versions mentions land. The link was a personal one – the willingness to fight could have had a good deal to do with this – and it was possible for a man to break this important bond by agreement. As long as there is no legal charge against

him and he is of good repute, he may 'seek', *sece*, a new lord. He cannot
be prevented from doing this: law codes of the tenth century make this
clear, and so important was the role of a lord in the legal process that a
lordless man must have one appointed for him.[13] As far as the law is
concerned, you could be under the protection of the lord of another area
which was far from where you lived, or place yourself under the protection of a new lord. Lordship was thus personal as well as territorial. Lords
were nothing without 'followers' or retinues, and this required investment: 'a young man, while still in his father's protection ought to do good
deeds, making liberal rich gifts, so that when he comes of age good
companions will stand by him, lend aid to the people when war comes'.[14]
Young armed men were a threat to order: their lords must control them
and their men must seek their permission before leaving their sphere of
influence. In an era when 'the state' had little in the way of power to
ensure 'law and order', powerful men with what would later be called
'affinities' could act as stabilising or destabilising elements.[15] From late
in the pre-Conquest period we learn of lords who control territories
containing 'many townships', and whose authority, possibly also whose
income, depends in some way on his control over them: 'If a lord has so
many men that he cannot control them he needs to install a trustworthy
agent, a *gerefa*, into each township on his territory who will be on terms of
mutual trust with the men there.'[16]

Anglo-Saxon commendation, a personal bond, was the antithesis of
the relationships intimately connected with landholding that will figure in
the final part of the book. The idealised image of 'good lordship' in the
early middle ages was very different from its later manifestations. It
derives from a lord's role as ensurer of order: *omnis homo credibiles faciat
homines suos et omnes qui in pace et terra sua sunt*: 'Every man shall make his
own men credit-worthy, as well as those who are *in his peace* and his
land.'[17] 'In his peace' expresses an idea which was very important in
medieval society: the responsibility of people in authority for public
order. Lordship was thus deeply involved with justice but not in the
sense that lords had private courts.[18] Almost the reverse was the case:
they had the responsibility to make sure that public justice worked. The
'lordless' man, who so troubled medieval authorities of all kinds, was a
threat not only to public order but to the very working of justice. It is
probably in this sense that we should understand an important strand in
the moral economy: every man must have a lord and if he has not got one
then his kinsfolk must find him one. They must do this at a public
meeting and make sure that he has a fixed abode where he will be subject
to the law. The importance of this was not because people in Anglo-
Saxon England were dedicated to social inequality but because lordless

men undermined justice: they were people who could not be found legally liable for any wrong: *ðe mon nān ryht ætbegytan ne mæg,* those from whom 'no one can get what is just'.[19]

Lordship and Rank

While lordship in all its forms had a deep connection with power, throughout much, perhaps most, of English history an equally important idea was rank, position in the social hierarchy. It brought with it expectations of what was due from, and due to, people of particular rank, what behaviours, what foods, clothes, and language were thought appropriate. Rank was, as always, expressed through behaviour and language in particular situations as much as through legal distinctions. In death as in life it was on the battlefield that nobility was particularly recognisable: it is by the elaborate weapons buried with him that archaeologists identify a male member of the elite, and women's dress and jewellery can be read by archaeologists as signifiers of their status.[20] The elite displayed their status in many other ways too. An often-quoted story recorded by Bede, writing in the eighth century, shows that one could always tell an aristocrat, even one who had fallen on hard times. A nobleman who had fallen in battle hoped to pass himself off as a poor peasant bringing food to the troops, but was recognised as of noble birth 'by his appearance, his bearing and his speech'.[21] The social status of peasants, in the sense of 'countrymen', 'rustics', 'farmers', must have been equally apparent. Everyone would have recognised peasants: they were country people who earned their living by the sweat of their brow. The term that Bede uses in this story is the one which was common throughout Europe to mean 'peasant': *rusticus.* The poem 'The Battle of Maldon', written in the manner of heroic Old English verse to record a famous defeat in 991, relates that an *unorne ceorl,* an 'ordinary commoner', distinguished himself fighting alongside his social betters, as if that were worthy of notice.[22] Everyday speech may have been rather different, and as far as we can tell from the meagre evidence that we have, peasants do not seem to have been subject to the kind of abusive language that was to become engrained in European culture in the later middle ages: *ceorlisc* does not seem to have meant 'churlish' in the later sense of 'fit to be despised because low and coarse'. When King Alfred famously distinguished 'those who work' from 'those who fight' and 'those who pray', he was describing the three essential supports for his kingdom, not denigrating peasants.[23]

In any terms in which historians and archaeologists care to define them, as they were in their own terms, Anglo-Saxon lords were members of a recognisable elite – they were *ealdormanna, drythenes, hlafordas*. Not 'lords and peasants' but 'the powerful and the poor' are the groups into which the French historian Jean-Pierre Devroey divides French rural society at the time covered by this book.[24] English peasants were not necessarily poor, but his approach reminds us of an essential truth: however important peasants might be in their own townships and localities, in the world at large, lords were 'the powers that be'. However, although lordship in Anglo-Saxon England was a strong and multifarious bond, it was not yet, as it would come to be, fixed in the private ownership of land.

Notes

1 Colgrave and Mynors, *Bede's Ecclesiastical History*, iv. 24, 416–7, translation of O.E. in Hamer, *Choice of Anglo-Saxon Verse*, 122–3.
2 Loyn, 'The term ealdorman'.
3 Willamson, *Environment, Society and Landscape*, chapter 4.
4 The following section draws heavily on chapter 6 of Banham and Faith, *Anglo-Saxon Farms and Farming*.
5 Oosthuizen, *Anglo-Saxon Fenland*.
6 Stenton, *English Justice*, 148–211, quotation at 157.
7 Barrow, *Kingdom of the Scots* has provided a model on which much subsequent work has been based, including Faith, *English Peasantry*, chapter 1. Small *scirs* have become a controversial topic: Molyneux, *Formation of the English Kingdom*, 100–4 discusses them primarily with reference to the services they owed. A recent study of Hampshire is Eagles, '"Small shires" and *regiones*'.
8 The legal aspects of *ealdormen*'s authority are now fully explored in Lambert, *Law and Order*, 124–8, 138–49.
9 Loyn, 'The term ealdorman'; Thacker, 'Some terms for noblemen'.
10 Alfred 37: Attenborough, *Laws*, 80–1; Liebermann, *Gesetze*, i. 70 where the Latin translation of *boldgetale* is *mansio*. The revenues which lords could accrue from justice are very fully discussed by Lambert, *Law and Order*, 124–36.
11 *Swerian*: Liebermann, *Gesetze*, i. 396–9.
12 Wormald, *Making of English Laws*, 383–4 at 384; Whitelock, *Beginnings of English Society*, 31–5 at 33; Stenton, *Anglo-Saxon England*, 483–4; Baxter, *Earls of Mercia*, 219–25, 277–86.
13 V Æthelstan 1.1, II Æthelstan 2.1 and 2: Attenborough, *Laws*, 152–5, 128–9; Liebermann, *Gesetze*, i. 166–9, 150–2.
14 Swanton, *Beowulf*, 34–5.
15 For a critique of the historical tradition of a strong Anglo-Saxon 'state' as exemplified by the work of James Campbell and Patrick Wormald, see now Lambert, *Law and Order*.
16 Liebermann, *Gesetze*, i. 453–5.
17 III Edmund 7: Robertson, *Laws*, 14–15; Liebermann, *Gesetze*, i. 191.

18 For private justice in pre-Conquest England: Maitland, *Domesday Book and Beyond*, 332; critiqued by Wormald, 'Charters, law and the settlement of disputes', 163, and Lambert, *Law and Order*, chapters 3 and 6. The origins of the manorial court are discussed here in Chapter 13.

19 II Æthelstan 2: Attenborough, *Laws*, 128–9; Liebermann, *Gesetze*, i. 150–1.

20 'Furnished' graves, those with objects buried with the dead, are not found after the end of the seventh century, after which this type of evidence comes from finds on excavated sites and discovered by metal detecting.

21 Plummer, *Venerabilis Baedae Opera Historica*, iv. 22.

22 While the fact that all free men were liable to pay *fyrdwite*, a fine for neglecting a summons to military service, has been interpreted as evidence for a universal obligation, Abels, *Lordship and Military Obligation*, 11–42 argues for a much more limited liability. Peasants undoubtedly had other obligations connected with warfare, however: Faith, *English Peasantry*, 95–9. Alfred's provision for half the army in the field to return home at intervals could as well be interpreted as aimed at protecting agriculture by releasing serving farmers as a measure of defence.

23 This is thought to be the first reference to the idea of tripartite division of society, which became a commonplace of later medieval thought. It occurs in Alfred's additions to his translation into Old English of Boethius' 'Consolation of Philosophy': Keynes and Lapidge, *Alfred the Great*, 32; Abels, *Lordship and Military Obligation*, 66, 132–4; Powell, 'The three orders in Anglo-Saxon England'.

24 Devroey, *Puissants et Misérables*.

3   Our Island Story

One particularly powerful 'legitimising notion' in early England (and powerful throughout much of English history) was that people's rights, status, and even their ownership of property derive not from their current situation but from the remote past, even if this was often an imagined past. Many important ideas which northern European people had about themselves grew out of the circumstances in which the Roman world had come to an end. Each of the societies which succeeded it had its own mixture of Roman inheritance and 'barbarian' innovation, but they had this in common: they had been established by invasion by peoples from outside their borders. Throughout our period, conquest narratives played a very important part in forming an 'imagined community', a people's sense of their common identity, invoked particularly when the country was under threat. Among the people who came to be known as 'Anglo-Saxons' it was a long-lasting belief, however far this may have been from the historical truth, that their society was the result of invasion and conquest. Bede says of the people who settled in England that 'they came from three very powerful Germanic tribes, the Angles, Saxon and Jutes' but he knew that they also came from several other areas of northern Europe, including the Frisian seaboard and Scandinavia, each with their own sense of identity and history. Aldhelm, bishop of Sherborne early in the eighth century, and so living in an area likely to have been a cultural mix of British and 'Saxon' elements, identified himself as culturally 'Germanic', 'nourished in the cradles of the Germanic peoples'.[1]

Prosaically, the archaeological record suggests that this mixed bag of migrants to England were groups of working people, most of whom put down roots and made a living from the land: they became, overwhelmingly, peasant farmers. Migration certainly involved conflict, for the settlers were not moving into an empty territory, although it may well have been one in which the population had been drastically reduced by plague. But it was tales of war and conquest, not peaceful settlement and acculturation, that were preserved in oral tradition, although we know of this only through written narratives and poetry. For the tenth-century poet celebrating the battle of Brunanburh, which took place in 937 and was essentially part of a West Saxon campaign to extend their power in the north, 'nor has there on this island been ever yet a greater number slain, killed by the edges of the sword before this time, as books make known to us, and old and learned scholars, after hither came the Angles and the Saxons from the east, over the broad sea sought the land of Britain, proud warmakers, victorious warriors, conquered the Welsh and so obtained this land'. (The defeated British countered this with their own heroic narratives, which played an equally important part in their sense of identity – and gave them hope of the revenge to come.) Foundation myths were an important element in the ideology of kingship: the narratives of descent from Adam or Brutus that were woven into the genealogies of regional kings, and preserved in oral tradition until recorded in the ninth-century Anglo-Saxon Chronicle, all contain a 'first founder' figure.[2] Literary accounts which played an important role in how Anglo-Saxons liked to view their past are of heroic leaders taking bands of faithful warriors to dramatic victories and the seizure of territory and strategic places. They effortlessly merge myth with narratives which retain an element of historical fact. Hengest and Horsa, said to have been invited in by the British leader Vortigen to defend Britain against the Picts, were quasi mythic in that they were descendants of Woden (and named after horses), but it was common practice, in the shambles of the collapsing Roman Empire, to invite 'barbarian' mercenaries to defend the frontier.

The earliest English poetry feels not nationalistic but European. The poet in the strange poem *Deor* draws comfort in his affliction from the fate of figures of the European past, the Gothic kings Theoderic and Eormanric: 'that too will pass'.[3] Poems/songs like this would have been recited by the *scop*, the 'court poet', to his patron, and we can read them today because they have been preserved in a single prestigious compilation made in the late tenth century: how widely known they were outside elite circles is a matter of conjecture. The texts of many of the early Old English poetry we have come from a single source, the 'Exeter Book', a compilation of vernacular poetry, both sacred and secular, made about 97, in itself testimony to the enduring attraction of the poetry of the 'heroic age'. The *scop*, the court poet accompanying himself on the harp, seems at first sight a typically elitist scene, and *Deor* is a very sophisticated poem. However, Bede tells a story which might refer to what we would nowadays call a 'folk tradition' of just this kind of music-making and recitation. For much of his life, Caedmon, whose name may suggest that he was of British descent, worked on the farm of St Hild's monastery in Northumberland. This was in the 670s. The farm workers' custom was to get together after work and 'for entertainment' get some beer in (the OE translation calls them a *gebeorscipe*, a 'beership') and take turns in singing songs to the sound of a harp, much like the bard in *Deor*. The rule was that everyone must take a turn, a scene familiar to anyone who has spent an evening in a traditional Irish pub. We know nothing about the songs they sang, or recited, apart from the fact that they were secular and traditional and that Caedmon was unusual in not having learned any. One night, when the harp came round to him and he was called on to sing, he went out to the shippon, where it was his turn to check on the cattle. There he was miraculously inspired to compose Christian poetry, including the epigraph to this chapter, ending his days as a monk at Whitby.[4] Nor do we know in what language his fellow workers sang: they are more likely to have been of British extraction than of Anglian, and the Britons had their own heroic legends and songs. However, there must have been by the seventh century, in Northumbria at least, a folk tradition which included tales of the gods from the wider pre-Christian world. The eighth-century scholar Alcuin of York reprimanded the monks of Lindisfarne for telling tales of Ingeld, asking, 'What's Christ got to do with Ingeld, or Ingeld with Christ?' Ingeld was a figure from the Danish wars which are the background of the poem *Beowulf*, and although heroic fighters were certainly no model for Christian monks, that did not stop them being popular. Even the pious parents of local boys who became monks and priests at Durham in the ninth century named them after such heroes as Ingeld, Theodric, and Hunfrith. Thus although there was a great deal about the Anglo-Saxon church that was highly elitist, there are hints of a common culture that crossed class barriers and in which tales of the past were particularly popular. The highly learned Aldhem, bishop of Sherborne, said of his own poetry: 'No-one born of our race and nourished in the cradles of the Germanic peoples has laboured so greatly in this kind of pastime before our humble self', and he was said by William of Malmesbury to have known enough popular songs (and to have composed a hit himself) to entertain people coming out of church by singing at the wayside.[5] The heroic narratives of the conquest of Britain were not simply popular legends. For two 'old and learned scholars', Bede and Alcuin, the invasion narrative was a vital part of their political philosophy: it was because England had been won by conquest that it was important that it must remain ever cautious and ready to defend itself against threats from abroad. In Chapter 9 we find that this was to remain a vital part of the national narrative.

Traditions of Law and Lawmaking

It is a matter of guesswork to assume that, with a tradition of historical heroes, incomers had also brought with them customs and legal ideas of their own: the earliest surviving English written laws date from the late sixth to early seventh century, at least two hundred years after the advent of the first settlers. What is a little clearer is that while the Old English laws reflect many of the values of this older world, the period of the 'great migrations' of people from beyond the Roman frontier into western Europe, they were recorded in a society which had retained much less *Romanitas* than had much of continental Europe.[6] While they share some of the subject matter of the barbarian law codes, such as the 'Laws of the Salian Franks', they are not in Latin, but in the vernacular. They are very far from having the formal and analytic structure of classical Roman law, even the 'Vulgar Law' of the Roman provinces. Unlike Roman law, they have almost nothing to say about property. Their rhythmic and repetitive style gives the impression of their having drawn on customs which had been passed on by word of mouth, not learned from texts by law students. Rather than set out the principles on which a 'jurisprudential' decision should be based, as Roman law had done, they often incorporate long lists of penalties for particular offences which could be learned by heart, perhaps recited. They were very absorbent and could incorporate the ad hoc decisions made at meetings of the king's council, but could also preserve the new formal teaching of the church as it rooted itself in English society.

While the Old English law codes can tell us something about the political aims of converted Christian rulers such as Æthelbert of Kent and his successors, and of their powerful associates and literate churchmen, because, like the other 'barbarian' law codes, they have their roots in the customs of the people who had settled in western Europe in the aftermath of the collapse of the Roman regime, they can tell us too something about their embedded values and assumptions.[7] One of the most important of these was that there were two basic divisions in society. One, as common to western Europe after the 'fall of Rome' as it had been before it, was that between slaves and free men (almost all written law concerns itself with 'men' in the sense of 'people', although the terms used may often have implied the inclusion of women).[8]

Perceived ethnic difference added a new element to the concept of slavery in the Roman model. There is no agreement as to whether 'barbarian' settlement in England was a matter of mass migration or of dominance imposed by an elite, but although the situation must have varied from region to region, the upshot was that there was no social equality for most of the conquered indigenous inhabitants of Britain. The fact that *wealh*, the word for 'Briton', could also mean 'slave' is eloquent in itself. Michael Costen's work on Somerset argues that many people whose forebears had been slaves in the Roman regime remained oppressed through the post-Roman period characterised by the local power figures based in hillforts, Gildas' 'tyrants'.[9] Although political alliances may have been forged by marriage between members of the British and barbarian elites, among the general run of people there may even have been a kind of apartheid in the early settlement period. Many settlements which evidently remained British were distinguished by the place-name 'Walton', from *wealh*, Briton/Welsh and intermarriage discouraged.[10] The differences between the skeletons of males buried with weapons who were taller than those buried without have been interpreted as a real physical difference between the armed incomers and the disarmed Romano-British dead.[11] The laws of Wessex, which come from a time when the West Saxon kings were extending their power over the West Country, show that even British landowners who may have been important figures in their own society and region received less favourable treatment than their non-British equivalent.[12] From the Kentish laws we learn of a category of person whose forebears were slaves but who were themselves on the way to legal freedom: the *læt* or freedman and other people appear in the Kentish laws whose role as servants made them so subordinate to their masters that their distinction from slaves must have been nominal.[13] Many people whom we encounter in this book were living and working in conditions that amounted to near slavery. Nevertheless, the distinctive legal sense of slavery, of being the property of another person, remained important. Slaves were an important part of the workforce of Anglo-Saxon England, as they had been of the Roman world, and the legal category of slave, of a human being who could be owned by another, was still found useful until its end and after.[14] The concept of being free depended on there being a concept of being unfree.

The second main division, and again this is common to the English and the continental laws, was that among free men between *eorlisc* and *ceorlisc*, noble and non-noble. The rigid categories in which the written laws describe the social order could well have been out of line with what was happening in real life: 'nobles', *eorlisc* men, are highly visible in the laws much earlier than an elite becomes clearly visible archaeologically in 'furnished' graves (those in which the body is buried with objects) where weapons (other than knives) are taken as a sign of high rank.[15] Local elites could gradually have emerged in many informal ways, among which strong-arm tactics come to mind, rather than having been born into an hereditary class of nobles. Moreover, to be a noble was essentially to be a leader in battle. Social hierarchy was expressed in terms of the devotion of fighting men to the lord who leads them in battle. These are ideals, not descriptions of life as it was lived, but they were not necessarily only the ideals of the elite. The 'warrior-hero', nearly always a figure from the past, sometimes from the mythological past, could be a hero even among people who might well have been oppressed by a militarised ruling class, and some of the most powerful Old English poetry expresses the strength of this bond. Before the Viking invasions of the ninth century, when Alfred endeavoured to put together some kind of national military force, warfare was much more often a matter of bands of retainers serving under the command of a local figure of authority, to whom personal loyalty was owed. *Gesithcund*, 'of the rank of companion in arms', expressed the nature of their role, more important than noble birth. Relationships within the elite retained much of this personal flavour into the period when a *scir* force was levied under the command of the man in charge of the *scir*, the *ealdorman*.[16] Those who were neither slave nor noble were ceorles. The word itself derives from a Germanic root *karl*, simply meaning 'man' and although some translations of the law codes translate ceorles as 'free men', which is what they were, in the sense that they were free people (the word can mean women as well), in this book I have tended to leave ceorles as ceorles. Like all of Europe, Anglo-Saxon England was a society in which most people were peasant farmers and the English laws share the continental laws' attention to specifically rural offences and the compensation due for them: damaging to livestock, farm workers, and slaves, cattle theft, dangerous dogs, and so on. Although it is sometimes clear that a particular law is aimed at settling the kind of dispute that would only arise between people who were involved in agriculture, such as allowing stock to stray by neglecting hedges, the laws never employ any word specifically denoting 'peasant'.

While the laws are evidence of a binary distinction that was made *between* free people as either *eorlisc* or *ceorlisc*: noble or non-noble, rank *among* them is expressed more precisely in terms of their legal monetary value, their *wergeld* or 'man-price'.[17] To understand this we need to be aware of an assumption in early medieval England, which has always seemed alien, even 'primitive', to modern readers but is still common in some cultures today, that it is perfectly honourable for an injured party to accept a sum of money as reparation from the culprit rather than either personally seek redress or turn to the law to enforce the appropriate penalty. Theft, murder, breaking and entering, and personal injury, what we would call 'grievous bodily harm', are all covered. The system was an integral part of the moral economy of what was often a violent world, but there is no need to interpret *wergild* payments, as has often been done, as an alternative to feud. (The alternative to feud remained feud.) The reality was a great deal more sophisticated, and has at its heart what lawyers would later call tort: a civil injury rather than a crime. Tom Lambert's recent work has done much to advance the idea of tort, a wrong done to another, as opposed to crime, a wrong done to the state, being at the heart of Anglo-Saxon legal thinking. He has emphasised the fact that the rationale behind wergelds and other monetary compensations for offence was that they represented what an honourable man must pay, and what an honourable man (or his kin) could accept, as recompense for injury. The very administration of these rules involved some fairly sophisticated procedures to ensure a just settlement between the parties involved. But as to what should properly be paid, one of the benefits provided by the English written vernacular laws, as opposed to laws which could be preserved only in memory and transmitted by recitation, was that they recorded precisely what was due for every kind of injury, from the head down to the nail on the little finger, so no bargaining was needed.[18] Lisi Oliver has shown the rationale of what seems to us comical detail: the laws have a built-in mnemonic structure, 'they move from head to toe according to physiology, so the entire body of the laws move from head to toe according to status.'[19] In view of the importance of livestock, it is reasonable that something very like wergeld seems to have been applied in cases where livestock were injured: the horn, tail, and eye all have their value. Viewed as a rough-and-ready insurance system, wergeld seems less exotic than commonsensical. It remained in force for centuries, so presumably worked: a tariff of traditional compensations for personal injury, in even greater detail, sits happily in the pages of the Anglo-Norman lawbook, the *Leges Henrici Primi*.[20] Rank mattered of course: some people are worth more than others and offences against them are strictly graded, not only according to their nature, but to the status of the victim or injured party as well. In the Kentish laws the *wergild* of a nobleman was 300 shillings and that of a *ceorl* 100. The West Saxon laws have more elaborate ratings as they make special (and lower rates) for free British landowners. As they are themselves the property of others, slaves do not have wergelds: injury, killing, or rape of slaves entailed compensation to the owner, not the slave. The laws distinguished ownership of a slave from ownership of a servant. Sexual intercourse with another man's household servants incurred far higher penalties than intercourse with his slaves.[21] While there can have been very few people in this society who did not have a 'lord', of some kind, only the lowest had owners. Living in a country where a large proportion of the indigenous people had been deprived of freedom, however subordinated to others some peasants undoubtedly were, they were always able to see that there were other people who hardly belonged to society at all.

Notes

1 Orchard, *Poetic Art of Aldhelm*, 45.
2 'Battle of Brunanburh': Hamer, *Choice of Anglo-Saxon Verse*, 1–7: 'British' might be preferable to 'Welsh' here. Genealogies: Dumville, 'Kingship, genealogies, and regnal lists'.
3 Hamer, *Choice of Anglo-Saxon Verse*, 87–9.
4 Colgrave and Mynors, *Bede's Ecclesiastical History*, iv. 24, 414–19. The translation into Old English of the *Historia ecclesiastica* was probably made under the instigation of King Alfred: Mitchell, *Invitation to Old English*, 263–4.
5 Wright, *The Cultivation of Saga* discusses the continuing popularity of heroic traditions among people of all classes in early England. St Aldhelm as folk singer is at 21–2, the boys at 19–20. Orchard, *Poetic Art of Aldhelm*, 45.
6 Oliver, *Beginnings of English Law*, 16–20.
7 I follow Oliver, *Beginnings of English Law* for grammatical and other evidence for the dating of the Kentish laws. Although Barnwell, 'Emperors, jurists and kings' does not refer to England, his point needs to be taken into account here that there were some practices and attitudes, generally considered to be 'barbarian', which also had a place in the 'customary' Roman law administered in the provinces. Among these was financial compensation for injury. Hines, 'Social structures and social change', aligning the law codes with archaeological evidence, brings out some important shifts in emphasis between Æthelbert's code and Wihtred's, which brought in 'a new social vocabulary'.
8 Goetz, 'Social and military institutions', 457–62.
9 Costen, *Anglo-Saxon Somerset*, 74–9.
10 Hooke, 'Place-name hierarchies and interpretations in parts of Mercia'.
11 Härke, '"Warrior graves"'.
12 The West Saxon laws on the wergelds of the British are Ine 23.3, 24.2, 32, 33, Attenborough, *Laws*, 42–5; Liebermann, *Gesetze*, i. 100–103. Charles-Edwards, 'The making of nations in Britain and Ireland'.
13 Pelteret, *Slavery*, 294–8; Oliver, *Beginnings of English Law*, 91–3.
14 Rio, *Slavery after Rome* and Pelteret, *Slavery in Early Medieval England*, for the post-Roman situation.
15 Welch, 'The mid-Saxon "final phase"', 269–75. Burke, *Popular Culture in Early Modern Europe*, 157–9; Gurevich, *Medieval Popular Culture*, 57.
16 Stenton, *Anglo-Saxon England*, 299–303.
17 Hough, in Lapidge, Blair, Keynes, and Scragg, *Blackwell Encyclopedia*, s.v. 'Wergild' gives the regional variations and sums up the evidence from other sources.

18 Lambert, *Law and Order*, chapter 1,' The law before Æthelbert': Lambert's insights underlie much of what follows.
19 Oliver, *Beginnings of English Law*, 37 shows the organising principles involved.
20 *Leges Henrici Primi*, c.70, 219–23.
21 Pelteret, *Slavery* remains the fullest analysis of the vocabulary used for the servile and semi-servile in English contexts.

4   Honour and Respect in Peasant Society

Honour was an important and enduring element in the moral economy and mattered as much to ordinary peasants as it did to the nobility. Although the word came into English via Norman French after the Conquest, when it was associated with and eventually appropriated by the chivalric code which came to play such a large part in the moral economy of the nobility and gentry, a code which excluded peasants, 'honour' seems also to have retained something of the Old English notion of *weord*, 'entitlement', and peasants did have *weord*. Included in the legal system as members of the rank of *ceorl*, they were entitled to their legal compensation and obliged to render it when required: that is what they were *weord*, our 'worth', in the sense of 'entitled to'.[1] A text to be discussed in Chapter 9 and 10, *Geþyncðu*, is concerned with what degree of honour was considered to be due from and due to the different orders of society, including the lowest of the low and in the manor courts of the thirteenth-century peasants will be found insisting on their right to be treated *honorifice*, 'honourably'.[2]

Rank and Honour on the Great Estate

If the concept of worth played a part in early medieval England it was not because it was an egalitarian society but because it was a ranked one. One context in which differences in rank were most clearly articulated was that of the large aristocratic and ecclesiastical landholding: the great estate. Peasants played a wide variety of roles in relation to powerful landholders. The higher status of some derived from their closeness to the estate centre and their involvement with their lord's business: their very name, *geneat*, meant 'companion'. We find a detailed description of the kind of obligations they had, in the text known as *Rectitudines singularum personarum*. In the early eleventh-century revision of this text *geneatas* are shown personally responsible for making arrangements at estate centres such as preparing for the lord's visit, taking messages (they were sometimes 'riding-men'), driving pack-trains and droving, highly responsible jobs which might involve carrying substantial amounts of money. They must have been a highly recognisable elite, known outside the immediate locality. *Geneatland* is a category of land recognised in the ninth century and appears in place-names where it is found in proximity to an estate centre.[3] These are broad categories, and there must have been a great many people who were known locally to have been employed on estates in a variety of capacities. Domesday Book gives us occasional glimpses of people who had substantial farms but were nevertheless tied to service tenancies at the estate centre, like the reeve who held two hides from the monks of Winchester *quasi villanus* but 'could not go where he wished' to seek another lord.

All peasantries are themselves little hierarchies, and country people were concerned with distinctions between them. Owning a ploughteam itself conveyed status, and the ploughman heroically striding the land behind his team remains today an image of the farmer. In his 'Institutes of Polity' written in the early eleventh century, the highly educated archbishop Wulfstan made a distinction between the superior *yrthlingas*, 'men who plough', and the inferior *aehtemen*, 'men who work', a distinction familiar in medieval Europe and inherent in peasant culture.[4] Farming has always had winners and losers. Quite apart from sheer bad luck, the genetic misfortune of having no children to share the work of the farm, local environmental disadvantages like poor land, or the vagaries of the weather must have meant that many small farms gave a very poor living. At the other end of the scale, while the peasant farm was essentially one worked by the family, many farms were large enough to need extra hands: the household economy of these is discussed in Chapter 6.[5] Small farms, besides, do not need all the labour that family members could provide, and working off the farm has always been part of their economy: working for neighbours was a survival strategy. There was thus a hierarchy of esteem within peasant society which was based on economic circumstances: while some people worked their own land to support their own families, many others needed to supplement what they could grow by what they gained by working for others. Farmers and farm labourers before the Conquest no more regarded each other as social equals than their equivalents did in the nineteenth century or any of the centuries in between, or than they do today. However, while working for a powerful lord or a better-off neighbouring farmer was to be on a slippery slope which could lead to something very like slavery, no free person, however economically dependent, was as totally rightless as slaves were.

In many, if not all, rural communities an especially respected position seems to have been attached to particular people, not necessarily the richest, such as the veneration of local saints. These were often people who were not simply respected for their piety but were valued for what their piety could achieve for the community, perhaps by performing a miracle such as making a well appear. The Norfolk 'saint of husband-men', St Walstan of Bawburgh, was such a man. He renounced his inheritance and worked as a farm labourer. Venerated among the local people for his holiness, he had a respected role as the 'guide of their harvests', which may mean that he acted as the 'lord of the harvest' who supervised the work, and died at haymaking. He was reputed to be able to heal the wounds typical of harvesting, including reaffixing severed limbs.[6] Often a particular group of people is particularly esteemed. The 'older and wiser men', the 'village elders', are familiar from later medi-eval England (and are not altogether unfamiliar to anyone who lives in an English village today) and at least one Old English term for a man of authority, *ealdormann*, has 'elder' as its root. Peasant elites also became consolidated as a result of the countryside becoming formally organised from the mid-tenth century for the purposes of dealing with local matters, mainly crime and its policing. Tenth-century legislation (which Chapter 7 will discuss in more detail) both initiated and greatly expanded what we call now local government, but it did not do this in a vacuum: there were many ways in which rural people organised and policed themselves which grew out of the circumstances of their lives, not royal initiative. The reciprocal and communal arrangements that were imposed by the demands of policing and monitoring free-ranging live-stock long predate any formal legislation. In the tenth century the *scirge-mot*, the shire assembly, was becoming the forum for the legal business of the highest rank of society.[7] Perhaps for this reason, although all free men nominally had to attend, the county, as the shire was now called, seems to have signally failed to become as embedded in English rural life at the level of ordinary people as did the 'townships' which had their roots in working lives. A vill, OE *tūnescipe*, was the group of people belonging to a *tūn*: it is the same kind of word as 'fellowship' (or 'beership'). Cornish moorland farmers called their little hamlets 'townships' and the land that belonged to them the 'townland'; both terms remain in common par-lance, particularly in the north. Townships were the political worlds of the peasantry and the sphere in which peasant elites operated. They remained units of local government and consequently their boundaries were mapped in the early editions of the Ordnance Survey.[8] This makes it possible to gain an idea of what kind of area a township might be on the ground: in some parts of England a recognisable collection of neighbour-ing farms, in others a village and its surrounding fields, elsewhere, particularly in the north of England, large territories where settlements were few and dispersed. Whether this formal structure was an innovation imposed from above on an existing informal way of managing local affairs which had evolved from below remains a matter for debate in both England and Ireland, where the Anglo-Norman townlands pose a similar problem. However, while in Ireland many townlands are named from a single person or a family, in England townships are sometimes recognisable as groups of long-established farms or have boundaries which are seemingly much earlier. Thus what became administrative units often look as if their origins may have lain in long-established husbandry, possibly the joint cultivation of arable land, and in shared access to pasture.[9]

Mid-tenth-century legislation put considerable responsibility in the hands of local men with the formal grouping of the population into groups of ten, 'tithings', with mutual responsibility for good behaviour and adherence to the law, under a 'tithingman'.[10] (The term 'tithing' survived as an administrative area in what had been the West Saxon kingdom; elsewhere, the 'township' was its equivalent.)[11] While the primary responsibility of the tithingman was to ensure that all who should be in a tithing had been duly sworn in, it seems that he might also be thought of as a local headman. Certainly he was worthy of respect. According to a twelfth-century collection of Old English law, he had to bring to court (we are not told what court this is, but it is probably that of the hundred) 'disputes between townships and neighbours ... pastures and meadows, haymaking fights between neighbours and many other such which frequently arise.'[12] The *gerefa*, the 'reeve' of a township (the term was used for officials of many kinds), was also a person of some importance as a small player in the public sphere of local government.[13] Reminiscent of the responsibility of heads of household for their dependents' Christian observance, *tungerefas* and tithingmen, along with the priests, were made responsible for policing the much more stringent rules about almsgiving and religious observation that came in during the crisis of renewed Danish invasions in the late tenth century.[14] In 1086 the proceedings of the Domesday enquiry required that every vill should have a 'reeve' as one of the people sworn in to provide the information that was demanded. This was a highly responsible position to be in as evidence was given an oath and it demanded that accurate knowledge was given about each locality's tax liability in the form of its hidage. The township or tithing was the forum for much that was important in peasant lives and an essential part of how things were run in what James Campbell has called 'a curiously orderly world.'[15] The system produced and preserved its own local elite, as local government tends to do.

One reason for the rule that all free adult males should be in a tithing was to ensure that at the meetings of the larger administrative unit, the hundred, the tithingmen would be able to report that 'all the tithings are full'. Nominally at least, they would then be part of that assembly and subject to its procedures and rules. Again, the hundred as it appears in the legislation of the tenth century may be a newly formalised version of something much older. Many hundreds, particularly in Wessex, met at highly inconvenient but traditional places which have the hallmarks of assembly points which had long functioned as marketplaces, military rallying points, sites for horse races, and so on, which brought together the people from a wide area. Elsewhere, particularly in the Danelaw, they look like the result of much later organisation of the countryside for military or taxation purposes.[16] Legislation by Edward the Elder, although not explicitly naming the hundred court, is thought to mark the transition from these kinds of assemblies, in which disputes might well be heard and settled, to something much more like a formal court. This was to meet every four weeks, to fix dates on which to hear and settle lawsuits, and to ensure that all who attended were 'law-worthy'. Edgar's 'Hundred Ordinance' elaborated these rules, established panels of witnesses in each hundred, and made the bishop an essential participant. It is hard to envisage what manner of rural dispute or offence could have evaded the scope of the hundred courts.[17] They were recognised by Norman writers and reinforced by Norman rulers as an essential part of the way that England was run and later chapters will return to them.

Founding Fathers

'Founding fathers' were an important element in the political thought of early medieval England. Royal genealogies, lines of ancestors, some going back to Woden or Brutus, were an essential part of the ideology of the nascent kingships of the sixth and seventh centuries as recorded in the 'Anglo-Saxon Chronicle', a compilation which stemmed from the court of Alfred, king of Wessex, and thus became part of the founding narrative of his kingdom.[18] We are not dealing here with what can be known about the past from the archaeological and linguistic record, but with people's ideas about it. Even if in reality the population of pre-Conquest England was of mixed origins, the *idea* of a single English 'people' was an important one, an 'imagined community' in Benedict Anderson's term. Just as the issuing of laws was seen as a benefit conferred on a particular kingdom, as Æthelbert's were for the people of Kent, the most respected figures in the learned tradition were thought of as benefactors of an entire nation. Modern readers value Bede as the founder of historical scholarship in England, but to people who read him in early England he was a *deodwita*, 'wise man of the people': the term for a chronicler itself incorporating the idea of a people, a folk. Although the modern translation, 'The History of the English Church and Nation', has given it a title redolent of the established Church of England, Bede himself called his major historical work 'the ecclesiastical history of the English people' (or 'the people of the English'), *Historia gentis Anglorum ecclesiastica. Đeod*, 'people', 'nation', 'folk', is an element in a range of Old English words relating to authority, learning, proper mode of conduct, as if it were a fundamental property of how society should be. It is not hard, therefore, to understand the importance which people attached to the period of Germanic immigration, seen as the foundation era of the English 'people', as one of their 'legitimising notions', their 'island story'. Such notions were important to peasants too. That there had been 'founding fathers' to whom particular respect was due and from whom some kind of inherited authority derived, was a 'legitimising notion' which validated the peasant hierarchy. It is a powerful idea in pre-modern societies, and still plays a part in the modern world. Sixteenth-century Scottish clan chiefs had their forebears recited and praised by their household bards. However fictional these may have been, their recitation gave the chiefs the charisma of long-standing legitimacy, and that was a very important part of their claim to own the land of the clan and the rights they exercised over the peasant farmers who lived and worked there.[19] In England specifically peasant ideas of 'founding fathers' are much more difficult to trace. One clue may be that properties known as 'Old Austers', 'ancient hearths', seem to have been thought of as having a particularly revered status in some later medieval villages and this could be because they were regarded as those of the earliest inhabitants. The *astrier* was the Norman French equivalent of the OE *heordfast*, someone with his own hearth, so although the itself term cannot be pre-Conquest, the importance of the 'householder' in this sense was rooted in Anglo-Saxon values.[20]

Putting the Name on the Land

One way of looking at how Anglo-Saxon people at large may have thought about themselves in relation to the land of their origins is to look at the way they named ordinary places. England is a particularly good place to pursue this line of investigation, as there is a strong and continuing body of scholarship devoted to the study of English place-names of all kinds, from cities and streets to villages, fields and farms, woods and hills, and rivers and streams. What is hard to determine is when a particular name came into use. New names are always being coined, but most of the ones that we can be sure were in use in Anglo-Saxon England come from the very end of that period: they were recorded in 1086 when the commissioners responsible for gathering information for the Domesday survey were required to ask in each locality, 'What is the name of this place?' Officialdom requires stable names for large numbers of places in a way that the ordinary business of life does not, so this could well have been almost the first time that such a question had been asked in many parts of England.[21] Until the authorities demanded a single name for a scatter of hill farms, a straggle of woodland cottages, or a little hamlet all well known to people of the neighbourhood, why would one have been needed? And names could change: early place-names, especially of small places, were more likely to disappear than were later ones. In this way we may have lost many Brittonic or Latin/Brittonic names which may have been current in the early settlement period. Whether these disappeared because someone made a deliberate choice to rename a place or because Brittonic simply died out as a viable language is hard to tell, but the upshot is that the English countryside is today studded with names with Anglo-Saxon, not Celtic or Latin, roots. However, we can be sure that a certain number of names were in use before about the year 800 because they are found in written texts before that date.[22]

Whether places were named by the people who lived in them, or by the people who didn't, whether they go back to the origins of a place or were produced only when someone in authority needed a name for it, are very difficult questions to answer even for our own time, almost impossible for such a remote period. But we can learn something from the different *ways* in which place-names were created. Many places are named from natural features: the study of these by Margaret Gelling and Ann Cole has given us new insights into how people perceived the landscape.[23] Another way may tell us something equally interesting: how they thought about their past. Naming and claiming are closely connected processes. A great many English villages, towns, and farms are named after somebody, nearly always a man. This way of naming places was practised by the end of the settlement period and continued. We almost never know the date of this individual, whether his name had always been attached to this particular place, what kind of a place it was at the time, or what his relationship was to the people who lived there, but at some point he had 'put his name on the land'. Individuals are commemorated in some farm names too, and here we may be a little nearer to a specifically peasant point of view, for it is their owners and their neighbours who give farms their names.[24] But it is owners and neighbours who change them too and we do not know how to date most of the personal names embedded in either surviving place-names or farm names. However, it is hard not to see farm names like 'Wine's Worthy' (a worthy was a ring-fenced farm) on the Hampshire Downs as conveying some degree of respect for the fact that this was once Wine's own property, his to pass on to his heirs. It was not until the thirteenth century that the kind of records were kept which enable us to study the topic in any detail, but when we are able to get an insight into the way that these peasants regarded their land, we find that a strong emphasis was put on inheritance: 'keeping the name on the land', keeping the family land in the family's hands.[25] Although it was important in the workings of peasant society, the special status of what was seen as family land was not simply a peasant notion but was shared across class divides. Elite landowners too set a high value on the preservation of the patrimony and made a distinction between land they inherited from their ancestors and land they had acquired.[26] Even within the highly ranked society that was Anglo-Saxon England, some values were shared. Free legal status, a respected place in both the local and the political community, a strong hold on the family property, were equally precious to *eorl* and *ceorl* alike and all drew on notions of the past.

Notes

1 This is sense VIII in Bosworth and Toller, *Dictionary*, s.v. *weord*.
2 *Geþyncdu*: Liebermann, *Gesetze*, i. 456–8; Birrell, 'Peasants eating and drinking', 13–14.
3 Faith, *English Peasantry*, 156–7.
4 Rabin, *Political Writings of Archbishop Wulfstan*, 101–24, n.15.
5 Examples may be found in part II of Banham and Faith, *Anglo-Saxon Farms and Farming*.
6 St Walstan: Arnold-Forster, *Studies in Church Dedications*, I, 424–5.
7 Molyneux, *Formation of the English Kingdom*, 165–72.
8 Winchester, *Discovering Parish Boundaries*, 31–5.
9 Adams, *Agrarian Landscape Terms*, 62; Winchester, *Exploring Parish Boundaries*, chapter 5.
10 I Edgar ('Hundred Ordinance'): Robertson, *Laws*, 16–19; Liebermann, *Gesetze*, i. 192–4.
11 Winchester, *Discovering Parish Boundaries*, chapter 4.
12 *Leges Edwardi Confessoris*, 28, 28.1: Liebermann, *Gesetze*, i. 627–72.
13 Harvey, 'Manorial reeve'. These have many parallels with the late medieval 'trustworthy men' of Ian Forrest's *Trustworthy Men*.
14 VII Æthelred 2,5: Robertson, *Laws*, 110–11; Liebermann, *Gesetze*, i., 261.
15 Campbell, 'Some agents and agencies, 207–11 at 207.
16 Loyn, *Governance of Anglo-Saxon England*, 120–48.
17 III Edgar 5,2: Robertson, *Laws*, 26–7; Liebermann, *Gesetze*, i., 202–3.

18 For royal genealogies: Lapidge, Blair, Keynes, and Scragg, eds., *Blackwell Encyclopaedia,* s.v. 'Genealogies, royal'.

19 Dodgshon, *From Chiefs to Landlords,* chapter 4, 'Patterns of chiefly display and behaviour'.

20 Old Austers are further discussed in Chapter 6.

21 In the eleventh century, tax collectors had been required to collect the geld due from each township and this may have led to names of individual places being recorded. Only summaries of these rolls survive. Place-names appear in charters and occasionally in literary sources, but the most common earliest source for a recorded place-name is Domesday Book: Gelling, *Signposts to the Past,* chapter 5; Roffe, *Decoding Domesday,* 184–90.

22 Hall, 'The instability of place-names'.

23 Gelling and Cole, *Landscape of Place-Names.*

24 Banham and Faith, *Farms and Farmers* adopts this approach in chapters 6–11, where examples of identifiable farms are to be found throughout.

25 Faith, 'Peasant families'; for Wine's farm, Banham and Faith, *Anglo-Saxon Farms and Farming,* 233–5.

26 Williams in Lapidge, Blair, Keynes, and Scragg, *Blackwell Encyclopaedia,* s.v. 'land tenure'.

Part II

Reciprocity

5 Hospitality

Early medieval people rated very highly the idea of reciprocity: that every action requires its appropriate response and the idea of 'what is owed in return' permeated ordinary life. The elaborate compensation tariffs of the wergeld system expressed this principle: wergeld was what a free man could honourably accept in return for an affront.[1] That is not to say that reciprocity implied, or enjoined, social equality or economic parity between the participants: higher status brought an entitlement to receive higher payments. Reciprocity was required in every situation, whether making a counter-gift in exchange for a gift, avenging the death of a kinsman, or simply returning a favour. Here it is seen as the legitimising idea behind the system of supplying the travelling courts of kings and lords with produce levied from the countryside. *Feorm* was the Old English term for this Anglo-Saxon version of an institution which had a long history in medieval Europe. Such obligations were so evidently exploitative of those working to produce the food for these meals that they have been characterised as 'feigned reciprocity', Gadi Algazi arguing that in Germany by the later middle ages 'Lords and peasants ... need not have believed that their obligations were based on a general norm of reciprocity. It was enough for them to perceive the particular links between specific obligations and services as obvious and traditional.'[2] As regards the relationship between lords and peasants in his period and area of study he may well be right, but this chapter argues that in early medieval England the legitimation of *feorm* had not yet drifted apart from the legitimation of what people of all ranks owed as 'hospitality' and thus still retained a good deal of its reciprocal connotations.

In our culture hospitality is essentially a voluntary expression of good-will or social obligation. Yet the obligation to provide others with food from one's own household supply, and the entitlements that stemmed from this, underlay so many medieval situations and institutions as to suggest that 'hospitality' once meant more than good manners. Because of the importance of the idea of reciprocity to the moral economy, hospitality could be the acceptable face of appropriation. The word itself

49

implied reciprocity: Latin *hospes* means both 'guest' and 'host'. Well before the beginning of our period, hospitality had provided a metaphor for the appropriation of Roman estates in Gaul by barbarian invaders (whether these incomers acquired land or a share of revenues is still disputed) described as *hospites*, 'guests'. The language of hospitality thus perhaps saved face for the cultivated survivors of the Roman landowning class whose estates had been taken over: their dignified correspondence is a study in elegant euphemism. In a similar way, well after the end of our period, the agents of the counts of Barcelona afflicted their tenants with demands for food, accommodation, and possibly access to their women as well, all in the name of the 'hospitality' that the Count himself, should he visit, was entitled to expect.[3] We know very little about what forms power may have taken in England before similarly powerful individuals began to be regarded as 'kings' and controlled the areas which came to be known as 'kingdoms', but there are some possible parallels to be drawn. The work of Robert Dodgshon has shown that we can learn a good deal about early medieval England from what we know about late medieval Scotland where a rural world of clans and clan chiefs survived until the sixteenth century. An economy of small peasant farms, many of extremely low productivity, supported elites and rulers from the produce that their agents 'uplifted' from the subsistence farmers of the chiefdom. This 'uplifting' continued in Scotland and the Isles until the growing authority of the Crown facilitated the introduction of rent in the modern sense. More usefully still, early modern Scotland has much to tell us about the moral economy of such a society. Its essentially exploitative nature was mitigated by a strong tradition of clan membership, which might oblige chieftains, whose lavish feasts conveyed honour on the whole clan, to provide in hard times for those whose produce they appropriated. This expropriation of the poor to feed the powerful was couched in the language of hospitality.[4]

Hosting Lords and Kings

Anglo-Saxon kings and their entourages were supported by a system of 'uplifting' which, although on a larger scale, had an important characteristic in common with that of the Scottish clan chieftains. Outside the economic sphere of the minsters, which were already becoming small economic zones *sui generis*, they did not live in, and off, an economy which was geared to producing large surpluses of foodstuffs which could be stored and processed as needed. Instead, small peasant surpluses were accumulated and consumed. The royal court was itinerant; kings and their travelling entourages were provided with food and drink and fodder collected from the farms of the districts they travelled through. This obligation to provide what was essentially a forced levy of peasant surplus was called *feormian*, which meant 'to provide hospitality', and the goods themselves were *feorm*. Hospitality, both the entitlement to receive it and the obligation to provide it, has been an essential part of communication through many centuries of European history. (It has not yet vanished altogether from the moral economy: local councils have had until recently an obligation to provide sites for 'travellers'.) Anglo-Saxon bishops, who, like kings, were travellers who lived off the countryside, were enjoined to be 'content with the hospitality offered them', *doncfulle heora gæstliðnesse and feorme*, when visiting their flock and it is clear that they could expect this *gæstliðnesse*, 'guestliness', as their entitlement.[5] By the time we have any written evidence of the actual practice, from early in the eighth century, *feorm* had become formalised. (The earlier, Kentish, laws give us no information about it.) One of Ine's laws lays down in great detail what *feorm* in terms of loaves and cheeses, meat and beer, and fodder for the horses was due from every ten hides *to foster*, 'to feed', the king as he proceeded around his kingdom. We learn from a charter of about the same date which granted a huge territory in what is now Hampshire that their hidage, their assessment in hides, had already been assigned to the specific places which were liable to contribute to the *feorm*.[6] As to its origins, rather than anything radically new, this looks more like the regularisation, perhaps an idealised statement, of a well-established practice. It is hard to tell if supporting the powerful with deliveries of supplies from the countryside was an innovation, a return to pre-Roman arrangements which had become 'embedded' in the countryside and its people, or a practice built on Germanic traditions in the lands from which the Anglo-Saxons had migrated. It could equally well have been an inheritance from the immediate post-Roman period, when formal taxation had collapsed and 'uplifting' produce may simply have been a way, even the only way, by which powerful men could enforce control and express dominance over a large area – in plain language, pillage.

It would be thus perfectly reasonable to interpret the system of *feorm* as simple appropriation. But medieval appropriation took various forms, none of them simple. One important distinction to bear in mind is that between rent, tribute, and taxation. Owed to the king, not to a land-lord, *feorm* was not rent and the supplies to be delivered to the royal vill to await the visit of the king and his household are nothing like the many examples we have, admittedly from a much later period, of typical rents in kind. Nor are Ine's bread and butter and so on the kind of supplies which looting the countryside of a defeated rival would have produced as tribute. When victors levied tribute from territory which they had conquered, it was paid in money or valuables or herds of cattle driven off on the hoof. Taxation, in contrast, was levied from a ruler's own territory and it would be reasonable to interpret *feorm* as taxation: the renders of produce were assessed on the hides, just as other public obligations were. Nevertheless, there is a particular attribute of *feorm* which suggests that its 'legitimising notion' was hospitality. As the work of Debby Banham has conclusively established, the supplies were the ingredients of *meals* for the king, his family, and his entourage and fodder for their mounts and baggage train animals, for a set number of days.[7] The peasant families of the kingdom were expected, quite literally, to feed the king and his *familia* as if this remote group of high personages were literally their guests. Thomas Charles-Edwards has pointed out how important royal progresses were to the local elite, giving them a chance of personal access to the king and his entourage.[8] This seems unlikely to have been possible for the peasants who actually produced the food, yet the institution of particular groups being obliged to provide meals for visiting elites had such a strong and lasting presence in European culture that its tenacity is worth exploring. The uplifting of produce for the benefit of a powerful man could establish and reinforce feelings of identity. It was a Scottish smallholder's membership of a clan that legitimised his obligation to provide his chieftain with hard-won 'uplifted' food, and this membership gave him some claim to reciprocal support from him in hard times.

We don't know whether or not Anglo-Saxon peasants ever identified their interests with a dominant figure and supported him in this way but we do know of a category of names of areas ending in *ingas*, 'the people of', which associate a group of people with an individual.[9] These names cannot tell us when this association of the people of an area with an individual began, what it meant, or how its meaning may have changed over time, but they can tell us that it was once part of the way that people thought. They tended to identify themselves, and the place where they lived, with an important man (none of the *ingas* names is female). By the time we have any written evidence, Anglo-Saxon rulers had begun to identify themselves as 'kings', not chiefs, and their territories as kingdoms. But we do know that some kingdoms had been cobbled together by rulers who had successfully quashed the independence and appropriated the territories of rulers of small areas. The physical identity of these smaller areas derived from the fact that they contained a variety of resources, the arable and pasture and woodland that the inhabitants needed, and their political identity lay in the fact that they had 'central places' around which the district came to be organised. Hillforts sometime played this role. It may have been nothing new to the people of these small regions to hand over produce to support a dominant figure with whom they felt a strong connection. Although they no doubt used strong-arm tactics as well, it is possible that when the agents of the Anglo-Saxon (or in Kent, Jutish) kings began to organise small regions for their support they could draw on this tradition of provisioning. It had a striking longevity. Nellie Neilson's study of the rents and obligations owed by peasants on later medieval estates traced some of these back to the 'early rights of progress and quartering' which had been part of 'the past order of things'. Royal and aristocratic parties on the move continued to be supplied from the countryside right through the Anglo-Saxon period: Hereward the Wake on the run in the Fens could count on being fed from the *feorm* he was entitled to there, and supplies were still being delivered to the court late in the twelfth century.[10] What economic effect the system of provisioning the royal court, which came to be called 'the farm *(feorm)* of one night', had on the people who were obliged to supply it is another matter. While some farmers must have found it a burden to give up anything at all from their carefully husbanded resources, Ine's list of what was due to the king's court from every ten hides did not in fact represent a large transfer of surplus if the burden had been distributed among several farms, but it took 'surplus' away from people who may have had very little to spare. People whose livelihood depended on a small peasant farm would certainly have experienced supplying it as a burden.

Provisioning an itinerant court which turned up from time to time was a very different matter from supplying a landowner who remained in one place. From the late seventh century on, an enormous amount of land was coming into the hands of minsters, communities of monks or nuns, by grants from the king, either directly or through donations from the greater aristocracy. What the king gave was the right to the produce which would otherwise have gone to him as *feorm*. Moreover, on the great monastic estates, arrangements to supply the *feorm* to feed a permanent community of consumers – the monks and nuns – led to the people on those estates being organized so as to exploit them more efficiently. Minsters had the literate and bureaucratically experienced people who could record and collect supplies on a regular basis, and very large landowners, although we know very much less about them, may have been in much the same position. Even so, the terminology of hospitality still seemed to be what was thought to be appropriate for relationships between landowners and the peasants on their land. From the late tenth century we have a document which describes in great detail the obligations and entitlements of all the different kinds of workers and tenants that might be found on a great, probably ecclesiastical, estate. This is *Rectitudines singularum personarum* and it will play a large part in Chapter 9 because it seems to describe an idealised world which was thought to be in jeopardy.[11] It depicts a highly organised estate, with a workforce of highly dependent people, including slaves. However, the language of hospitality was used for the arrangements made for the key points in the farming year, haymaking and harvest in particular, when extra hands might be needed to get the work done before the weather broke or the crops spoiled. Just as any farmer might need to call on his neighbours for help at such times, landowners 'prayed' the people of the neighbourhood for extra help to get the jobs done in time. These were known as 'boon-ploughings', 'bid reapings', and similar phrases, the elements *bid* and *boon* both coming from OE words for 'to pray or entreat'. The entitlements due from these 'prayed for' kinds of work are described in the vocabulary of hospitality: *winterfeorm*, Easter *feorm*, *benfeorm for ripe*, harvest boon *feorm*, *gytfeorm for yrde*, drink-*feorm* at ploughing, *mædmed* mowing-reward, *hreacmete* rick-food, *æt wudulade wæntreow* a wain-tree at wood-loading, *æat cornlade hreaccopp* at corn carting 'rick-cup' (the equivalent of 'topping out' for building workers) 'and many things which I cannot recount'. These were local custom, not the landowner's rules, and the compiler of the document is anxious to make the distinction between the two: it is the responsibility of 'whoever has the *scyre*', the authority or the office, to 'always know what is the *ealdlandrædan*', 'the longstanding rule of the estate' and *hwæt ðeode ðeaw*, 'what the local custom'. Reaping or haymaking, rick-building or ploughing when an estate owner 'prayed' for help, even with these customary entitlements to food and drink, must have been a good deal less voluntary than helping out a neighbouring farmer, for which you might expect his help in return. Boon- and bid-works were to become a compulsory element in the obligation of many manorial tenants by the twelfth century and they may already have been so when this document was compiled. Nevertheless, the compiler evidently thought that the work at the boons and the food or drink provided were essentially different from the compulsory obligations and allowances of cottars, labourers, and specialist farm workers like the shepherd and dairy workers. He did not consider them to be 'estate custom' but 'local custom'. That what was effectively the appropriation of peasant labour was described as 'requested', 'prayed for', not demanded as of right, and that the meals the landowner was obliged to provide were described as *feorm* shows the important place the notion of 'hospitality' still played in the moral economy of landowner and peasants alike.

Hospitality, of course, is a two-way relationship: just as *hospes* means both 'host' and 'guest' and being given a meal in someone's house is understood as obligation to provide one in return. The days, if they ever existed, when a powerful man's peasant subordinates would have entertained him at their own hearths were long gone by the time that we have any evidence from eighth-century England. By this time *feorm* had become bureaucratised and, literally, taken out of the producers' hands with provisions for itinerant courts being delivered to collecting points and then, presumably, taken to wherever the court was.[12] They were emphatically not for meals at which the people who provided the ingredients might have had the pleasure of the king's company. In better-documented cultural traditions, such as those of Scotland, Wales, and Ireland, the lavishness of the feast laid on for powerful people conferred and confirmed the high status of both the chief who 'provided' it and the people who shared it, and England is not likely to have been very different. This is where elite politics took place: attendance at the table of an important person literally gave access to the 'seat' of power and a chance to meet him face-to-face.[13] When we do have evidence of people having access to 'high tables', it was a privilege of an elite: great Anglo-Saxon 'halls', like Heorot in *Beowulf*, were not built to entertain the local peasantry. Nevertheless, as the work of Jean Birrell has shown, when are able to get a glimpse of the values and aspirations of peasants after the Conquest, the right to an important meal in the company of the social superior whose good living, after all, their labour had provided, was often seen as a valued entitlement. As Birrell emphasises, late medieval manorial 'custom' represents the result of negotiation between lords of manors and their tenants, not what 'has always been the case.' What was recorded may simply be what was current practice, not what had been true 'time out of mind.'

What people believe to be a custom is important and hospitality continued to provide a language in which social relationships, even exploitative ones, might be expressed in a way which preserved people's sense of worth. Attending the Christmas feast at the table of the lord of the manor was considered a 'custom' on many Oxfordshire manors in the thirteenth century, although the tenants sometimes had to provide part of that feast themselves.[14] The 'tenants' dinners provided by Oxford colleges, institutions whose revenues, after all, came out of their tenants' hard work, were a valued entitlement. Looking back from late in the eighteenth century, the Scottish economist Adam Smith described the moral economy of a world long gone, or rapidly going, in his lifetime, but which still had a hold on his imagination. At the heart of it was the notion of hospitality. Before commerce and manufacture 'gradually introduced good order and good government ... the inhabitants of the country lived in a continual state of war with their neighbours, and of servile dependency on their superiors ... and a great proprietor, having nothing for which he can exchange the greater part of the product of his lands which is over and above the product of the cultivators, consumes the whole in rustick hospitality at home.' If his estate could produce enough to feed a hundred or a thousand men, he can make use of it in no other way than by maintaining a hundred or a thousand men. He goes on to describe the vast retinues of the middle ages, when 'Westminster Hall was the dining-room of William Rufus and might frequently, perhaps, be not too large for his company.' And if hospitality on this scale became unworkable, then the surplus must be consumed by his tenants and 'as he feeds his servants and retainers at his own house, so he feeds his tenants at their houses. The subsistence of both is derived from his bounty, and its continuance depends upon his good pleasure.'[15] For weak and strong alike, hospitality was part of the shared language of a still remembered moral economy. The very fact that offering and receiving hospitality often provided a language in which to describe what essentially was systematised appropriation shows its enduring power. We could perfectly well dismiss hospitality as a blatant piece of 'false consciousness' intended to make exploitative economic relationships acceptable, but there was more to it than that. Reciprocity in the moral economy ensured that, even in essentially exploitative relationships, the weak retained some dignity while at the same time advantage, and the right to it, remained with the strong. And as on the farm so in the wider world: food mattered.

Notes

1 Lambert, *Law and Order*, 35–9.
2 Algazi, 'Feigned reciprocities', 125.
3 Sarris, *Empires of Faith*, 58–68; Bisson, *Tormented Voices*.
4 Dodgshon, *From Chiefs to Landlords*, chapters 2–5.
5 Colgrave and Mynors, *Bede's Ecclesiastical History*, iv. 5, 350–3; Old English Bede 260–2.
6 Faith, *English Peasantry*, 40, for a fuller discussion of this aspect of *feorm*.
7 Banham, 'Knowledge and use of food plants'.
8 Charles-Edwards, 'Early medieval kingships', 30–3.
9 Gelling, *Signposts to the Past*, 109–12; Bassett, 'In search of the origins of Anglo-Saxon kingdoms' in Bassett, ed., *Origins of Anglo-Saxon Kingdoms*, 18–23.
10 Johnson, *Dialogue of the Exchequer*, 40–1; Neilson, *Customary Rents*, 15.
11 Liebermann, *Gesetze*, i. 444–53 from Corpus Christi College Cambridge ms 383, a mid-twelfth-century ms compiled at St. Paul's where it has no title, and a Latin translation in the twelfth-century legal collection the *Quadripartitus*,

where it is given the title *De dignitate hominum*. Douglas and Greenaway, eds., *English Historical Documents*, ii. no. 172, 813–16. Harvey, '*Rectitudines singularum personarum* and *Gerefa*', the authoritative discussion to date, considers it to have been a revision, probably by Archbishop Wulfstan of Worcester and York, of a document originally written in the tenth century and based on the practice of a particular estate. It is discussed further in Chapter 9.

12 Stafford, 'The farm of one night'; Lavelle, 'Royal estates'; Bourne, 'Kingston – the place-name and its context', 271–2, has shown that Kingston place-names have a strong association with major routes and quotes Stenton to the effect that 'food rents', by which is meant *feorm*, was delivered to 'king's *tun*' to await the arrival of the royal party.

13 Charles-Edwards, 'Early medieval kingships', 29–30.

14 Birrell, 'Manorial custumals', 14–15.

15 Smith, *The Wealth of Nations*, 260–2.

6   Hearth, Household, and Farm

James Scott has singled out two principles as basic to the moral economy of the peasantry that 'all are entitled to a living, even at the cost of loss of status and autonomy'. Closely involved with this entitlement was a concomitant range of obligations: as well as being able to support itself, 'a household needs a certain level of resources to discharge its necessary ceremonial and social functions'.[1] Both entitlement to a living, and the public obligations of the household are ideas which have reciprocity at their core. Both provide us with insights into working and family life where many, perhaps most, relationships were, then as now, no doubt taken for granted and unspoken. Early medieval households of all kinds had 'ceremonial and social functions' to fulfil, and households of all kinds centred on hearths. This chapter illustrates the importance of reciprocity in the household, around the hearth, and on the farm: here too reciprocity legitimised social hierarchy and here too food played an important part.

Hearths

Long after houses, and the way that people lived in them, had changed entirely, the hearth continued to have great symbolic importance. As an emblem of domesticity, 'hearth and home' still do today. The word *heard, heord* was used for the domestic fire and a house and it would probably have been impossible to think of one without the other. Before chimneys became common, most people sat, ate and drank, and slept not in front of fireplaces but around hearths, which in great halls and in Anglo-Saxon peasant farmhouses alike were in the middle of a single living space. It may have been of crucial importance that the fire always remained alight, banked up at night and 'uncovered' in the morning. As the only source of warmth and food in peasant and elite households alike the hearth carried great emotional weight: in a story told by Bede, the household around it came to stand for human life itself. A king's retainer, pondering the appeal of the new faith of Christianity with its promise of

an afterlife, likens 'the present life of man on earth' to the experience of
the king sitting with his retainers in the hall in winter: 'the fire is burning
on the hearth in the middle of the hall and all inside is warm, while
outside the storms and wintry tempests are raging'. A sparrow flies into
the hall through one door and out again through the other. 'For the few
moments it is inside the storms and wintry tempest cannot touch it, but
after the briefest moment of calm, it flits from your sight, out of the
wintry storm and into it again. So the life of man appears but for a
moment: what follows or indeed what went before we know not at all.'[2]
Far apart though they were in possessions and status, both the elites and
the peasantry held the hearth as central to their values: the hearth was the
emblem of the household. Beowulf's men were his *heorð-werod*, 'hearth-
band', of 'hearth-knights', *heorðgeneatas*: they owed their place at their
leader's hearth to him and he, in turn, had obligations towards his
followers. What would become the Civil Service started out as the royal
household, and what would become offices of state originally had very
domestic titles: the king's butler, his steward, his chamberlain. The
twelfth-century text which describes in minute detail the working of the
king's household, *Constitutio Domus Regis*, lists the (refined) loaves to
which his officials, as his 'loaf-eaters', were entitled.[3]

While the elite household lived off the produce of other households'
work, it is central to the moral economy of the peasant household that its
members constitute the labour force for the farm.[4] Without the produce
of the farm, the household would starve; without the work of the household, the farm could not produce food. These are good practical reasons
why hearth, household, and land were so firmly linked in Anglo-Saxon
minds, but Scott's 'ceremonial and social functions' bring a broader
perspective. Having a hearth of one's own was a crucial signifier of status,
even at the bottom of society. A *heorðfæst*, 'hearth-fast', man was a
resident, someone who belonged to a household, as opposed to a *folgere*,
a 'follower' or someone attached to another's. To be hearth-fast entitled
a person, however poor, to a place in the public world and subject to its
obligations, rather than living as the slave did, perhaps sometimes more
comfortably, in the private world of an owner. Hence in the view of the
church the hearth was a unit of taxation: the dues in corn paid to the
church at midwinter were reckoned on the hearth. Eleventh-century
cottagers with smallholdings were dependant in the extreme, and often
burdened with compulsory work for the landlord, but they were nevertheless 'hearth-fast' on their small plots, and owed dues to the church 'as
any free man should'.[5] Behind this is the status attached to having both
home and land: however poor they were, only those paid tithe who had
land on which to grow titheable crops.

The hearth, with its fire alight, was long taken to symbolise the owner-ship of land. In the seventeenth century it was the hearth, not the householder, that was the taxable unit, used in place of counting indi-vidual taxpayers for the down-to-earth reason that hearths 'remove not as heads or polls do' but the association of hearths and ownership of land has a deeper and longer history. To be 'hearth-fast' was essentially to claim, or gain, a share in one of the most valuable resources of a rural community and one which has already been stressed earlier in this book, rights to pasture. Driving their cattle, sheep, and pigs from rural settlements to sometimes distant pastures brought people into contact with people from other small communities who also had rights in there. But this was not a free-for-all: common land was available to 'commoners' whose stock had a right to be there, not to the world at large. Such rights were almost never absolute but were always linked with the ownership of property, on however small a scale.[6] This associ-ation had an extraordinarily long history, albeit one embroidered with popular myth. The linkage seems to have been behind the situation in two Somerset villages studied by the late Mick Aston and the late Barry Lane. In these villages, particular properties known as 'Old Austers' are thought to have taken their name from the Norman French word for 'hearth', *astre*. Their French name must be post-Conquest, but the OE term *heord* was used locally to mean a dwelling and its land, so it is likely that 'old austers' were established farms well before 1066. Unlike the other properties in the village Aston studied, where most common rights were strictly limited or 'stinted', ownership or tenancy of an 'old auster' conveyed *unlimited* rights of common. Auster rights may thus date back to a time in a community's history when there was no need to ration this precious resource.[7] Like nations, peasant commu-nities may have had their own 'foundation myths' in which these 'ancient hearths' may have been thought of as those of the 'founding fathers' of the village: whether or not they actually date from its estab-lishment is another matter. Perhaps they indicate something else as well. A fire implied a hearth, a hearth a household, and a household implied mouths to feed. Old austers take us back to the principle which, in James Scott's words, was embedded in the peasant moral economy the right to subsistence: 'all are entitled to a living'. Rights of common for the household's livestock were a vital part of that living, particularly in a pastoral economy such as that of medieval Somerset, and the Old Austers were a solid expression of this principle. It is not surprising that the hearth had symbolic as well as economic importance: to 'close down' a hearth permanently meant a crucial event had taken place in the life of a household.[8]

Households, Hides, and Free Status

Living as they did in a countryside of family farms, people at all levels of
Anglo-Saxon society measured and valued land in terms of hearths and
households. Literally so: when they needed to give a rough idea of an
area, even to make a rough guess at the extent of a huge region like 'the
land of the West Saxons', they expressed it in terms of the number of
hiwisces, that is to say, families, households, or houses that it contained,
today the equivalent would be 'family farms.'[9] As the 'hide', the *hiwisc*
became a unit for measuring land in Anglo-Saxon England. We learn
from Bede that 'the English' in his time reckoned land in terms of the
number of 'families' it could support.[10] The English were not the only
northern European people who were beginning to measure land in this
way. The Roman terms *jugum* and *jugera*, which derive from the word for
'yoke' and connote measurements of ploughed land, were beginning to
be replaced by the OG *hof* and the Latin *mansus*: both are words for
places where people live. (That Bede refers to the way 'the English'
reckoned land may imply that he knew about the Roman terms.) There
was more to hides than land measurement. As it was on hides that
taxation was assessed, and as the land measured in hides, 'hidated',
was the land whose owners owed service in times of war, to own a hide,
the land to support a family, was fundamental to the status in society of
the man whose family land it was.[11] It meant that he was a free man, not a
slave, and this brought with it obligations in the wider world, to the king
and to neighbours and strangers. That the entirety of England was
thought about in terms of family farms goes a long towards explaining
why the laws make no distinction among the ranks of the non-noble: the
land that supported the free population was the land subject to the public
law.

Hides, though a seemingly rough-and-ready way of reckoning land,
proved to be an adaptable and astonishingly long-lived one. That they
came to be used in so many different contexts could well be that people
were comfortable with reckoning land in terms not of acres but of farms
and people. The hide was used in conveyancing to indicate the amount of
land conveyed: charters, which record grants of land by the king, very
frequently described its extent as 'of x hides', although other terms were
also used. In Domesday Book (1086), the number of hides a place was
assessed at, what it 'answered for', meant its liability to taxation (very like
the 'rateable value' of modern Britain before the introduction of the
community charge), and hides provided the unit of assessment for various systems of taxation and public obligation until the twelfth century.[12]
At the point at which this book ends, around 1200, fractions of the hide

had become units on which rents and services owed to a manorial landlord were assessed, but even then it retained its old connections with freedom and public obligation. Even when they had become tenants of the lord of a manor the owners of even a quarter of a hide – the 'yardlanders' – continued to enjoy, or claim, a particular standing in rural society. This connection of land, status, and public obligation is something we will continuingly revisit, for it remained at the heart of the moral economy of early medieval rural England.[13]

The Family Farm

It seems that when Bede referred to the hide as 'the land of one family' he was referring to land belonging to a group of some kind. But *familia* often meant something other than our biological family: it was used in the middle ages for many groups of people with no blood relationship but who had some kind of bond, like the members of a religious community.[14] It is equally appropriate for the work-group which supported the farm and was supported by it. While the peasant farm is by definition a family farm, the amount of labour needed, and hence the size of household that a farm could support, must have varied enormously. It may be helpful to bear in mind that nowadays a family with modern equipment can cope with thirty-five to fifty acres of mixed farmland, but that is with modern equipment, not with animals as the only form of traction.[15] There were many farms of this size in pre-Conquest England, and on these family labour was essential, not only of the adults but, as in the nineteenth century, 'For the small farmer ... children were an essential part of the workforce.'[16] From our period we know more about children at play than about children at work: none of the delightful pictures which show children are of working youngsters. From later evidence we know about some jobs even quite young children could have done around the farm such as crow-scaring and leading the cow out to graze, but the crucial point must have been when a boy or girl was strong enough to do an adult's work, in particular ploughing. Anthropologists have long recognised the stages in life, and transition from one to another, as important. Burial evidence which might illuminate this is only available from the period when it was still the custom to bury articles with the dead, 'grave-goods', a custom which ended late in the seventh century. This seems to show that there were two distinct 'coming-of-age' times for a boy: the first was when he was about twelve and the other was when he was about eighteen.[17] Could the first signal a boy who has achieved adulthood? We learn from the law codes that vis-à-vis the law he then became responsible for his actions as a member of the adult world and had to become a member of a tithing, the smallest unit for local peace-keeping. Perhaps this was also the age at which he achieved adult status as far as taking on his share of men's work was concerned: did he learn on the job by ploughing what in twentieth-century Oxfordshire was called 'Boys' land'?[18]

Some demands are inherent in peasant life. One is risk-avoidance. All Anglo-Saxon farms were mixed farms, growing food crops as well as raising livestock. This was itself a basic risk-avoidance strategy: before the development of an effective market for basic foods, people would have starved if they had not been able to produce all, or nearly all, they needed of both cereal and animal products. This was true of rich and poor alike. Even the smallholdings which supported the poorest agricultural workers and the freed slaves who worked on the estates of landlords were tiny mixed economies, with a cow and a bit of land.

Risk-avoidance meant that two jobs were essential, irrespective of the size of the farm and the social status of the farmer. One is caring for the stock, the other is feeding the workforce. Some members of many farm households were away all summer with flocks and herds on distant pastures and others (probably many more than we currently know about) were off the farm droving, fishing, working in mining and forestry. But every kind of outdoor job took a pair of hands away from the farmstead during daylight hours, and someone was needed there to manage the poultry, spin and weave, nurse the baby, keep the toddlers from falling into the fire, and, most important of all, feed the workers. This is why headship of a household at every level of society is associated with providing food. What came to be terms for members of the elite, 'lord' and 'lady', came from Old English words which stood for male and female heads of households in a more practical sense: a lord is a *hlaford*, a 'loaf-keeper', a lady a *hlædige*, a 'loaf-kneader'. An ordinary non-noble person, a *ceorl*, too was thought of as a provider of food for his household and 'loaf-keepers' and 'loaf-kneaders' of any social rank might have their own *hlaf-ætas*, 'loaf-eaters'. To be someone's 'loaf-eater', in the language of the law codes, was to be their dependant. The term would only make sense if the loaf was the food provided within the household, even if we have to extend the term 'household' to include people who got their food from the hearth and slept in a separate building nearby (and 'loaf' to include other kinds of food). As is often the case, Ireland and Wales provide better, and much more vivid, illustrations of how systems like this worked, or, which is just as important, were supposed to work. In the Irish laws, the employer had an obligation not simply to provide food for his tenants but to see that 'they consume it with him'. In medieval France, Marc Bloch observed, full membership of the family, which conferred the right to inherit, belonged only to those who had lived in common with its members: those who had not, the *forisfamiliati*, were 'outside the bread'.[19]

From the mid-Saxon period on, farming in some areas was becoming much more capital intensive, and as none of the operations on the farm (except milling) was in any way mechanised in our period, that meant that it was becoming more labour-intensive too. There was more careful animal husbandry, with both sheep and cattle kept nearer the farm. The cultivated area was expanded and reorganised and a type of plough was beginning to be adopted on some farms which would have needed a team of at least two oxen, probably six, to pull it, and one (strong) person to 'follow' or guide the plough and another in front to manage the plough-beasts. Rural life has probably always seen some farms thriving and some failing, but the likelihood is that there was now beginning to be a greater differentiation between types of farms and between types of farm house-holds. Peasant houses were changing from the mid-Saxon period and this suggests that the households which they held were changing too, at least in size. Early settlers, like those at Mucking on the north bank of the Thames below London, could well have had a specific age profile, possibly a group of kinspeople. The domestic buildings there in the early settlement period had only one room and an indoor space of between about 180 and 720 square feet. In mid- and late-Anglo-Saxon England, larger houses appear which were much more recognisably *farm*houses than their predecessors had been, having about the same amount of living space as the substantial Wealden houses of solid Kentish yeomen or the timber-framed houses of medieval Hampshire. They were now more likely to be embedded in groups of buildings, with droveways and pad-docks, and some were in enclosures of a kind.[20] Changes in building form may indicate not only that people were beginning to value a close connection between their farmhouse, its household, and their land, but also were beginning to think about the household as a little world of its own. Larger farms like this could well have needed more labour than the family alone could provide.

Farm Workers

On other farms, there were more mouths than the farm could feed. While in this book 'peasant' stands for people who were supported by the land that they worked, we need to bear in mind that many people making a living in the countryside were not substantial farmers but smallholders. Although some farmers took advantage of the changes in the equipment and methods of arable farming that made it possible to get better yields, it is likely that many continued to grow grain, the most essential job of all, on a very small scale and in traditional 'low-tech' ways.[21] Preparing the tilth with an ard or even a spade, broadcasting the seed, scaring off the birds, cutting the ripe corn with a small sickle, threshing it with a flail, grinding it on a quern, baking bread on a flat stone, although hard and heavy work, needed neither large numbers of people nor traction animals. In the jobs associated with small-scale animal husbandry, reliability, skill, and experience were what was needed for taking sheep or cattle out to graze, milking, and cheese making. A family of a couple and a child could probably manage to support themselves, but 'surplus' children who were old enough to take on an adult's workload were also old enough to need an adult's food. Many must have left home to join what has always been an important strand in rural England: farm workers. They are among the least-studied people in rural history and their housing has made very little showing in the archaeology or rural settlements, but we meet them throughout this book. A law of Ine of Wessex (688–729) calls to mind the 'tied cottages' of later England in a rare recorded intervention by a king into the realities of rural life This itself may suggest that there was a new situation, one not covered by custom, about which his ruling had been sought. Ine's reign was at the start of a period when the elite, granted large estates by the king, were beginning to shift from being a warrior class to being a class of landowners. Secure possession of land, which was beginning to be assured by formal written grants from the king, would have allowed many lords to establish headquarters at what would later be called the *caput*, the 'head' of their possessions.[22] We know very little about how they managed their properties in order to support themselves in style. For the recipients of large grants of thirty hides or more the *feorm* due from the farmers on their newly acquired land, which now came to them instead of to the king, would have been essential when they were travelling about their possessions. While lords of lesser lands did not have access to *feorm* from a large areas, all the members of the unproductive elite needed regular supplies of everyday goods, many of them (malt, beer, meat, fish) perishable. To keep this kind of production going demanded a reliable labour supply. Slaves were one source, but were probably not available everywhere, or in large enough numbers, even with enough agricultural skills to supply the demand for labour. The vocabulary of the law codes suggests a source: *folgeres*, people who are not 'hearth-fast' but 'followers', *conducticii, stipendarii*, 'hired men (and women)', and who are more likely to have been wage-workers, possibly migrants, who 'lived out', but who knows if they were entitled to food while at work?[23] There were also evidently landless people (and it is tempting to suggest that many may have been Britons) willing to supply labour, or labour and some kind of render, in return for being 'outfitted': set up on a smallholding, with the small stock needed to work it. Ine's law ruled that people in this situation were free to give up these labour tenancies and leave if they wished: but if the landlord had provided them with housing they were from then on tied to the estate.[24] Nothing better exemplifies the importance of being 'hearth-fast' than this law. The link between housing and rural employment was to have a long history in rural England. These smallholdings and cottages, stocked and built by the lord, bring to mind the farm labourers' cottages and allotments of much later England, when losing your job would mean losing your home.[25]

Boarders

Domesday Book reveals how important farm workers were to the rural economy in 1086. It classifies as *bordarii* over 40 per cent of the recorded numbers of people in four counties and over 20 per cent in nearly all the rest. The Latin term *bordarius* was a new word in England. It Anglicizes the Norman French term *bordier* which in eleventh-century Normandy was used to describe a category of peasants who were considered inferior to those with substantial farms, and who often had duties connected with the lord's household. *Bordarii* were not a category that the commissioners had been instructed to count, but they evidently found English people of a kind that they considered to be the equivalent to *bordiers*, although they sometimes found it difficult to distinguish them from cottagers. A later description of the enquiry says that they were required to count both 'those who live in *tuguria*, shacks or cottages, and those with houses and fields', so their having a farmstead and the land belonging to it, and the household to maintain it and be maintained by it, might have been the criterion which distinguished the farmers of a township from the *bordarii* with cottages. In eleventh-century Normandy the term was used as a rough description of lesser peasants, but in England it may have acquired a more precise one: Judge Bracton in the thirteenth century may have been voicing contemporary opinion that the term *bordarius* derived from *borde*, 'table', and that *bordarii* were part of the lord's *dominium*, the land reserved for supplying his table.[26] Modern translations of Domesday Book translate *bordarii* as 'smallholders' and while it is true that they certainly had very slender resources, they were more like very small-scale peasants with arable land than the small mixed enterprises that the term suggests to us today. Reginald Lennard's work revealed that if Domesday *bordarii* had a ploughteam at all it was of one or two oxen, and when their land is described it is seldom more than five acres. Working for others may well have been what stood between them and destitution.[27]

While many must have worked at the centre of a large estate and the term came to be associated with these, the numbers of *bordarii* are so large and their distribution so wide that it is likely that many worked on the larger farms of their more prosperous peasant neighbours and were entitled to their food, their 'board', from the farm's hearth. This book uses the familiar modern word 'boarder' to translate Latin *bordarius* in order to make this point and that an obsolete word, 'hind', for a farm labourer comes from the Old English *higan, hiwan* (member of) a household, brings home how important a part this unregarded class has played in the rural economy. The experience of the men and women in much later periods who worked for local farmers was that working for a peasant farmer could be as hard work, if not harder, than working for a great landowner. Even today the perquisites of a job, particularly those connected with food and drink and the conditions in which these are taken, are highly prized and often contested. In our period, people working for a local farmer could well have found that they had no set entitlements like the fixed customary doles of food and drink they would have received on a large property like the one envisaged in the description of a model estate in the text known as *Rectitudines singularum personarum*.[28] The farmer's wife, with an eye on feeding her family and making ends meet, was in no position to be an over-generous 'loaf-giver'. Harold Fox's work on farm servants in early fourteenth-century Somerset convinced him that the reason that 'service in husbandry' was popular among the better-off peasants was that it could be cheaper to hire and house a neighbour's son and send your own out to work on another farm, than to keep him at home. Possibly 'service in husbandry', as it came to be called, while indubitably hard work, formed part of a country boy's training, as service in a lord's household did for the young nobleman. Even the most exploited slaves and farm workers had an entitlement to be fed, and came under their employer's protection, his *mund*.[29] It is from the laws that we know this, and that is a sign that the household was not only a domestic group and a workforce: it was also a legal space.

The Household as a Legal Space

A household, of whatever social rank, was a group with its own moral order whose members each had their own expectations and obligations. It may have been the very fact that the viability of this small self-sufficient world was ensured by strong feelings about the protection of its private space that the law codes were careful to ensure that it was not therefore outside the sphere of public law. Within it, legal responsibility was strictly assigned. The head of the household, the lord of this private sphere, was held liable for keeping law and order within it. A law of Wihtred of Kent shows how serious the implications of this could be. If the head of a household stole with the cognizance of his household, including any children of ten and over, they would all go into slavery. He was legally responsible for the behaviour of anyone under his roof, even someone there temporarily like a travelling chapman or family members home for a visit. It was not simply providing shelter but feeding the visitor, 'giving him food from his own store', that triggered the householder's responsibility. A person whose drinking companions, those in his 'beership', caused trouble, whether by rowdy behaviour like taking someone's 'stoup', his drinking vessel, or drawing a weapon, owed a fine *to the houseowner* as well as to his victim and a penalty to the king. Even the head of what might have been a very poor household had his right to compensation from people who fought under his roof. Just as much as his superior, a dependant *gebur* or a *gafol-gelda* was entitled to compensation for fights that broke out in his house. Destructive gossip like calling someone a perjurer (a very serious insult) or verbally abusing him, (perhaps the kind of 'fighting with words', or flyting, which was the next best thing to, and probably often the precursor of, a regular punch-up) incurred the same penalties. Shedding blood in someone's house was more serious yet: the person responsible owed the owner his *mundbyrd* and the king 50 shillings.[30] A person's *mundbyrd* was his 'protection' and by extension its monetary value. It is a concept which appears in the very earliest English laws, those of Æthelbert of Kent and recurs through those of his Kentish successors.[31]

The evidence of the law codes suggests that while the idea of protected spaces may have been deeply embedded in the Anglo-Saxon moral economy, under the influence of changing ideology rulers were able to extend and manipulate them. Æthelbert's laws were issued in the early stages of the conversion of his subjects to Christianity and are concerned with the protection of a new kind of space, that of the church. As Christian practice came to be more energetically promoted among the population at large, domestic space too was missionized. The head of a household was coming to be seen as the head of a small Christian community. The tenth-century laws which required this might remind us of the responsibility of later heads of households to conduct 'family prayers', which included the servants. He had to ensure that the feasts of the church were respected, a rule that must have been difficult to enforce when it meant taking someone off a vital job. Feeding his household during a fast was forbidden and he had to make sure that all his hired men (*omnis hyremannus suus*) gave a penny in alms. Even the smallest cottage owner owed the 'church-scot' due from 'every free (i.e. non-slave) hearth'.[32] The household itself had a version of James Scott's 'ceremonial and social functions' and was an important transmitter of the values of the moral economy. It was important, for instance, that children growing up in the communities described by Sue Oosthuizen in her recent book on the Anglo-Saxon Fenland should know exactly what needed to be done to maintain dykes and ditches. Sharing the work as soon as they were able, they would in time pass their knowledge on to the next generation.

The importance of the household as a social unit meant that it was important for it to be clearly identifiable as a physical one. Boundaries and proper enclosures were thus vital and references in the laws echo the emphasis both the barbarian codes and the Irish laws put on the farm enclosure, the *les*, the ditch and bank, and the area immediately surrounding it. In the Kentish laws a man's *tūn*, his *edor*, or house-enclosure, must be kept up, and 'piercing through' the 'proper house-shield', the *rihthamscyld*, incurs due compensation. The *ceorl*'s *wordig* in one of Ine's laws 'must be enclosed, winter and summer'.[33] We are still a long way from being able to envisage what these terms meant at the time, but they all refer in some way to the idea of a protected and legally visible space around the house. We can see the beginnings of an articulated view of the Anglo-Saxon equivalent to the *les* on the ground. Changes in building form may indicate not only that people were beginning to value a close connection between their farmhouse, its household, and their land, but were also beginning to think about the household as a little world of its own: Helena Hamerow has detected an increased emphasis on enclosures on some farm sites, including around the farmhouse, in the mid-Saxon period which had not been apparent in the early scattered settlements.[34] Place-names may be relevant here, although it is not at all clear what contemporaries meant when they called a farm or small hamlet 'X's *tūn*', giving us the many place-names in 'ton' like Cola's *tūn*, now Collaton, and its neighbours in South Devon. Was it their protective enclosure, perhaps the forerunners of the colossal banks and walls around some Devon farmyards, that made these places distinctive?[35] Practical considerations, like managing the livestock and poultry kept near the farmhouse, must have been a consideration in constructing enclosures, but the privacy of the home evidently mattered, perhaps even more. The four households who, sometime before the Conquest, set up house in a valley at Brown Willy on Bodmin Moor enclosed the arable and took in some of the surrounding moorland: all this belonged to their little 'township' but the houses of the township families were built with their doors turned away from the communal space at its centre.[36] Of course some more practical considerations must have been equally important. At Yarnton, Oxfordshire, for instance, cattle in the middle Saxon period were evidently beginning to be kept in a more systematic way: hay was grown which would have provided better winter feed for cattle than rough grazing and what may have been cattle pens were erected near the farmstead. But there is no hard-and-fast line between what was done for practical reasons and what had other meanings too. If people were keeping their livestock in a more household-oriented way in mid-Saxon England, that may be because the individual household and its economy were coming to be more important in the way people thought about the world.

Passing on the Farm

If to be the head of a household entailed moral and legal responsibilities, then one of the most important was the most basic: to provide an heir.[37] This mattered to lords and peasants alike and long continued to do so. While the disposition of land and goods was ruled by different customs in different periods and areas, it was universally acknowledged that family members had the prior, generally the sole, claim.[38] In claiming thrones, too, family mattered: William I claimed to be Edward the Confessor's rightful heir and it was because they recognised the strong feelings that the English had about inheritance and wanted to emphasise the continuity of their regimes with those of the Old English rulers they had displaced that both Danish Cnut and Norman William gave their assurances that the rights of heirs would be respected. Issued in the immediate aftermath of the Conquest, William I's London charter was intended to reassure the London elite that he wanted them to continue to enjoy the rights of the previous regime. Part of this promise was that 'it is my will that every child shall be his father's heir, *yrfenume*, after his father's death.'[39] Although we know much more about the way that the land of major landowners passed from one generation to another than we do about peasant practice, we know little enough about even that. Our knowledge of what the major landowners thought was important derives from the surviving charters and wills which record the transactions which were designed to bring this about. The majority of those were designed to transfer land to the church, and one view of why these elaborate written records were introduced into England in the first place is that this was precisely the intention: 'bookland', land granted by charter, *boc*, could safely go to endow the chosen institution and escape the claims of the family members who otherwise had a claim to it. Family claims were still evidently thought primary: a law of Alfred rules that someone who had inherited land, even bookland, must not 'give it out of his kindred' if there was express provision against this. A remark of Bede suggests that he thought family property would normally be divided among family members, and it may be that it was precisely because the general principles of the moral economy of inheritance were so well known that the law codes have virtually nothing to say on the matter.[40] Taking on a farm, like taking on a kingdom, means taking on responsibilities and to run either demands experience. To be the head of any household, as we have seen, brought its own legal burdens. Secure inheritance passing on property to someone who would run it in the interests of its 'stakeholders' was not simply a preoccupation of the elite, such as the 'bishop, portreeve and burgesses of London' to whom William's writ-charter was addressed: it mattered to peasants too.

When it comes to how the peasant farm was passed on to the next generation, we have a wealth of rules from both Irish and Welsh laws but almost nothing from the English. What we know about other European peasant societies suggests that while all the children of the owner had rights of some kind, there were advantages of knowing that the farm, in normal circumstances, would go to one son and also there were advantages in knowing which son, if there were more than one, that would be. The death of the head of a farm household brought not simply a question of who should inherit the land. It was an important moment for the household members whose work kept the farm going and who expected that it would feed them in return. What would happen to this understanding when their 'loaf-giver' died? Would their entitlement continue? The entitlement of family members to be supported from the family land in return for work arose from a permanent problem: how to balance the numbers of mouths to be fed with the numbers of pairs of hands needed to do the work. Although English peasant inheritance custom in the thirteenth and fourteenth centuries is richly illustrated and has been intensively studied, there is no pre-Conquest English written evidence which can match that from France, Italy, and Spain. This gives a very good idea of what a range of different strategies was available – there was no such thing as a universal peasant practice.[41] However, the different strategies do seem to share a common characteristic: they recognise that *all* family members, under certain circumstances, have entitlements. Work was the crucial factor. In cases where a single heir was deemed to be entitled to inherit the entire farm, a difference was sometimes drawn between those non-inheriting children who, on reaching adulthood, stayed on the farm and those who decided to leave. The first continued their entitlement in return for work, the second were entitled to a portion of family moveables which they could take with them: some of the livestock, cash, or other goods are all found. Some strategies involved dividing the family land among heirs, either by physically splitting it up or by working it as a jointly owned holding, and where this was the local practice we find extremely elaborate rules about who was entitled to what. For the needs of the farm to continue being paramount, rather than people inheriting the farm, it was the farm that inherited the people.

As much as who owns the farm, what matters is who runs it and is responsible for crucial decisions. In many peasant societies, and still true today, this is a source of conflict between fathers who wish to hang on to authority, and sons and daughters who want to claim it. Whoever prevails, well before the owner dies it needs to be known who the rightful heir is. There is a hint that this notion of a single nominated heir was seen as important in pre-Conquest England. A law of Ine provides for the fatherless child. The mother is given supplies for her maintenance and the relatives keep the house until the child is of age: *gewintred sie*, until he is 'wintered'. He is then entitled to the *frumstol*, the 'first seat'. It seems as if the heir had, literally, 'pride of place'. The evidence from early Anglo-Saxon graves (which, we need to bear in mind, cease to give us the evidence of grave-goods after the late seventh century) does seem to show that reaching eighteen brought a boy to an important stage in life. In the eyes of the law he was already an adult: this may have marked the stage at which his father retired and he could marry and take over the farm from the old man.[42] Ideas about inheriting property may have been connected with ideas about death and burial. In the early settlement period, single large cemeteries served a wide scattering of small settlements, as if they were the dead of the people of quite a large area. To go to a burial then would have meant meeting strangers from other places, some quite distant. In mid-Saxon England the dead were becoming more neighbourly, buried in smaller cemeteries nearer to individual settlements. Presumably they were buried by their descendants who still lived there, just as many of the graves in a village cemetery today are visited and cared for by relatives. The fact that people were now living closer to their own dead has been interpreted as a new attitude to death, but it might also be interpreted as a new attitude to land, with a stronger notion of the connection of a small group of people and their ancestors with the land that immediately supported them. What is in no doubt is that, high and low, family claims to family land mattered. An important tenet of the moral economy was shared across classes: family land belonged in family hands. When we come to look at the situation after the Conquest we will be able to appreciate the resilience of this basic belief.

While the household continued to be the basic unit at all levels of society, in the last two centuries of Anglo-Saxon England the experience of being a member of a peasant household was very diverse, and becoming more so. The small community around the hearth of a substantial peasant farmstead, under the rule of the farm's 'lord' and 'lady' and 'fed from the same pot', might consist of blood relatives only, or it might also include slaves and farm workers also entitled to their 'board'. This is the kind of group that would in later centuries be known as 'in mainpast', the legal responsibility of the head of the household.[43] Supported from the produce of the farm which their work had produced, and living surrounded by the land of the farm, in a sense they were part of its social identity. Members of peasant households with holdings which were part of the inland of an estate owner, whether that owner was an individual lord or a religious community, lived very different lives. They depended on the produce of land and livestock which were not an inalienable family possession but an 'outfit', granted complete with dwelling and tools in return for their labour and rent in cash and kind. The lord's land and livestock had prior claim on their skill and labour over their own land and livestock, for its primary function was to supply the lord's table. They lived in the ambit of a notable residence, one that was, from the tenth century on, increasingly likely to be marked off from the landscape of peasant farms. On the eve of the Conquest, then, just as there were two very different kinds of land, warland and inland, there were now two very different peasantries: those within the ambit of independent farms, and those within the ambit of the great estates. It was not necessarily an economic divide, for a living scratched on a small independent farm could have been very meagre and even a slave on a great estate was entitled to rations. It was a divide between people whose living depended on land liable to public obligations, and thus enjoying free status, and people whose living depended on a lord's will.

Notes

1 Scott, *Moral Economy*, 5, 9.
2 Colgrave and Mynors, *Bede's Ecclesiastical History*, ii. 13, 182–5.
3 Johnson, ed., *Dialogus de Scaccario*, 129–35.
4 See Appendix: 'The family farm in peasant studies'.
5 *Rectitudines singularum personarum*, 3, 4: Liebermann, *Gesetze*, i. 446.
6 Pollock and Maitland, *History of English Law*, i. 620–3.
7 Lane, 'Westbury-sub-Mendip, Somerset'; Aston et al., 'Medieval farming in Winscombe', 112–15 and 140n.149. AND, s.v. *astrier*. I am greatly indebted to the late Mick Aston and to the late Barry Lane for their information about old austers. Maitland associated the practice of inheritance by the youngest

child with his being the *astrier* or 'fireside child' who stayed at home to work on the family holding: Pollock and Maitland, *History of English Law*, ii. 271, 285. *Frumstol*: Ine 38: Attenborough, *Laws*, 48–9; Liebermann, *Gesetze*, i. 104–7.

8 Hamerow, *Rural Settlements*, 46, 48.

9 These names come from the 'Tribal Hidage', the name now given to a list of the 'land' of different peoples, the *Westerna, Ciltern saetna*, etc. assessed in numbers of hides, reckoned in hundreds and thousands. It is printed in Bassett, *Origins of Anglo-Saxon Kingdoms*, 225–30. It is often interpreted as a 'tribute list', probably because the hide was the unit on which various obligations and taxes came to be levied. However, as the only Anglo-Saxon version of this document which survives is in an educational work, an eleventh-century grammar book, it may once have served, in an era without maps, as a geographical text.

10 Colgrave and Mynors, *Bede's Ecclesiastical History*, II.9, 162–3.

11 Charles-Edwards, 'Kinship, status' and 'Early medieval kingships'. That the hide was used to assess the basis of public burdens, possibly including the cash render known as *gafol*, long before the era of the land-tax known as geld and heregeld, should modify the argument of Wareham, 'Fiscal policies', that England before the tenth century was a 'domain' economy, in which the king basically lived off his estates. Wickham, who characterises it as one from which 'tribute' was exacted, seems to elide the distinction made by Charles-Edwards: that while renders such as the public burdens laid on the hide are due from the realm of the ruler, tribute is essentially extracted from a conquered people. Wickham, 'The other transition'.

12 It was not until later that a single hide acquired a notional areal equivalent of 120 acres: this being reckoned as the total area that one ploughteam could plough over a year.

13 This is treated more fully in Faith, *English Peasantry*, chapters 4 and 5.

14 Herlihy, *Medieval Households*', 44–59; Stanley, 'The *familia* in Anglo-Saxon society', 42–7. Charles-Edwards, 'Kinship, status'. No statistical evidence can be produced of the acreages of Anglo-Saxon peasant farms, but the volumes of the Darby *Domesday Geography* series give, where these are available, the numbers of ploughteams, ploughlands, and *villani* in each county. In some counties the numbers of teams, or ploughlands, 'of the *villani*' are given in individual manorial entries. Lennard, 'The economic position of the bordars and cottars' collates this information for those two categories. Part 2 of Banham and Faith, *Anglo-Saxon Farms and Farming* identifies some individual farms with pre-Conquest origins.

15 Howkins, *Reshaping Rural England*, 38.

16 Reed, 'Peasantry of nineteenth century England'; Howkins, *Reshaping Rural England*, chapter 2.

17 Stoodley, 'Childhood to old age' in Hamerow, Hilton, and Crawford, eds., *Oxford Handbook of Anglo-Saxon Archaeology*.

18 I am grateful to Murray Maclean of Collins Farm, Frilford, Oxfordshire, for this information.

19 Charles-Edwards, 'Kinship, status', 12–14; Bloch, 'Personal liberty and servitude', 41; Herlihy, *Medieval Households*, 58–9, argues that, together with decline of slavery, the emergence of the 'family farm' itself led to the formation of 'commensable' households in western Europe. Many peasant households in Anglo-Saxon England, however, probably themselves contained slaves.

20 Hamerow, *Rural Societies*, 78–94.

21 Banham and Faith, *Anglo-Saxon Farms and Farming*, 44–51 (ploughs and ploughing); part II *passim* for small arable areas.

22 I owe this observation to Tom Lambert.

23 An anonymous reader has made the interesting suggestion that these 'followers' may have been, like the 'followers' in the *Rectitudines singularum personarum*, ploughmen. Ploughmen had such heavy responsibilities in caring for their beasts which must have tied them to the farmyard, however, that I think the broader sense is more probable here.

24 Ine 67: Attenborough, *Laws*, 58–9, Liebermann, *Gesetze*, i. 118–19. Thomas Charles-Edwards' discussion of this law in 'The distinction between land and moveable wealth' remains fundamental to much that is said in this book.

25 Newby, *Deferential Worker*, 178–94.

26 The Norman French origin of the term *bordarius* is more fully discussed in Chapter 11. For their representation in Domesday Book: Darby, *Domesday England*, 69–72. For the term in Normandy: Musset, 'La tenure en bordage'. AND, s.v. *bordarius* citing Delisle, *Classes Agricoles* who notes that their services were predominantly domestic: Faith, *English Peasantry*, 73, for this aspect. *Bordier* is interpreted as having derived from *borde*, 'plank', on the grounds that bordars lived in wooden cabins by Harvey, 'Evidence for settlement study', 107–9, and Lennard, 'Economic position'. Most rural buildings in 1086 were made of wood, however, and *borde*, in Norman French and then in English, also meant 'table'. In *The English Peasantry* I interpreted *bordarii*, following Bracton, with reference to people servicing lords' 'table-land': the two explanations need not be contradictory if they also were people entitled to food provided from his table and they were fed from peasant tables too: Halliwell, *Dictionary*, s.v. 'borde'. The use in the Phillimore edition of Domesday Book of 'smallholder' for *bordarius* is accurate in the sense that *bordarii*, when this can be investigated, as was done by Lennard, had smallholdings and equipment but it does not convey their connection with other people's tables.

27 Lennard, 'Economic position of the bordars and cottars'.

28 *Rectitudines singularum personarum*: Liebermann, *Gesetze*, i. 444–53. For entitlements to food and drink at boonworks: Birrell, 'Peasants eating and drinking' and 'Manorial custumals reconsidered'.

29 Fox, 'Exploitation of the landless'.

30 Ine 7; Attenborough, *Laws*, 38–9, Liebermann, *Gesetze*, i. 92; Hlothere and Eadric, 11–15; Attenborough, *Laws*, 20, 21, Liebermann, *Gesetze*, i. 10–11. For the growing monetary interest of kings in the legal process, through entitlement to fines, see now Lambert, *Law and Order*.

31 Æthelbert 8, 13, 14: Attenborough, *Laws*, 4, 5, 6, 7, Liebermann, *Gesetze*, i. 3, 4. Wihtred 2: Attenborough, *Laws*, 24, 25, Liebermann, *Gesetze*, i. 12; Ine 6.3: Attenborough, *Laws*, 38–9, Liebermann, *Gesetze*, i. 3–4.

32 Wihtred 14: Attenborough, *Laws*, 26–7, Liebermann, *Gesetze*, i. 13. Edward and Guthrum 7.2: Robertson, *Laws*, 106–7; Liebermann, *Gesetze*, i. *Rectitudines singularum personarum*: Liebermann, *Gesetze*, i. 444.

33 Æthelbert 32; Ine 42: Attenborough 8–9, 42–51. Liebermann, *Gesetze*, i. 5, 106–7, Rivers, *Laws of the Alamans and Bavarians*, The Bavarian Laws IX.8; 25, XI.1 at 148, 150–53. For a different interpretation of *rihthamscyld*: Oliver, *Beginnings*, 97–8; Ammon, 'Piercing the *rihthamscyld* – a new reading of Æthelbert 32'. However, both authors' interpretations depend on reading the ms as having given *rihthamscyld* in error for *rihthæmedscyld*. Their argument rests partly on the placing of this law in the context of adultery and physical assault, but it is also grouped with three offences involving breaking enclosures. I am grateful to Mark Atherton for his help here. *Les*: Kelly, *Early Irish Farming*, 363–4, 368–9.

34 Hamerow, *Rural Settlements*, 72–83.

35 Faith, 'Cola's *tūn*'.

36 Peter Herring, pers. comm.

37 I have here followed Siddle, 'Inheritance strategies'.

38 While much information about peasant inheritance customs in the later middle ages can be derived from manorial records and has been extensively researched, such information for the pre-Conquest period is extremely sparse. It has been discussed by George Homans with reference to the influence of continental practice in 'Rural sociology of medieval England' and Faith, 'Peasant families and inheritance customs'.

39 William I, London Charter: Robertson, *Laws*, 230–1; *Yrfenume*, like many terms for property, derives from a Germanic term for cattle: Bosworth and Toller, *Dictionary*, s.v. *irfe-nume*.

40 Alfred 41: Attenborough, *Laws*, 82–3; Liebermann, *Gesetze*, i. 74–5.

41 Homans, *English Villagers*, Book II remains the widest survey of local custom.

42 Ine 38: Attenborough, *Laws*, 48–9; Liebermann, *Gesetze*, i. 104–7. Graves: Stoodley, 'Childhood'.

43 Belonging to the same household in Norman England was known as being one of those 'for whom the same pot boils', *eorum crocca towallet*: *Leges Henrici Primi*, 94.3a and 88.18; Homans, *English Villagers*, 109–10.

Part III

Reputation and Witness

A person's reputation in modern society is constructed in part by people who do not know him or her. In early medieval society it was constructed by people who did. Writing about the opposite of good reputation, shame, Alice Coven perceptively argues that this 'has to do with the life of the community ... it involves a notion of worth bound as much to how one is treated by other people as to whether one knows one's actions to be right or wrong.'[1] This chapter looks for the 'notions of worth' involved in the multifarious everyday transactions between people in 'the life of the community'.

There is no reason to think that Anglo-Saxon farmers were any less independent-minded than their counterparts are today. The ethos of the family farm, after all, was self-sufficiency and dispersed farms with names that we still use today, like Eadda's worthy at Yadsworthy and Cola's *tŭn* at Collaton, refer to individuals long gone.[2] Yet even the most independent-minded of farmers depended on their neighbours. Of all the work done on the farm, growing food crops was the most vital and the most labour-intensive operation, and cattle were any farmer's most valuable piece of capital. The laws concerning cattle reveal a good deal about the moral economy of the farming world.[3] Their principal use was for traction – pulling ploughs, harrows, and carts of various kinds – rather than for meat or milk, for they were too valuable to eat and most cheese and butter was made from sheep's, not cows', milk. Working oxen, castrated male cattle, were expensive to keep, needed training for the work they had to do, and when worked hard needed good fodder and long rests. They were generally worked in teams, but many small farmers made do with a single ox, or a pair, and evidently some could not afford even this. One of Ine's laws gives us a hint of how they might manage without this essential resource. One was to hire a neighbour's team, paying him in fodder. 'Let people be canny', *gesceawige mon*, that the full amount due was paid; if he cannot manage this, then he may pay half in fodder and half in some other form of payment. This was not a charitable transaction, but it was not a purely commercial one either: as plough oxen were valuable, and could easily be put out of action by injury, it is hard to see how the owner could make a profit from the arrangement. The law is careful about where responsibility lies: it is for the owner to make sure that he did not lose out from it.[4] All farmers are careful to ensure against risk, and it is no coincidence that there was a raft of steep compensation payments due for injuries to cattle. There was another reason for common vigilance. Because it fuelled the principal means of traction, the ox, animal fodder was as important in Anglo-Saxon England as oil is in the modern world. While spring and summer grazing was plentiful, the availability of winter fodder governed the numbers of livestock that could be kept. This meant that when hay began to be deliberately cultivated, as it was at the Oxfordshire settlement at Yarnton in the eighth century, it was extremely valuable. Hay meadow needed to be protected when it was growing, although animals were often put out to graze the 'aftermath' after it was mown. Another of Ine's laws demonstrates that farmers who depended on this valuable common resource and shared its benefits shared too the responsibility of maintaining it. It deals with the problem of a group of farmers who have fenced off some land as 'common meadow or other share-land'. They were jointly responsible for the fencing and anyone who has neglected to fence his share with the result that animals get in and eat up the common crops or grass owes the others compensation at a level to be sorted out between them. (Yarnton's 'lot meadows' were used as a 'common meadow' into the nineteenth century: a tradition which goes back at least to the middle ages.)[5] As so much depended on others, peasant farmers could not afford to trust anyone who was not of good reputation. Even livestock needed a good reputation: hedge-breaking animals which persistently strayed out of control and damaged growing crops were an even more serious problem: anyone whose corn-land was damaged by one had the right to take it and kill it.[6] Ine's laws, giving us a glimpse into the kind of dealings between people that were probably very common causes of conflict, show us that it was the conditions of production that bound people together. Fair dealing and the common good were important in the moral economy of working life not because transactions between neighbours were altruistic, nor even necessarily friendly, but because they were essential. Livestock husbandry provides a good example of this.

Livestock and Community

Whether in the Iron Age or in twenty-first-century Britain, raising livestock imposes connections between people. James Rebanks' recent popular account of sheep farming in the Lake District shows how much, even in the era of mobile phones, he depends on neighbouring farmers, and they on him. Trudging up the mountain to check his flock under heavy snow, 'I pass my neighbour doing similar work. A little nod says he's seen me and knows where I'm going. That little nod may keep me alive later. No-one else knows where I'm going.'[7] Often remote, common grazing of all kinds on moor and mountain, fen and marsh, appears as an essential feature in the formation of many kinds of early territory. The previous chapter argued that the early forms of authority held by *ealdormen* were exercised 'top-down' over *regiones, provinciae,* or *scirs*. But the imperatives of rural life were important long before we see them in their administrative role and for the people who belonged to those territories, and to whom these resources 'belonged' in the sense that they had established use-rights over them, 'bottom-up' descriptions are more appropriate. When the hundred and the township come into the written record, it is clear that matters relating to livestock took up a great deal of their time and were the chief source of disputes in the country-side.[8] Some small regions seem to have evolved into the administrative units known as hundreds, and many hundreds met at places which show that they had a traditional role in livestock management. Swanborough Tump, the meeting-place on the Marlborough Downs for the Witshire hundred of Swanborough, was the 'herdsmen's mound'. When the hun-dred met, a good deal of its time must have been taken up settling any cattle disputes which hadn't already been sorted out on the spot when they occurred. Some hundred meetings were very likely also the *ceáp-dæg*, the 'market day', at least for livestock. Witness and reputation mattered more than ever when buying and selling animals, and still do. It would be many centuries before distinct breeds of domesticated animals were established in England, but any small herd or flock will need to import new genetic material from elsewhere to ensure enough genetic variation to keep them healthy. Anyone buying in a ram or a bull would be wise to find out its reputation for siring good stock. Buying and selling needed witnesses and sureties, so their owner's reputation needs establishing too, and this means that stock owners must meet one another. A good deal of Æthelstan's and Edgar's lawmaking was a response to problems which must have come up time and time again in any society with which ran its livestock in open country: one law com-plains that 'many heedless men do not care where their cattle wander'. It is the local community which administers and polices this most conten-tious area of rural life. The hundred and the township both have duties. A township might have its own herdsman, who had responsibility for his neighbours' cattle as well as his own. Stolen animals always caused problems. Neighbours knew whose animals were whose. In fact, it seems that, as can still be true today, the cattle in a community would have been as recognisable to everyone as the people were. Anglo-Saxon cattle were much less uniform than the carefully bred cows we see today, and very likely each one would be known by its distinctive markings: newly bought stock had to be 'introduced' when brought back from market for precisely this reason. And known by its footprints too: part of the responsibility of the township was to produce a tracker to follow the hoofprints of stolen animals and to turn out to help with the search. Boundaries mattered and were known to all. In the case of the tricky situation when the stolen stock crossed the hundred boundary, if anyone follows a trail from one *scyre* to another his neighbours must help until the *scyre gerefa*, the 'shire reeve', is informed. He takes the posse on to the boundary where the reeve of the other *scyre* takes over. It is pretty clear that the *scyre* here is the same thing as the hundred: in a later version of the same law it is the men of the one hundred that follow the track into another hundred and it is the hundredman that take over the search. Not just theft but all dealings involving livestock were carefully monitored under the eye of the community. Proper procedure, witness, and reputation were important: if someone claimed that his stock had been stolen, and 'attached' them (took them until the dispute should be settled), he needed to have five men nominated from among his neighbours, his *neahgebura*, from whom he must choose one to swear with him that he was doing this in accordance with *folcryht*, the 'customary law'. If the animals were worth more than twenty pence, he must choose two men out of twenty. Even exchanging cattle needed respectable witnesses and even a cow could have a bad reputation as a known hedge-breaker or a poor milker.[9] When the tenth-century kings proclaimed laws for the running of local society, then, they were building on a moral economy which had long valued good reputation and personal knowledge and in which cooperation mattered. And it was these deep roots established by practice in the small localities of the hundred and tithing that made it possible for formal law and administration to do their work.

Disputes and Dealings

In the sense that membership of a group brought with it a bundle of recognised and reciprocal rights and obligations, the moral economy of the small world of hearth, household, and farm had much in common with the moral economy of the larger world. What becomes more evident in this wider world is the importance of good reputation and witness. The OE word *witness* meant something closer to 'having knowledge of' something or someone, rather than the modern sense of having personally observed an event. When disputes or offences came to court, witness could, as today, be testimony to the facts of a case. But witness to someone's reputation was equally important. Anglo-Saxon justice was a very public affair. Courts, 'moots', were essentially meetings where judgements were arrived at as the decision of the entire assembly of the court, the 'suitors', or settled by arbitration if the court could not decide.[10] What gave weight to legal settlements was not the sanction of punishment by the state but swearing an oath to the truth of what you say. As God is the ultimate witness, sworn oaths were vital to establish truth and oathbreaking was a terrible sin. While a great many private agreements may have been sealed by a handshake, a *borh-hand*, as they are today, transactions which involved valuable property, or which involved an accusation brought into court, needed something much more solemn and, importantly, more public. Throughout the middle ages a great many legal and commercial transactions would depend on people who were prepared to act as one another's guarantors or 'sureties' and bind themselves by oath. Standing surety for someone, becoming a 'pledge' for the truth of their evidence, could involve one in loss. Consequently, while today personal knowledge of the accused disqualifies anyone from serving on the jury which is to pronounce on their guilt or innocence, in the small, face-to-face society of medieval England personal knowledge of the accused was essential: witness consisted of people who would risk damnation by swearing on his behalf. An accused *ceorlisc* man, a non-noble, could clear himself of an accusation by finding three of his *heafodgemacena* to swear for him: the word seems to mean variously 'equals', 'fellows', and 'chief mates' and all imply personal knowledge. In a very serious case, that of stealing another's man (presumably a slave) another ruling has it that an accused man must have a number of 'free witnesses', to 'swear for' him: of whom one must be from his home township.[11] Being able to produce these 'oath-helpers' in court was a way of making one's reputation publicly known, not only as someone of 'good repute' but as a free man. Only servile people depended on the witness and pledge of security of their lords or their owners. The reputation of a slave was not something the wider community could swear to because unfree people were not part of that community. What added legality to their economic dependence was that they were often living away from their 'natural' community of family and neighbours who could stand surety for them. Their working lives were lived out not under the eye of neighbours but of their owner, and as part of the little legal world of his household they needed his *borh*, his pledge. To pledge someone, to take on responsibility for his good behaviour, could incur a cost and was not done lightly. The social world of a substantial farm may not have differed in this respect from the prestigious households of the nobility. Farm servants were regarded as much a part of their employer's household and thus legally 'under his pledge' and could be sworn for by him, as were the 'knights, chamberlains and cooks' who in the later middle ages were under a baron's pledge. The people who were in turn under the pledge of the esquires and servants of these great men are, in turn, likely to have been under theirs.[12]

Land and Witness

The witness of neighbours was vital when it came to questions of land. The land transfers that we know most about from early and mid-Saxon England were donations on a scale large enough to found a minster or endow a high-ranking royal servant. This is where the 'small world' of peasant society met the greater world. At this level, land changed hands at formal occasions, meetings of the king's council attended by important people, both lay and ecclesiastical.[13] A long tail of their names as witnesses, each 'signed' with a cross, typically ends the Latin section of the dispositive section of the charter which was the formal record of the gift. But it is unlikely that the owners of these names had much idea of what farms and meadows, small woods and clearings, ploughed land and pasture were actually changing hands 'on the ground'. In early donations, this was less of a consideration. When the king of Mercia gave land to support a new minster to be founded early in the eighth century, rough guidelines using large landscape features were enough to delineate a sizeable chunk of the west Midlands: 'between the Stour and ... (the forests of) Morfe and Kinver'.[14] In the ninth and tenth centuries, many land transfers, at least the ones for which we have charters, were on a much smaller scale and lesser landmarks, of the kind only known to local people, were becoming essential. Boundaries also mattered increasingly from the tenth century on, because that is when there began to be a more systematic collection of tithe, a tenth of all 'natural increase' in crops and animals due to the church. This 'natural increase' came from peasant fields and pastures, so accurate knowledge of, and agreement about, who owned what was vital. Only neighbours knew where one man's farmland ended, which tree marked the edge of another property, where the common meadow or the king's hedgebank was, what the little brook was called. Thus many charters from the ninth and tenth centuries have very detailed boundary clauses which delineate the boundary by means of such landmarks – from Wine's tree to Effa's farmland, to the king's deer park ... all 'according to the *ruricoli*', the 'countrymen'. Some of these were added at a later stage from the detailed knowledge which only local people could provide.[15] It could even be said that this countless anonymous rural population have literally named rural England for us for, while everyone in the locality knew where Cola's farm, or Ecca's meadow, or 'the slough' was, it was a charter that gave these an 'official' name. Some boundaries could simply have been recited verbally, but if those attached to a charter were perambulated this could well have been a ceremonial occasion, perhaps like the Rogationtide perambulations that were beginning to be part of the ceremonial year.[16] The witness of peasant neighbours was thus a vital element in the development of a concept of legal title.

The relationships and practices, conflicts and ways of resolving them, which governed the way in which life went on in the countryside on both the small scale and the large, had an enduring influence on the organisation of public life in the wider world. The units, both areas of land and groups of people, known as tithings and townships are an example. These small political worlds were the setting for negotiations between neighbours and between neighbours and strangers. Being sworn into a tithing was a kind of rite of passage into adult society: it brought the obligation to attend the hundred court, held monthly, and so meant being both subject to the public law, liable to the punishments handed out to adults, and at the same time a member of the group which formed judgements. Although the written law was inaccessible to the majority of people, highborn as well as lowborn, Lambert says of this local legal world that 'Anglo-Saxon legal discourse ... does not seem to be that of a distinct group of legal experts. There is little to suggest that it would have been beyond the comprehension of anyone who had the sort of basic legal knowledge accessible to those who attended local assemblies.'[17] At the same time as becoming a full member of local society, the new member became part of the larger political world. This too was a world structured around personal loyalty: a general oath of loyalty to the king, which first appears in written form in III Edmund, 'all shall swear ... that they will be faithful to King Edmund even as it behoves a man to be faithful to his lord'.[18]

The way the countryside was becoming organised linked peasant farmers into the political world. They became more formally part of the financial system from 1012, when *heregeld*, a tax to pay the army, was levied. A land tax, this was levied at so many pence in the hide and the hide was the unit used to distribute the burden of *heregeld* among its members. Each county's obligation was divided among its constituent hundreds, then among their constituent townships, and within the township was assessed 'according to the hides'.[19] The hide was divisible into fractions: generally of four quarters called *virgatae* or 'yardlands', and their fractions (the Danelaw equivalent, the carucate, had eight bovates) and the sum due from the township was probably divided likewise. It is likely that it was the township's responsibility to see this carried out whether collectively or through the *tungerefa*, the 'reeve of the township', with each paying according to the amount of land he had. A 'top-down' exaction it certainly was, but *heregeld* was a progressive tax, and assessing liability to it fairly, or at least in such a way that it stood a reasonable chance of being collected, was a complicated business which would certainly have needed negotiation and local knowledge. That very large sums could be collected in this way from the rural population may owe a good deal to the practice in the townships of people settling matters for themselves.

Notes

1 Coven, *'Byrstas* and *bysmeras'.'*
2 Banham and Faith, *Anglo-Saxon Farms and Farming*, 246–51; Faith, 'Cola's *tŭn'*.
3 Banham and Faith, *Anglo-Saxon Farms and Farming*, chapters 4 and 5.
4 Ine 60: Attenborough, *Laws*, 56–7, Liebermann, *Gesetze*, i. 116–17.
5 Ine 42: Attenborough, *Laws*, 48–51, Liebermann, *Gesetze*, i. 106–9.
6 Ine 42.1: Attenborough, *Laws*, 50–1, Liebermann, *Gesetze*, i. 106–9.
7 Rebanks, *The Shepherd's Life*, 185.
8 Banham and Faith, *Anglo-Saxon Farms and Farming*, 158–62.
9 VI Æthelstan 8.7: Attenborough, *Laws*, 162–9, Liebermann, *Gesetze*, i. 178–81. The legislation is discussed in more detail in Banham and Faith, *Anglo-Saxon Farms and Farming*, 160–1.
10 Wormald, 'Charters, law and the settlement of disputes'.
11 Hlothere and Eadric, 5, 8; Wihtred 21: Attenborough, *Laws*, 18–9, 20–1, 28–9, Liebermann, *Gesetze*, i. 9–10, 14.
12 Hudson, *Formation of the English Common Law*, 62.
13 Roach, 'Public rites and public wrongs'.
14 Sawyer, *Anglo-Saxon Charters*, no. 89.
15 Jenkyns, 'Charter bounds'.
16 Blair, *Church in Anglo-Saxon Society*, 486–7.
17 VI Æthelstan: Attenborough, *Laws*, 157–69; Liebermann, *Gesetze*, i. 173–83. III Edmund: Robertson, *Laws*, 12–1; Liebermann, *Gesetze*, i. 173–83. Lambert, *Law and Order*, 15. The tithing in Æthelstan's 'London Ordinance' looks as if might already be partly territorial as there are more people in some tithings than in others. Later medieval tithing groups became territorialised in the sense of becoming attached to particular holdings in the village: Schofield, 'Land, family and inheritance'; Morris, *Frankpledge System*, 10–14.
18 Lambert, *Law and Order*, 210–13.
19 S. Keynes, *'heregeld'*. Lapidge, Blair, Keynes, and Scragg, *Blackwell Encyclopaedia*.

8   Markets and Marketing

It was E. P. Thompson's study of the behaviour and beliefs of the people involved in the market for grain in the eighteenth century that led him to the concept of the moral economy, and James Davis' work on markets in the later middle ages has enabled him to add an earlier dimension, concluding, 'The marketing of food and foodstuffs remained subject to traditional moral scrutiny into the eighteenth century ... in the name of the good of the commonwealth.'[1] In the 'face-to-face' peasant society of the tithing or township individuals were known to one another and neighbours could be called on as sureties. Where country people were most likely to encounter strangers was at market. This chapter provides a glimpse of how the traditional values of the moral economy fared in an increasingly commercialised world.

Early medieval England, like most rural societies, was permeated with transactions, large and small, in which people exchanged goods and services with others. We are used to thinking of transactions, whether on a vast international scale or at the level of the domestic economy, in terms of the market: willing buyer meets willing seller, commodities change hands, or services are rendered, for an agreed price and there is a mutually acceptable currency in which this price is paid. Using a nationally and internationally recognised currency is the only way of making transactions that we recognise in 'developed' economies today. It is not the only way. Evidence from early medieval northern Europe shows that people then had ideas about transactions that were very different. One is the proper place for money. We think it is appropriate to use money, or its equivalents, in all kinds of transactions: that is part of what we consider a transaction to be, and monetization, in this sense, is essential to our view of 'development'. But some early medieval people who were familiar with coins thought that they were appropriate only in certain situations, or spheres. Some, who had no access to coins at all, or very limited access, were perfectly capable of carrying out transactions nevertheless. Northern Iberia had a very active land market, in which peasant proprietors transferred parcels of their land to monasteries, but not for money, as there was no coinage at that time. There was a coinage in Ireland, but, to judge from the laws, the court was thought to be the only appropriate sphere for using it. There were coins, although not many, in Iceland, but, to judge from the transactions recounted in the sagas, the one thing they weren't used for was buying and selling. The Scandinavian countries were short of coin but deeply involved in international trade. People in Anglo-Saxon England shared some of these attitudes, but there were many more coins circulating in early medieval England than there were in Iceland, Ireland, or Iberia and in that respect it resembled Francia more closely than any of these.[2]

Owning Things

If early medieval ideas about money were very different from those of today, it is also worth bearing in mind that ideas about the value of *things* could have been very different too. In the modern world a tool is an object designed to do a job. In early medieval society, the tools which were essential to life carried symbolic meanings too. Among the military elite, swords certainly did: some had names and their own history. The tools on the peasant farm were well-regarded in early medieval Europe: the coulter was specifically protected against theft in one of the barbarian codes and awarded the protection of the saint in the rule of St Benedict.[3] In early medieval England, similar respect appears to have been attached to the tools essential to provide the bread grain for the household, *hwetstan* and *cweorn*, 'whetstone' and 'quern': one to sharpen the sickles for reaping, and the other to grind the corn. Both querns and whetstones were made of hard stone which would stand up to years of use and could not often be found, or worked, locally. Some querns are found made from stone which came from quite nearby; one came to a Buckinghamshire farm from about 16 kilometres away. Whetstones were made of much harder stone, often sourced from the Pennines and the Lake District but they too also came from the Continent. Stone is heavy stuff, and working it a specialist craft. So whetstones and querns were everyday essentials which were also 'traded goods'. Allen J. Frantzen has assembled and interpreted the current published archaeology of quernstones in Anglo-Saxon contexts in an illuminating way, arguing that when buried with women they had 'meaning' which we can no longer recover (and about which archaeologists disagree). Querns do not seem to have been regarded as prestigious, possibly because grinding by hand was work for women and slaves. But what is not in doubt is the investment they represented in terms of the cost and labour of excavating and transporting the stones and the skill in processing and fitting them up: they were a piece of valued technology, whatever their other significance may have been.[4] If hearths and loaves had value and meaning, the quern must surely have had value and meaning too.

The whetstone, although also an everyday object, nevertheless seems to have had a particular charisma. A highly sophisticated whetstone topped by a stag, sometimes interpreted as a kind of sceptre, was found in one of the 'princely' graves at Sutton Hoo. There was something special about smiths, not only because of their magical association with Weland the smith, smith to the gods. Smiths looked after those vital attributes of powerful men – their weapons. A lord leaving his estate was entitled to take with him three servants who were essential to the proper maintenance of his station: his children's nurse (perhaps a wet-nurse), his *gerefa* ('steward'), and his smith.[5] Horseshoes are not found in England before the eleventh century, so the smith's role in this case is likely to have included keeping his master's personal armoury in good metal (or as we spell it now, mettle). A whetstone may have been something personal to its owner. If people are using sickles they must stop to sharpen them, and when they are working as a group they all must do this at the same time, so each reaper needed his or her own. For peasants, whetstones were essential to keeping an edge on the item most likely to have carried meaning: the knife. This was an essential tool around the house and the farm – how else to cut a loaf or a cheese, a thread, a withy for binding a fence, butcher a slaughtered animal or stick a pig, or reach for if a quarrel grew into a brawl? As far as we can tell, their sickles, ploughshares, and spade-ends were not buried with peasant farmers in the way that their weapons were with elite men (although if made from iron ore forged locally they had a very poor chance of survival). But knives very frequently appear in graves of people of both sexes, including some children.[6] We have already seen that objects buried with the dead may have signalled crucial stages in life, possibly marking out twelve and eighteen as crucial stages in an individual's role in the adult world at which he or she first became an adult in the eyes of the law and then someone fit to inherit. If a knife could be a cherished personal possession and peasant men, women, and children sometimes took theirs with them to the grave, just as a nobleman might take his sword, it is possible that the same kind of thinking was at work: these are not simply tools, but *emblems* and they carried a meaning, although not one that we can understand today. For *eorlisc* and *ceorlisc* alike, value appears to have involved a good deal more than monetary worth.

Means of Exchange

How could essential items like querns and whetstones have arrived on distant farms unless money had changed hands? Was coin an essential element in every transaction? It is possible that people in the past were capable of much more flexible ways of thinking about money than we are today. A great deal of what we know about the means of exchange derives from what we know about coins, and we know a great deal more about coins than we do about money in the broader sense of a medium in which transactions are carried out. We also, of course, know much more about the official and regulated use of coins than we do about their unofficial, informal, and unsanctioned use. There is very little archaeological evidence of any kind of what was going on in the countryside in the fifth and sixth centuries after the end of the Roman administration and the collapse of the villa-based lifestyle of the landowning and administrative class. With that collapse went the ending of the demands of the state for taxation in cash and kind, the *annona*, which had appropriated so much peasant surplus. With the withdrawal of the army in the early fifth century, no more Roman coins were minted in Britain. However, there were still plenty about. Even when the highly regulated coinage of the Roman world was a thing of the past, its coins may not have lost their credibility at a stroke: some were hoarded and may have been used for transactions between people who had learned to trust them long after there had ceased to be an 'official' currency backed by the Roman state. They did not apparently use them as jewellery, a common non-monetary use of coins, although, like other Roman coins found in early Anglo-Saxon graves, they may have been regarded as valuable objects rather than useful currency. In an era when there was no longer any official supervision of the currency, or taxation to fund civic institutions, no longer any attractive consumer goods to buy, and no villa-owners to sell to, there was a very steep decline in production for the market: very few manufactured goods are found from the fifth and sixth centuries.[7] However, the end of official markets and marketing need not have meant an end to everyday, small-scale monetary transactions, even if there was no longer an officially sanctioned coinage. It is possible that people went on using out-of-date coins because, over time, they had learned the usefulness of coin in small local transactions.[8]

Thinking only in terms of an officially sanctioned currency may be a barrier to understanding early medieval attitudes to money. Real-life practice may have been more flexible about money than what official statements prescribe. Using coin as a base by which to reckon value is not the same as using coin as money for commercial transactions. Thus monetary tariffs could serve as a guide to the seriousness of an offence. The earliest laws we have, those of Æthelbert of Kent, set penalties in shillings, a gold-based coin, at a time when, as far as we can tell from the evidence of finds, there was very little gold coinage actually in circulation. Compensation payments, wergeld, were owed for various types of injury, and *wites*, fines owed to the king, were also reckoned in shillings. To stand surety for someone meant to be prepared to pay up if he defaulted on the payment of a fine. An extremely aggressive attack, say in an alehouse brawl which left the wounded man minus an eye and with a fractured skull, could let the aggressor in for a fine of more than 60 shillings. The shilling was supposed to be the equivalent of the Roman gold *solidus* but it was a unit of account, not an actual coin. People seem to have found it useful to *reckon* in shillings even if shillings were nowhere to be had. If so, this implies a considerably sophisticated attitude, widely held. A new low-denomination coin, the tiny silver penny, sometimes known as the *sceat*, was introduced in large numbers late in the seventh century, followed by a larger and easier to handle 'broad penny' from the eighth century.[9] A likely context for this is a general revival in the northern European economy. Where direct witness and local reputation were not easy to come by, a trusted currency was vital. The kind of commerce we know most about is cross-Channel, between Frankish and Anglo-Saxon traders, carried out through many intermediaries and in at least two languages. At this level, trading partners do not need to know each other personally, although many probably did: what they need is a trusted medium of exchange and if this medium is a currency, then it is one which, whatever its design and provenance, has an agreed-upon and carefully regulated content of precious metal. Numismatists have provided a very advanced body of knowledge about what, it now appears, was a highly advanced system. From the later eighth century, Anglo-Saxon rulers – probably in emulation of, and in cooperation with, their Frankish counterparts across the Channel, and the people they traded with across the North Sea – instituted a coinage which was highly controlled in terms of its weight, which was manipulated to be compatible with continental issues. From the late tenth century, standards were maintained by the periodic recalling of an old currency and the issue of a new one, henceforth the only legal tender.[10] The *idea* of legal tender was energetically promoted. A tale known as the 'Legend of the Seven Sleepers' can be read as propaganda for such a view. Seven men who had fallen into a deep sleep in the reign of one emperor woke up many years later in the reign of another. Going to market to buy food, they offered coins to a trader who, recognising that these were not current currency, shopped them to the authorities. As to actual practice, the only kind of evidence which can give us anything like a firm date by which individual coins were in use is that from hoards of coins deliberately deposited together, generally buried. These cannot have been deposited until after the date of the latest coin they contain. As most hoards contain coins near in date to the date of deposit and few that are out of date, their evidence shows that, by and large, official standards were effectively imposed.

Markets Official and Unofficial

Public scrutiny was one way of patrolling and controlling the officially sanctioned use of coin, and rulers in the tenth century appear to have made continuing efforts to ensure this, limiting all transactions to 'ports' (the word was not confined to seaports) or to public meetings such as the hundred court, *folcesgemot*. Laws from the first half of the tenth century rule that transactions of buying and selling of goods worth more than 20 pence must be carried on in a *port*, that is to say in the milieu most closely under official control of town officials, the port-reeves, and, in the case of some market towns, where the mint was.[11]

The growing royal control of both coinage and markets at the level of both international and inland trade is evident from numismatic evidence and from legislation, but how coinage and markets worked at the level at which they attracted legislation may not be the most helpful approach to the peasant economy. The situation in the countryside could well have been much less tidy. Although tenth-century kings issued laws to regulate trading there, the cattle market at the hundred court already seems a long way from the world of regulated mints and authorised coinages and of authorised markets or 'ports'. Well away from the regulated world, a great deal of buying and selling must have gone on. People did not only go to goods: goods came to them. Away from major routes, country people could buy portable goods 'up-country', perhaps in places like the 'chapmen's dell' on the Hampshire Downs. *Ceapmanna*, 'chapmen', might be put up on their travels in people's houses where local people could come round to see what they had for sale. The possibilities for dispute that such petty trading could give rise to could have been why the householder was made legally responsible for chapmen lodging under his roof.[12] For some essential commodities, pottery being the one we know most about owing to its presence in the archaeological record, peasants and elites alike depended on major distribution systems. In the mid-Saxon period, what amounted to mass-production began in Ipswich, and fragments of Ipswich ware are found on rural sites throughout East Anglia and beyond (although in much of western Britain people seem largely to have managed without pottery). Fragile goods such as pottery and heavy goods such as querns were likely to have been moved in bulk by water: possibly they were bought and sold at riverside markets. The saltways brought this essential preservative by known routes used to supply large-scale consumers. But small consumers needed salt too, and place-names like Salthrop may have arisen for places where the salters stopped to trade with people of the locality. Peasants were largely self-supporting in food, but the peasant economy was involved in both urban and rural markets. Growing towns needed provisioning: towns-people were a market for meat and other goods brought in from the countryside How did peasants pay the chapman, the pottery merchant, or the salter?

The supply of cash in peasant households must have fluctuated a good deal, largely due to the fact that marketing in the rural economy had its own seasonality, set by the rhythm of the farming year.[13] From the mid-Saxon period some peasant farms were producing wool for the market, albeit on a small scale, and when they had sold their wool (possibly in advance) to a broker, many people could have had coins in their pockets (or purses). Working for wages as *hyringmanna* on a labour-hungry estate like Ely could bring in cash, and Ely was in the market for small amounts of corn and small numbers of sheep which look like purchases from small local producers.[14] Autumn sales of cattle not worth keeping through the winter, or surplus corn after the harvest, may have been traded at small, probably seasonal, and unregulated places beyond the orbit of official-dom in the regulated market towns. Many of the coins (and other small metal objects) which have been dropped and lost and found again at what have been called 'productive sites', those where exceptional numbers of metal-detected finds have been made, could have come from peasant purses. Some of these places look like informal cattle markets: an ingeni-ous piece of place-name scholarship by Ann Cole has identified, from 'nettle' place-names, sites where large numbers of animals were gathered, their droppings enriching the nitrogen content of the soil, on which nettles thrive. Place-names may also, she suggests, indicate drove roads which brought cattle and sheep to market: one such name, *heord-wic*, now Hardwick, is much too common to have been an officially recognised market.[15] These were places where in addition to gambling and drinking, themselves two important aspects of marketing, a large number of transactions had gone on. While those with money enough to be able to deposit in a hoard appear to have respected the letter of the law as to what was legal tender, people with small amounts of cash may have been a good deal less scrupulous about using out-of-date coins. Although there is no way of telling when the coins found at such places had been lost and so no means of telling whether or not they had been used long after they were no longer officially acceptable, it seems likely that away from the regulated world of towns and town officials, mints and money-ers, these might have been places where people took a more relaxed attitude towards what was legal tender.

There was certainly money about. Numismatists claim to be able to work out how much. They tell us that were more coins in England in the late seventh century than in the twelfth, a time when both economy and population had increased and inflation had set in. But the supply fluctu-ated. Shortages of silver mined abroad very quickly resulted in shortages of coin, and Scandinavian finds reveal that large numbers of coins were moving across the sea from England. Peasants needed cash.[16] Pennies were needed to pay the geld and while small tenants and workers on estates were exempt, peasant farmers with their own land would have had to dig into their purses. And pay they did, as the thousands of pounds which were raised testify.[17] Even slaves had *peculium*, their personal savings. Records of manumissions in the 1070s show them paying as much as 2 pounds to buy their freedom from the religious houses that owned them. 'Every free hearth' owed church dues, and a money pay-ment called *gafol* of a shilling a yardland appears in some lists of peasant obligations.[18] We have no records of peasants' land transactions until well after the Conquest, although it is hard to imagine that none ever bought an extra acre or two, or sold off a field in hard times, as great landlords did. Yet there were never enough coins in circulation for every petty transaction to be accompanied by money changing hands. More-over, Anglo-Saxon coins were of too high a denomination to have been used for petty sales and purchases. The only actual coin in circulation was the silver penny, and that was too valuable for the humdrum business of acquiring a pot or a pig, standing a round for the beership, buying a dozen eggs, selling a calf, or renting a piece of land from a neighbour. Nevertheless, it is fair to assume that this was the area of life where small transactions were common. How did people manage? Credit is likely to have been an important part of the answer, as it was in later medieval England, when 'running up a tab' and money lending and borrowing on a small scale were essential to the economy of the rural community, but early medieval England has no evidence that might record this.

People did not manage by abandoning the *idea* of money. All that is necessary to make possible the transactions that people make with one another is that they agree on a unit of value. Coinless transactions are not those in which money plays no part at all: on the contrary, as a unit of value a coin is a very useful mental tool, particularly if its silver content is known to be policed by the authorities. A farmer buying a cow needed to be sure of its value in terms of a unit that the seller recognised too. And if the cow were to be traded on to another farmer, then it would be necessary that he, too, would recognise the chosen unit as a reliable way of reckoning value. The unit of value could be a coin, but neither of the buyers would need to have enough coins to make up a 'price', as long as each had, or could get hold of, enough of the chosen unit or its equivalent in goods, and as long as all the people involved recognised the value of the chosen unit. What made such 'commodity money' work was that it was socially recognised and respected. While many transactions in the peasant economy may have taken place without official scrutiny, when it came to buying and selling, peasants could not afford to take a relaxed attitude to fair dealing, witness, and reputation. Even in modern society, money is not culturally neutral; the imagery of royalty and cultural icons on banknotes and coins testifies to what items are felt to be of value. Rome had once taken pride in being able to give all its citizens bread and the weight value of Roman money was based on grain: the carob, barleycorn (and later the wheat) grain. In Anglo-Saxon society the idea of value was embedded in the importance attached to cattle. The Old English word for 'cattle', *feoh*, meant property in general. The words for markets and marketing, buying and selling, *ceap*, *ceapstow*, all derive from the word for cattle, *ceap*. So does *yrfe*, 'inheritance'. If people needed a way of expressing value, it is likely that livestock would have been their choice. In Debby Banham's words: 'wealth must overwhelmingly have consisted of livestock'. This may be why the law code of Ine of Wessex, which has given us other glimpses of the peasant economy, contains, under the heading 'About the worth of a ewe', a law which appears to be setting price: 'A ewe with her lamb is worth a shilling until fourteen nights (i.e. a fortnight) after Easter'. The same attitude to value appears again, two hundred years later, in a law of Æthelstan which settles the *ceapgild*, the compensation which could be claimed for a horse, ox, cow, or sheep. It would be a poor farmer who thought one sheep was worth as much as any other, or a good milker not worth a great deal more than a cow who went dry early after calving, a good riding horse far more than an unbroken colt.[19] Royal laws seem to sit very well with farmers' ideas of worth.

Although Anglo-Saxon England was a commercialised world, it was one which nevertheless was short of enough coins for every transaction and those there were had to circulate at high 'velocity'.[20] In such a world, the means of payment could be anything which both parties agreed was of value. People seem to have been comfortable with making payments in both cash and kind if both parties had agreed on the mixture. It does not seem to have been the case that the rich used coin, the poor commodities. This might remind us that while price and means of payment are standardised in modern economies, in many countries which are also part of the modern world a transaction is not such a cut-and-dried affair but involves bargaining and negotiation. Nowadays bargaining is generally about the price to be paid, but in the Anglo-Saxon world it may also have been about the means of payment. In Æthelbert's code, if someone kills a man he can pay either in coin or 'in property about which there is no question of fraud (*unfacne feo*)'. From Ine's laws we learn that people who rented out rights in woodland for foraging pigs might pay the owner in bacon or in pigs, and that the hire of an ox from a neighbour could be paid for in cash, or fodder, or a mixture of the two.[21] The laws about the value of animals suggest that they may have been part of a system of 'commodity money' in which a 'sheep's worth' could have been a way in which people thought of the value of things other than sheep. A protracted negotiation about land acquired by the Abbey of Ely included the abbot's paying as part of the final settlement *xx solidos ovium et palfridum pro x solidis*, 'twenty shillings-worth of sheep and a horse worth ten shillings'.[22] Nor were coins the only form in which the value of gold and silver were recognised. James Campbell collected from charter evidence some telling examples of how land changed hands between members of the Anglo-Saxon elite, or at least those of enough status for their dealings to be recorded in documents that have survived. The 'price' might be made up of a range of desirable domestic goods: beds, linen sheets, slave girls, gold cups, and jewellery, whose value was calculable by their weight as well as their design and/or 'as much silver as he can lay his hands on'. Rory Naismith has amplified Campbell's work, finding that although gold was the most highly valued, 'payments partly or entirely in commodities other than gold and silver continued throughout the Anglo-Saxon period'.[23] In much the same way, peasants probably 'bought' goods and services with other goods and services and as much cash, or its equivalents in units of account, that they could lay their hands on. Among people who knew one another, what mattered was that both parties agreed to the 'price', in whatever terms that was expressed, that the transaction was duly witnessed, and that both parties were vouched for by others who would stand the rap if they defaulted. In the 'real' economy, despite the sophistication of its currency and its regulated markets, people across Anglo-Saxon society were able to conceptualise value in very flexible ways. What is equally important is that, for *eorlisc* and *ceorlisc* alike, when it came to the market witness and reputation were of great importance.

Notes

1 Davis, *Medieval Market Morality*, 417.
2 Scandinavia: Kilger, 'Wholeness and holiness'; Ireland: Davies, 'Sale price and valuation'; Ireland: Gerriets, 'Money in early Christian Ireland'.
3 Le Goff, *Time, Work and Culture*, 81–3.
4 For hand grinding: Banham, *Food and Drink*, 17–18; querns and whetstones: Frantzen, *Food, Eating and Identity*, chapter 4; Arnold, *An Archaeology*, 133. Palmer, 'Hinterlands of three southern English towns', 56.
5 Ine 63: Attenborough, *Laws*, 56–7; Liebermann, *Gesetze*, i. 118–19.
6 Knives in graves: Arnold, *An Archaeology*, 100; Stoodley, 'Childhood'.
7 Dark, *Civitas to Kingdom*, 214–16 interprets the distribution of Roman coins as evidence of payments as part of British diplomatic strategy while no longer in use as currency.
8 Dark, *Civitas to Kingdom*, 200–6.
9 Naismith, *Money and Power*, 4–9.
10 Metcalf, 'Variations in the composition of the currency'. The argument that the English coinage was as effectively regulated as this is critiqued by Molyneux, *Formation of the English Kingdom*, chapter 4. I am grateful to Elina Screen for her help with coin evidence.
11 1 Edward 1; II Æthelstan 12–14; Attenborough, *Laws*, 114–15, 134–5, Liebermann, *Gesetze*, i. 138–9, 156–7.
12 Hlothere and Eadric, 15, Attenborough, *Laws*, 20–1; Liebermann, *Gesetze*, i. 11.
13 Spufford, *Money and Its Use*, 382–4.
14 Naismith, 'Ely memoranda', 362.
15 Cole, 'The use of *netel* in place-names'; 'The use of ON *nata* in place-names', 'Searching for early drove roads'; Blackburn, '"Productive sites"'.
16 For peasants' use of coin: Naismith, *Money and Power*, 278–82.
17 Keynes, heregeld. Lapidge, Blair, Keynes, and Scragg, *Blackwell Encyclopaedia*, s.v.
18 Pelteret, *Catalogue of English Post-Conquest Vernacular Documents*, 90–5.
19 Ine 55, 59: 54–5, 56–7, Liebermann, *Gesetze*, i. 114–15. VI Æthelstan 6, Attenborough, *Laws*, 160–2, Liebermann, *Gesetze*, i. 176–7. The much more detailed laws, dating back to Ine's time, about the injuries that might affect the real value of individual oxen and cows – broken horns, damaged tails and eyes – make it likely that there was also a sort of 'wergeld' for livestock. Banham and Faith, *Anglo-Saxon Farms and Farming*, 84–7 at 87.
20 Nightingale, 'The evolution of weight standards'.
21 Ine 49.3: Attenborough, *Laws*, 52–3, Liebermann, *Gesetze*, i. 110–11. Æthelbert 30: Attenborough, 8–9, Liebermann, *Gesetze*, i. 5.
22 Blake, *Liber Eliensis*, 88; Fairweather, *Liber Eliensis*, 111–12.
23 Campbell, 'The sale of land', Naismith, 'Payments for land and privilege', 313.

Part IV

The Wolf Sniffs the Wind

9   *Hwilom Wæs*: Archbishop Wulfstan's Old Social Order

He called himself 'The Wolf', a pun on his name, and his voice comes from the heart of the late Anglo-Saxon establishment. Wulfstan (d. 1020) spent his working life as an important churchman who moved in the highest circles of the political world. As a theologian and moralist whose career spanned the transition from the reign of Æthelred to Scandinavian rule under Cnut, he was a powerful influence on the legislation of both. In Wulfstan's time England, which had enjoyed over a hundred years year free from threats from outside in the shape of Viking raids, was again facing a Scandinavian threat but this time not from raiding parties but from Danish armies and fleets. In the seemingly more ordered warfare of the earlier Scandinavian invasions in the ninth century, formal negotiations and agreements had been sealed by written treaty between Alfred and the Danish leader Guthrum. Then Danes had negotiated equal compensation for people of roughly equal status, Danish freedmen being reckoned equal to English *ceorls*. Now, in Wulfstan's view, in this 'world turned upside-down' the ranks are reversed and if 'any slave runs away from his master and ... becomes a Viking (i.e. fights for the Danes) ... and if the slave kills a thegn, no wergeld is paid to any of his kindred, but if the thegn slays the slave whom he owned before, he shall pay the price of a thegn'.[1]

Wulfstan's 'Sermon of the Wolf to the English', from which this passage comes, was possibly preached at the time of the raids, so to an audience who knew well what violence was. He draws no distinction between sinful behaviour and natural disaster that war brought with it: 'devastation, famine, bloodshed, stealing and killing, sedition and pestilence, murrain and disease, spoliation by robbers ... grievous taxes, bad seasons, crop failure ... treachery and abuse of sanctuary'.[2] Like all churchmen of his era, he thought that it was not simply power politics that had brought the horrors of invasion and bloodshed, but sin, for which these assorted ills were the punishment. The remedy lay not simply in military response, but in the renewal of Christian behaviour, specifically by prayer. In this he was conventional enough: the leaders of any Christian country at that time would insist on mass prayer campaigns, increased insistence on church attendance, and so on, as part of the 'war effort'. But what is interesting and original about Wulfstan is not his view that during his time there had been a great falling away from the Christian behaviour of the past, which too is conventional enough. What troubled him as much as the English people's failure to attend church or pay their tithes, or their routinely sinful misbehaviour, was the collapse of the values embedded in the old social order. This is the point of view from which this part of the book approaches Wulfstan's work, in this chapter looking at the private worlds of lords' estates and peasant farms, in the following chapter at the public world of courts and warfare.

Wulfstan was knowledgeable about rural life. It is a sign of this that one of his political works, now called the 'Institutes of Polity', differentiates *yrþlingas*, 'men who plough', from *aehtemen*, 'men who work'. This is a distinction which was crucial in the middle ages, between people who would be called in France *manoeuvriers*, 'manual workers', and *laboureurs*, 'people who plough'.[3] He was here quoting his contemporary and friend Ælfric, abbot of Eynsham, another prestigious cleric who also knew a good deal about life beyond the cloister. Ælfric composed a question and answer exercise, a 'Colloquy', to teach novice monks Latin, in which the student asks workers in different occupations to describe their jobs. While outside the monastery a man ploughing his own land behind his own team was in the upper ranks of the peasantry and could make his own decisions about what work his team should do, estate ploughmen were commonly slaves. Ælfric's ploughman is a slave who works on an estate for a lord and owes a set amount of work, an acre or more a day, and even in freezing weather dare not stay at home for fear of the lord. His work is hard 'because I am not free'.[4] Men like Ælfric and Wulfstan knew what was going on in the countryside. Yet all Wulfstan's writings about rural life, practical although they are, are imbued with the same moral ideas as his advice to kings and bishops, extending them to the principles of estate management to exemplify what Patrick Wormald has called the 'holiness of society': the structure of society was not simply a matter of social function but of moral order. Wulfstan spent his working life involved in the administration of the estates of two of the major landowners in England: the cathedrals of London and Worcester, as well as one in difficulties, the archbishopric of York. Stephen Baxter has illuminated the way that his involvement in management decisions was not simply because he had a head for business but stemmed from his belief that the church's property was 'God's property'.[5] As bishop of London and then archbishop of York, a post which he held in plurality with the bishopric of Worcester, he was the lord of the thousands of acres which made up the church's estates so, like other prelates in pre-Conquest England, he needed to be knowledgeable about estate management. Wulfstan appears to have been exceptionally so, the first known to us in a tradition of bishops who took an informed interest in the episcopal estates. In the work associated with him, and probably owned by him, *Be gesceadwisan gerefan*, the eponymous 'Canny Steward' must be knowledgeable about the work that needed to be done on a large property, how farming strategies needed to adapt to local conditions, how the estate workers should be supervised. He may have been writing from direct experience, gained early in his career.[6] The vast episcopal estate at Fulham, one of its earliest acquisitions, was rated at forty hides on the eve of the Conquest and was always treated as one of the 'demesne manors', kept in hand to provide for the bishops and their households rather than leased out. In bishop Theodred's will of 942, not long before Wulfstan's time at London, it appears as a smooth-running concern with its own established ways of working: 'at Fulham everything is to be left as it now stands' and a labour supply which included unfree people 'unless one wishes to free any of my men'. This may in fact have happened, for there are no slaves in the Domesday entry for Fulham.[7] There we glimpse something of the workforce which replaced them: cottagers, some with gardens, some with tiny amounts of land, and boarders. There were also *villani* with a hide of land, others with half or a quarter of a hide, people with other people 'under' them, sokemen and 'Frenchmen', and London burgesses. Domesday records a different era, of course, and we cannot know what changes had taken place, both before and after 1066, at Fulham. What makes it interesting in the context of Wulfstan and his work and ideas is that it shows what a wide range of people an estate could contain: from people with involvements and obligations in, the wider political world like sokemen and burgesses, to farmers ranging from the well-provided to the very ill-provided with land, down to people managing on a combination of the produce of their own small plots and farm work.[8]

In spiritual and secular life alike, in Wulfstan's view, order and regularity are best ensured by getting things down in writing. His influence on the laws of Æthelred and Cnut stemmed as much from of his moral philosophy as did his homilies. His rules, which read more like exhortations, for canons, for the clergy, for kings and lay nobles, for *ealdormen* and their duties, have many of the same concerns with the social order as do his vivid evocations of the threat that young armed men presented to social order and national defence. His own view of the moral economy also permeates what he has to tell us about the administration of a great estate. A vernacular document of great interest to Wulfstan takes us into that world.[9] The Latin translation in the early twelfth-century legal compilation *Quadripartitus* gave it the titles *De dignitate hominum* and *Rectitudines singularum personarum*: 'Concerning the ranks of men' and 'The rules of each kind of position in life'. P. D. A. Harvey, building on the work of the Wulfstan experts Dorothy Bethurum and Dorothy Whitelock, was able to set out what has remained the authoritative analysis of this text and Wulfstan's connection with it. In summary: it was derived from a text written in the tenth century, Harvey favours the mid-century and believes that the original compiler wrote from his experience of a particular estate. Wulfstan revised this text, and this revised version is the one preserved in the *Quadripartitus*. Most of *Rectitudines singularum personarum* describes in great detail the obligations of the different categories of people who might be found on an estate, and the entitlements due to them. It has thus always been of great interest to historians of rural society and as a work of estate management ranked as 'estate literature' alongside the work of other practical churchmen like the 'Rules of St Robert' by Bishop Robert Grosseteste of Lincoln. Because it contains such detail about how many days labour are owed, what rent paid, how many acres to be ploughed, it has often been taken as an early example of a custumal, a record of the tenants' obligations on a particular estate, many examples of which survive from the twelfth and thirteenth centuries.[10] However, there is a significant difference. *Rectitudines* has no personal names at all: it does not purport to record what individuals owe, but what different categories of people typically do.

If its sole purpose, however, had been as a guide to what the lord of a large estate in the late pre-Conquest period was properly entitled to demand from the people who worked there, and what he was properly obliged to provide them with in return, this would not explain two further features of *Rectitudines*. The first is what it tells us about at the very beginning: the duties of thegns and geneatas. The passage regarding the thegn is one of two, the second being about the *geneat*, which appear to have been added to a text which was already in existence. If they are the work of the same reviser, these could well have been additions made by Wulfstan himself. If that were the case then, having dealt with the obligations of nobles in his 'Institutes of Polity', Wulfstan would here be addressing the next levels down in lay society, starting at the top with the thegn. The thegn's duties are reciprocal: he owes them 'for his book-right'. The title is *Thegenes lagu*, 'the *law* concerning the thegn', perhaps because the thegn's bookland is within the realm of public, not estate, law. The thegn's law is that he should be 'worthy of his bookright' (his holding his land by charter) and that he should do three things from his land: *fyrd* (army) service, *burh*-work, and bridge work. Liable to the these 'common burdens' of army service and bridge and defence work, he also had duties connected with the lord's person and his residences and military affairs: 'And from many estates, *landum*, further estate obligations arise by the king's order, such as deer hedging at the king's dwelling, *sceorp to friðscipe*, guarding the coast, guarding the lord and military watch, almsgiving and church scot and many other divers things'.

The Rules of the Estate

Next comes *Geneatas riht*. This is 'what is correct', rather than 'what is the law', for it concerns the *geneat* whose obligations are within the private realm of the estate. His duties, and those of the people whose obligations and entitlements follow, vary according to 'what is established on the estate: on some he must pay *land gafol*, land-due, and a yearly pig for pasturage, ride and do carrying service and lead loads (i.e. be in charge of a packhorse train), work and provide food for his lord, reap and mow, cut deer hedges and construct "stands", build and hedge the *burh*, bring strangers to the *tūn* (the lord's dwelling), pay churchscot and alms, keep guard over his lord, look after the horses and take messages near and far as he is bid.' Many of these duties were to continue well into the later middle ages. Involving riding and transport, carrying cash, and having access to the lord's household, as well as obligations, they remained, as they are here, marks of free and superior status of a category of people who have particular obligations to the owner of an estate.[11]

Next is the cottager, *kotsetla*, who has a cottage holding of at least five acres 'or more if it is the custom on the estate: ... it is too little if it is less because his work is frequent'. His duties also vary according to the estate: on some he must work first for his lord every Monday throughout the year, or three days each week at harvest. He does not pay land rent, *landgafol*. Poor and hard-worked but considered free, 'he owes his hearth-penny every Holy Thursday as every free man does'. The cottager owes the duties at the lord's hall and at the hunt and is liable to be called out for coastguard duty like the *geneat* and the thegn. Cottagers were part of what must have been a very useful pool of farm labourers for estate owners, available for off-farm jobs like coastguarding. By granting them small plots of land, and with no obligation to provide them with food, lords obtained from cottagers a regular supply of weekly labour and were guaranteed extra hands at harvest. Yet in their small way the cottagers remained heads of households, and free.[12]

Also provided with land, but significantly less independent, are people whose *riht*, their obligations and entitlements, looks back to the tied tenants of Ine's law, who having been housed and 'outfitted' by the lord, are tied to the estate. These are the *geburas*.[13] Like the cottager, the *gebur* is legally free so must pay the hearth-penny, due from 'every free hearth', to the church. The lord has provided him with two oxen, six sheep, and *vii æceras gesawene on his gyrde landes*, 'seven acres of his yard of land already sown', and the necessary tools and domestic utensils. He must cultivate three acres of this as his *gafol-land*, sown with seed from his own barn. All these obligations come into force when he has had for a year the land on which they are owed. As when he dies it all returns to the lord: 'let the lord take back what he leaves'; his children had no right to inherit (although in practice may well have done so). The advantage to land-owners of such tenancies had always been that they could be used to secure reliable supplies of labour. The *gebur* is part of the essential workforce of the estate. His obligations, which are given in great detail, are extremely onerous. 'On some estates' he owes two days' unspecified labour, 'weekwork', each week, every week of the year doing 'whatever he is ordered', and three days a week from Candlemas to Easter. He owes ten pence *gafol*, twenty-three sesters of barley at Martinmas, and two hens, and at Easter a young sheep or two pence. From the beginning of the ploughing season until Martinmas, he must plough an acre a week and collect the seed for sowing from, or possibly deliver the seed to, the lord's barn. He ploughs three acres as boon-work and two more for extra pasture. In spite of their name, these 'boons' could well already have been virtually compulsory on many estates when *Rectitudines* was composed: those that the *gebur* owes are among his compulsory duties and what Domesday Book records as *consuetudines*, 'customs', could very well have included this invaluable source of labour which could be called on when needed. While the text insists that practice differs between estates, on some heavy, on others light, these obligations have very close parallels with those of the *geburas* listed in a survey of an estate at Tidenham in Gloucestershire, also drawn up before the Conquest. Harsh though these conditions are, the logic of reciprocity prevails: while the economy of the *gebur* and his household are subordinated to the needs of the lord and his household, this is in return for the 'outfit' he has been granted.

Geburas have always been important in debates about the origins of serfdom, for good reason. The package of renders and work which they owed in return for their land, particularly the regular weekwork, has a great deal in common with the lists of the obligations of villein tenants with customary holdings in the later medieval manor. This fact has played an important part in interpretations of rural England which would date the origins of the manor to the early Anglo-Saxon period.[14] Certainly, *Rectitudines* in itself suggests some very long-standing and widespread conditions, and what we know about the origins of the conditions of tenure of the *geburas* shows such a class to have been an essential element of private landholding from at least the eighth century. They were in all essentials like the people in Ine's law, who had fallen into dependence by accepting housing, land, tools, and livestock in return for rent and labour. But they cannot be taken as typical of the peasantry at large: *geburas* were a particular category of peasant whose economy was embedded in the history of private landowning. Like the ploughmen, shepherds, and oxherds in Ælfric's Colloquy, the *geneatas, kotsetlas,* and *geburas* described in *Rectitudines* are people with particular roles because their holdings were part of the lord's inland, their arable physically closely integrated with, if not actually part of, the arable of the lord's home farm. It was the regular weekwork of the *gebur* which made the inland economy viable. T. H. Aston's suggestion that they lived in physically distinct spaces which had been laid out as tenancies 'which bear all the marks of lordly policy' has been amply borne out by subsequent archaeological work revealing planned elements and regular small plots in pre-Conquest settlements.[15] They were subject to an insecurity which was inherent in the terms of their tenure. Granted land, part already sown, livestock, and tools, they have been set up in tenancies which will return to the lord at their death. These conditions set them apart from even the poorest peasant farmers, whose children could count on inheriting their farms and their livestock, and may well have undermined their standing in the community at large. Although some may have had better housing and conditions than the general run of farm workers, *geburas* had no security because if they lost the job, they lost both home and land.[16]

Next are the specialist stockmen and women, the shepherds, cowmen, beekeepers and the like whose work involved them with care of the most valuable asset of any landholding: its livestock. Caedmon, in Bede's story about his miraculous gift of song, was this kind of worker, a cowman housed near the shippon and with the duty of checking the cattle at night. Such people were skilled workers, who needed to live near the animals in order to care for them. In the case of cattle used in traction, as well as being responsible for their well-being and productivity, they needed to be able to train them. They continued into post-Conquest England as permanent estate workers, or *famuli,* a term which in classical Latin has strong servile associations. Their entitlements are closely linked to their jobs: they are more like perquisites than rations. A valued perk might have been permission to keep one's own animals in with the lord's so they would be better fed and housed. The swineherd in charge of the demesne herd can have a styed pig as well as a slave's rations. Two workers with particularly important roles get shoes and gloves: we can equally well interpret this as simply being provided with the gear they needed for their heavy work in the fields, or as something more akin to a gift. The oxherd can put two of his own cattle in the shared pasture and receives shoes and gloves: he has care of the plough oxen The *folgere*, the ploughman, gets shoes and gloves (he was the one who held the plough and walked in the furrow, as opposed to the boy who led the oxen and walked on the turf) as well as two acres of land.[17] The shepherd gets twelve nights' dung at Christmas, a lamb, and the milk of the flock for a week after the equinox and a bowlful of whey or buttermilk all summer. The cowherd gets the beestings, the colostrum-rich milk, of an old cow for a week after calving, of a young one for a fortnight, and so on. These are perks tied to the jobs carried out by specialist workers who had smallholdings of their own and partly supported themselves from them.

Lastly, slaves. Slaves were a very important part of the labour force, still about 10 per cent of the population in 1086, and could be found on every size of agricultural enterprise, from the great estate to the family farm.[18] Some had, in the chilling phrase, 'sold their heads', that is to say had forfeited their legal freedom, 'for food.' As far as we know from the very inadequate archaeological record of housing at this level of society, they did not live in barracks as classical slaves did. They may have had no productive land at all, or very little, as they were entitled to slave rations, *metsunge*. These were for men twelve pounds of good corn, two sheep carcases, and one good cow, for women eight pounds of corn, one sheep or a penny for winter food, one sester of beans for Lenten food, whey in summer or one penny. The slaves' rations are an example of the fact that *Rectitudines* is as precise about entitlements as it is about obligations. While it is about what custom entitles lords of estates to demand from the people who work for them, and it is also about what they are entitled to receive from the lords in return. This part of the text concludes: '*Land-lagu*, estate law, varies, as I said before, nor do we set down these customs for all districts, as we said before, but we set down what custom is where it is known to us. If we learn better, we will delight in maintaining it, according to the district in which we are then living.'

Local Custom

The final part of the text is different in several ways from what has gone before. It begins with a distinction. Someone in authority, 'he who has the *scyre*', should 'always know what are the *ealdlandrædan*', 'the long-standing rules on the estate', which is what the preceding sections have set out, and *hwæt deode ðeaw*, 'what is people's custom'. What follows appears to be this 'people's custom'. This distinction was clearly very important to Wulfstan and his contemporaries and this, along with the fact that it is different from the main part of the text, makes it tempting to ascribe it to him. This section also records entitlements and lists a number of meals awarded for particular tasks, but it reads as if the information has been garnered not from a particular estate which was well-known to the writer, but from a much broader source. *Feola sindon folcgerihta*, 'local people's customs are manifold', and, it points out, what is recorded may apply only in particular communities, *on sumre ðeode*. Two meals, at Easter and Christmas ('winter'), are not connected with the transfer of labour but with the traditional cycle of the year, this recalls the responsibility of the heads of households to ensure observance. The remainder are rewards for the boon-works, the labour supplied at peak times by the peasantry of the neighbourhood when 'prayed for' by a lord. They differ from district to district and use the vocabulary of *feorm*: '*on sumre ðeode*, 'among some people' *winterfeorm*, 'winter *feorm*', Easter *feorm*, *benfeorm for ripe*, food for harvest, *gitfeorm* for ploughing, *mædmed*, 'mowing-reward', 'rick-reward' at stacking, 'at wood-loading a wain-tree' 'at corn carting a rick-cup' 'and many things which I cannot recount'. These meals are described in the language of proper reward, not of doles or rations. *Feorm, feormian*, are terms which we have encountered already as the obligation of owners of hides to provide food for the king, as well as the sustenance with which a household sustained its members. The obligations of reciprocity evidently remained an essential element in the moral economy of the countryside, in which 'hospitality' in the form of food and drink played a prominent part.[19] The *feorm* and the *med*, the 'rewards' in *Rectitudines*, are the meals, or the components of meals, owed as part of a mutually recognised (though by no means equal) relationship and are the long-established local customs of an area, *folcgerihta*, not the *landrædan*, the conditions of service on a particular estate. *Ealdlandrædan*, what the landlord could legitimately demand from the people on his estate, still had to take account of *folcrihte*, the customs that expressed what local people felt that they were entitled to.

This final part of the text ends: 'This is a memorandum of peoples' provisions and all that I have enumerated before.' I think this means that the author feels he has satisfactorily dealt with the customary food entitlements of all the various categories of people. The implication is that these were considered as important as labour and rent obligations. A landowner's *gerefas*, his reeves and bailiffs, would have run his estates day to day, so one purpose behind the compilation of *Rectitudines* might well have been to ensure that they paid due attention to traditional obligations and entitlements. It also contains several admonitions that they need to be aware of local conditions, and in 'Institutes of Polity' Wulfstan addresses the shortcomings of 'reeves', *gerefas*.[20] (The word had a wide range of meanings, and broadly conveys the sense of 'agent', someone who is working for a superior: it is only later that a 'reeve' came to mean exclusively the man who worked for a manorial lord.) His concern is always with the defenceless: as their only protection in the public realm was a proper administration of the law, so in the private realm of the estate it was only strict adherence to custom. Therefore, when he writes, 'It is right that reeves work diligently and always provide for their lords aright. But now it has happened that since Edgar died, even as God willed, there are more robbers than righteous men; and it is a wretched thing that those who should be shepherds of the Christian people are robbers', he could well have had this kind of agent in mind. That may be why there is such an important distinction made between estate rules, *rædan*, and local custom and why it is the responsibility of 'he who has the *scyre*', authority/office, to 'always know what the *ealdlandrædan*, the longstanding conditions on the estate, are and *hwæt deode deaw*, the local custom'. By their nature they are both from the past, the era of *hwilum waes*, 'once there was'. For Wulfstan, to preserve past certainties was to guarantee social peace. To record the traditional obligations and entitlements of the most exploited *gebur* was for him no less important than to admonish kings and *ealdormen*, bishops and priests, thegns and nobles, to respect their own traditional obligations. In keeping with his proscriptive approach to the whole of society, *Rectitudines* is typically Wulfstanian. If we read it as a description of lay society, from near the top to the very bottom, in terms of the reciprocal obligations and entitlements of the different ranks within it, despite its prosaic subject matter we may find that there is something of the 'holiness of society' about *Rectitudines singularum personarum*.

Free Men and their Property

If *Rectitudines singularum personarum* portrays a well-ordered society, where having land brought both duties and rights, the 'Sermon of the Wolf' portrays this link as under threat from within. *Frige men ne motan wealdan heora sylfra, ne faran þa hi willað, ne ateon heora agen swa swa hi willað. Ne þraelas ne motan habban þæt hi agon on agenan hwilan mid earfeðan gewunnen, ne þæt þæt heom on Godes est gode men geudon, 7 to ælmesgife for Godes lufan sealdon.* 'Free men are not allowed to keep their independence, nor go where they wish. Nor to deal with their own property as they wish, and slaves are not allowed to keep what they have gained by toil in their own free time, or what good men have granted them in God's favour, and given them in charity for the love of God.' Wulfstan may simply have been

referring here to bullying by powerful men, but these phrases do seem
to convey his belief that 'free men', whatever their social status, were
independent landowners and that even slaves had a right to their small
savings. These two sentences, found in only one of the manuscripts of
the Sermon, have been taken as evidence of the beginning of what
would be a profound change. The phrase *ne faran þa hi willað*, 'nor go
where they wish', has been interpreted as evidence for constrictions
having been imposed on a man's right to commend himself to a patron
of his choice, the kind of relationship which Domesday Book would
record as 'he cannot go with his land where he will'. Dorothy Whitelock, who made this point, thought that this passage might be early
evidence that 'difficulty is being felt in keeping clear the distinction
between personal commendation and the actual dependence of
tenure.'[21] The next chapter will argue that 'actual dependence of
tenure', strictly speaking a result of the post-Conquest settlement, was
still in the future when the Wolf preached his sermon and would indeed
turn out to be at odds with the bonds of personal commendation, but if
property rights were important to him and seemed to be threatened in
the chaos of the time we need to pay attention to this. We have already
encountered his views on the violence and abuse of power, the breakdown of proper order, and the rule of law. The phrase 'their own
property' or 'what is their own' seems to stem from a different concern,
with a change in property relations, not personal conduct. We need to
consider whether, quite apart from the dislocations of war, deep
changes may have been taking place which had led him to these concerns. *Rectitudines singularum personarum* and another text associated
with Wulfstan, *Geþyncðu*, are about the great church estates and the
doings of the political class, but what about changes lower down?[22]
What changes in relations between people concerning property might
have led Wulfstan to think, 'Free men are not allowed to keep their
independence, nor go where they wish. Nor to deal with their own
property as they wish'?

If this little piece of text really is as important as Dorothy Whitelock
considered it to be, then looking as closely as we can at what Wulfstan
may have meant by 'free men', 'their own property', and 'go where they
wish' might give us a glimpse into the social structure of rural society on
the eve of the Conquest. To begin with, 'free men', as slaves had done,
have lost rights they once had over 'what is theirs'. As is so often the case
in the language of the law codes, this phrase seems to encompass all free
men, those who 'have their own property', not a particular class or rank.
That makes it difficult to know what kind of free men and what 'their
own property' was. Most of what we know, or think we know, about the

property of lay Anglo-Saxons is based on the evidence of charters which granted or leased land to individuals, and of their wills. This evidence brings its own problems. It confines us from the start to areas for which charters and wills survive, which broadly speaking excludes England north of the Humber and much of the Danelaw. Charters have a much better chance of survival if entrusted to the care of a religious house and convey land in its zone of influence. Many families of great local power and importance may have been supported by 'old family land' never chartered, which had simply been handed down over the generations. And they are a textual net which has caught and subjected to intense analysis an unknowable proportion of those who had bookland: only one thousand charters survive from the five centuries. Nevertheless, however patchy their survival and coverage, charters were important in conveying a distinctive form of land, 'bookland', to people who would surely have thought about it in terms of exclusive ownership.

Although charters survive from the late seventh century to the eve of the Conquest, there is a marked concentration in the mid-tenth century These are for markedly smaller amounts of land than had been granted to the early minsters, often grants by kings to reward faithful 'public ser-vants' or ministers. Very few convey amounts of land under five hides, which may be significant. Although it is very seldom that we can put a known owner into a known site, or link a site with a charter conveying the land on which it sat, it is now becoming more possible to envisage what in another text associated with Wulfstan, *Geþyncdu* is the proper setting of a thegn: 'If a *ceorl* prospered so that he had fully five hides of his own land, church and kitchen building, bell-house and *burhgeat*, entrance to his courtyard, a seat and special office in the king's hall, then he thenceforth was worthy of a thegn's rights.' His status thus lay not solely in land, but in visible assets. His superior lifestyle was signalled by a prestigious dwelling, where the cooking was not done on the central hearth but in a detached kitchen, and a priest was either resident or on call to his private church. Its surrounding palisaded enclosure made its mark on the countryside by what was becoming a traditional sign of status: privatised space, and the bell in his bell-house could aurally extend that space still further. He had, in short, what contemporaries would have recognised as the dwelling of a significant person in the locality and called it his 'hall'.[23] The growing archaeological record of the built and settled environment of Anglo-Saxon England has recently been comprehensively assembled by John Blair, and Mark Gardiner has used textual evidence, some from Wulfstan's own works, to take us into the manor house and its buildings and some of the elements in the aspirant thegn's setting are becoming identified.[24] Blair has identified a distinct change in the kind of houses that were being built: 'domestic sites of a character comparable to later "peasant" or "yeoman" status until well into the tenth century, but often tended to assume a "seigneurial" aspect thereafter'.[25] One thing is certain: these proliferating halls were the homes of settled households which needed to be fed.

Lords with their halls and bookland, then, are becoming recognisable in the tenth century, and so were their estates, inscribed onto the lands by boundaries both fixed in local minds and inscribed in written boundary clauses. How were they run? Charters granted land in perpetuity, with freedom of alienation and the grantees were 'land-lords', to adopt Tom Lambert's phrase, but to describe them as 'landlords' implies an authority over the inhabitants which we cannot assume. Wickham characterises the tenth century as 'the other side of the line from the eighth and early ninth in terms of the weight of rents from most of the estates in most of the country'.[26] If we include labour as rent, then it is as well to remember how little we know about the population of any bookland estate from whom this rent and labour might have come. It could have included a very wide range of people. In fact, considering the varied topography of England, and the diversity of the people who farmed it and the ways in which they did so, it must have done. This cannot but have influenced, even constrained, landlord policies. Even some of the most prestigious lords would have had difficulty in getting regular work from the local inhabitants. Some of the farms on the huge royal estate of Hartland in North Devon revealed by Domesday Book were several miles from the estate centre, which in 1086 was probably still run on slave labour. The distances were too great to assemble any size of workforce. It would have taken a man with a ploughteam the best part of an entire morning to reach the fields of the home farm (after which the team needed to rest before the slow journey home!). And there may have been competition for labour from local farmers who were likely to have been feeding considerable workforces, perhaps including slaves, in their own households. A bookland estate could comprise within its boundaries many such farms. In 942 King Edmund granted forty hides making up land at ten places west of the Trent in Staffordshire to Wulsige *Maur*, 'The Black', thought to be a member of the important local family who founded Burton Abbey. Such areas had valuable natural resources in terms of game and raw materials, and the donees in principle were entitled to receive the renders of the royal *feorm*, if they were able to enforce its collection. Beyond that, how they might have exploited their agricultural potential, let alone the labour and resources of the local farmers, can only be a matter of guesswork. A century and a half later, Domesday Book shows that all but one of the properties in Wulfsige's acquisition were now 'manors', each consisting of a small home farm set among large numbers of scattered peasant farms. Some of the outlying farmers were themselves substantial enough to have been employing their own workers: it is hard to imagine their labouring for anyone else.[27]

The complex human geography of the English countryside, particularly in areas of dispersed settlement, could always make estate management difficult for any lord who wanted available and reliable people to work his land for him and the small-scale bookland lord could well have found it particularly difficult. Wulfstan was writing not long after the mid-point between the date of Wulfsige's charter and Domesday Book. Neither will tell us what had happened to 'free men' and 'their own property' in the interim, but one thing is certain: because there were more land-lords in the tenth century, more peasants were being drawn into their orbit. This was happening in the aftermath of what is being regarded as something of an agricultural revolution. The consensus is now growing that from the mid-Saxon period Lowland England had been undergoing radical 'cerealisation': cereals were now being grown more intensively and more land was coming under the plough.[28] Arable farming involved by far the most labour-intensive operations in the rural economy: the heavy work of ploughing, harvesting, and processing grain. It was the most capital-intensive too: everything depended on the oxen that pulled the plough and the skills of the people who reared, trained, and drove them. Yields could be improved by 'piling labour onto the land': clearing off stones, weeding, and bird-scaring. For land-lords and farmers alike more, or more intense, cereal farming and grain processing meant that labour demands increased and traction animals became much more valuable. Larger operations such as *Rectitudines singularum personarum* describes could support an inland workforce with ploughteams on the home farm and *geburas* providing weekwork. Sally Harvey's work on the structure of late Anglo-Saxon and early Anglo-Norman lay estates shows major lay lords whose estates were similarly centred on a large and highly labour- and capital-intensive 'demesne' sector.[29] But such large-scale operation was unavailable to lesser land-lords with small inlands. Nor was it likely that they would have been able to summon the entire neighbourhood for customary boon-work on their fields: their powerful neighbours, especially those with ancient estates, would surely have had the prior claim. Yet these lesser land-lords were a growing class. Apart from slaves, where was their extra labour to come from? Was it because of lords putting pressure on the more vulnerable peasant farmers on their estates that 'free men are not allowed to keep their independence, nor go where they wish. Nor to deal with their own property as they wish'? While speculation as to what exactly he meant cannot reasonably take us any further, we can still pay attention to Wulfstan's concerns.

Notes

1 Alfred and Guthrum: Attenborough, *Laws*, 98–101; Liebermann, *Gesetze*, i. 126–8.

2 *Sermo lupi ad anglos* is translated in Whitelock, *English Historical Documents*, i. no. 240, 854–9 in 'a form in which we know that the homily existed in, or soon after, Wulfstan's lifetime' and edited by Whitelock as *Sermo Lupi ad Anglos*. The possibility of such a date has been suggested by Simon Keynes: 'An Abbot, an Archbishop and the Danish Raids of 1006–7 and 1009–12'.

3 *Laboratores sind de usbigleofan tiliað, yrðlingas and ætemen to ðan anum betæhte*: Rabin, *Political Writings*, 106 n.15: Bloch, *French Rural History*, 193–6.

4 Garmonsway, *Ælfric's Colloquy*, 20–1. Banham and Faith, *Anglo-Saxon Farms and Farming*, 56–7; Pelteret, *Slavery*, 194–200.

5 Wormald, 'Archbishop Wulfstan and the holiness of society'. Baxter, 'Archbishop Wulfstan'.

6 I am grateful to an anonymous referee for this suggestion and for drawing my attention to the importance of Fulham to the bishopric estate. At one point in the *Rectitudines singularum personarum*, with reference to the beekeeper's allowance, the author uses the first-person plural.

7 Rio, *Slavery*, 206–7, highlights the decline in the numbers of slaves recorded for 1066 and 1086 in Domesday Book, so this may have been part of a wider trend.

8 For Wulfstan as bishop of Worcester and his estate policies there: Baxter, 'Archbishop Wulfstan'. Fulham: *Domesday Book, Middlesex*, 3:12; Kelly, *Charters of St Pauls*, 90–4, 138–41, 228, 225–8. For his time at St Paul's: Kelly, *Charters of St Pauls*, 38–9, 43–6. Kelly points out (at 77) that the charters relating to the episcopal properties at St Paul's are all originals, while those of the canons are all copies. Did Wulfstan establish a better archive tradition for the episcopal documents? In his work on the duties of the bishop, *Episcopus*, the bishop's role in justice included responsibility for ensuring that correct weights and measures were in use throughout his diocese: Whitelock, Brett, and Brooke, *Councils and Synods*, i. 419. I am grateful to Lesley Abrams for this reference.

9 Liebermann, *Gesetze*, i. 444–53 from Corpus Christi College, Cambridge, ms 383, a mid-twelfth-century ms compiled at St Paul's, where it has no title and a Latin translation in the twelfth-century legal collection the *Quadripartitus*, where it is given the title *De dignitate hominum*. On the basis of Wormald, 'Archbishop Wulfstan and the holiness of society' in Pelteret, *Legal Culture*, 225–51 and Harvey, '*Rectitudines singularum personarum*', I am taking Wulfstan

as author/reviser. My translations of titles are via DMLBS, s.v. *persona* 2; *rectitude, singula*. Baxter, 'Archbishop Wulfstan', considers that *Gerefa* and *Rectitudines singularum personarum* may have been brought together and interpolated by Wulfstan early in his career, when he was bishop of London, as both are in a later St Paul's ms: Cambridge CCC 383.

10 Harvey, *Manorial Records*, 17–22, Birrell, 'Manorial custumals'.

11 Lambert, pers. comm.; Harvey, 'Domesday England', 82–5; Maitland, *Domesday Book*, 384–8, points out the similarity of their obligations to those of their counterparts in the Tidenham survey.

12 Lennard, 'Bordars and cottars'.

13 Aston, 'Origins of the manor'; Dyer, *Making a Living*, 38–40; and Stacy, *Survey of Glastonbury Abbey* all take the villein tenants of the post-Conquest manor to be the equivalent of the *gebur* of the *Rectitudines*.

14 Their 'yard of land' has been interpreted as a reference to a yardland in an open field system. For the interpretation here: Faith, *English Peasantry*, 76–84. The suggestion there that the *gebur*'s 'yard' of land was a single strip of arable, not a 'yardland' in the later sense of thirty acres, has recently received a good deal of archaeological confirmation in Banham and Faith, *Farms and Farming*, 274–9, with many examples of small-scale strip fields as the precursors of open fields.

15 Faith, *English Peasantry*, 78–80, Blair, *Building Anglo-Saxon England*, 304, 408–9, Ashton, 'Origins of the manor', 13.

16 I am grateful to Roy Townsend of Finstock for his help with this topic.

17 Banham and Faith, *Anglo-Saxon Farms and Farming*, 57.

18 Darby, *Domesday England*, appendix 3.

19 Birrell, 'Peasants eating and drinking'.

20 'Institutes of Polity', x: Rabin, *Political Writings*, 111–12.

21 Whitelock, *English Historical Documents*, 856n.4.

22 *Geþyncdu* is discussed further in the following chapter.

23 Williams, 'A bell-house and a *burhgeat*'.

24 Blair, *Building Anglo-Saxon England*, chapter 10; Gardiner, 'The origins and persistence of manorial buildings in England'.

25 Blair, *Building Anglo-Saxon England*, 377.

26 Wickham, *Framing*, 349.

27 Hartland: *Domesday Book: Devon*, 1:30; Edmund's grant: Sawyer, *Anglo-Saxon Charters*, 479; *Domesday Book: Staffordshire*, 1:11, 1:12, 1:20,4:2, 4:4, 10:3, 1:29, 1:39.

28 McKerracher, *Farming Transformed*.

29 Harvey, 'Domesday England', 115–21.

10 Land, Law, and Office

Peasants encountered lords in many ways other than on their estates and in their fields. They met on occasion as players in the public world, and here too, in Wulfstan's view, the ground was shifting in disturbing ways. What concerned him was a principle which we have already met over and over again in the previous chapters: what is due from the various orders in society, and what is due to them. Inevitably we bring some of our own preconceptions about the past when we translate documents which come from that past. This has consequences. *Geþyncđu* is an example. This is the title given to one of his best-known works, or rather a work preserved in manuscripts known to be connected with him.[1] Its Latin translator, writing early in the twelfth century, gave it the title *De promotione*, 'Concerning advancement to office, promotion' and modern commentators, following his lead, commonly refer to it as 'The promotion law' or 'A tract on status'.[2] *Geþyncđu* could be read as a tract deploring social mobility, which indeed it is, and what it does. However, a person's position in a social hierarchy in society falls very short of what Wulfstan meant by *geþyncđu*. When he was writing, this was a word suffused with connotations of honour and dignity. From the Mother of God herself, queens and saints, bishops and distinguished scholars are awarded the *geþyncđu*, the dignity and honour which they have earned by their virtue.[3] It takes us nearer to understanding the moral economy of his time to see Wulfstan's work in the light of what we can learn from some of his other writings: in these, due reward in return for due obligations was one of his major concerns. For him, the idea of rank is always accompanied by the idea of the appropriate honour which each rank deserves. *Geþyncđu* looks back to a time when such standards applied to all the people who did the business of government: 'in the laws of England *leod* and *lagu*, people and law, went by rank and the councillors of the people were *wurđscipes wurđe*, considered worthy of honour each according to his status, whether *eorl* or *ceorl*, noble or commoner, *degn* or *đeoden*, thegn or prince.' His picture is not of a static society. Wulfstan knew very well that people wanted to rise in the world of high politics, that both churchmen and laymen were

117

constantly looking for advancement and that the route to power lay through the king's hall: he had followed that route himself. By his time the business of government had proliferated. Now there was a recognised social difference between the king's *ðegen*, his 'servants' who do the king's business, and the mass of ordinary people, *ðeoden*.[4] There is no reason to believe that he would have thought there was anything wrong with getting on in the world. But for him advancement is more than simply a career path: political authority, in his view, must always be supported by both land and a visible expression of status: 'If a *ceorl* prospered so that he had fully five hides of his own land, church and kitchen building, bell-house and *burhgeat*, entrance to his courtyard, a seat and special office in the king's hall, then he thenceforth worthy of a thegn's rights.' He looks back to a time when 'in the English laws' five hides had been recognised as the property that was the proper size to support a thegn who played a role in administration and could act for his superior in a lawsuit. *Geþyncðu* takes account of one of the realities of the political world: someone at the centre of power and in frequent attendance on an itinerant king would always need to delegate and delegated authority too needed land behind it. 'If a thegn prospered so that he attended upon the king and rode on his business in his retinue, if he had a thegn who followed him who had five hides for the king's service and had attended his lord in the king's hall and had gone on his business three times to the king, then (his thegn) might from then on represent his lord with his fore-oath in various obligations and legally make his case wherever he is obliged to. And he who had no such agent who has thrived swore for his rights himself or lost his case.'[5] A man who held office in the public realm, even as a deputy, must have land behind him when he appears in court.

Was Wulfstan here noting a tendency of what had been public courts to become more exclusive and look a little less public?[6] It is not clear what kind of court he had in mind in which a thegn with five hides might 'represent his lord with his fore-oath in various obligations and legally make his case wherever he is obliged to'. In his time, the shire court was the forum for the legal business of all ranks of society. Since the business and disputes of the elite, lay and clerical, were settled there, the 'shire reeve' or sheriff attended in the interest of the king and the bishop those of the church. While all free men nominally had to attend, lords represented by thegns acting as their agents would have been a powerful presence there. Access to the hundred courts too was tending to reinforce distinctions of rank. Possibly the fact that so much hundredal business, and so many rural disputes, involved cattle and that cattle were central to the economy of every farm above the size of a smallholding, would have ensured that most of the farmers of any locality would have looked first to the hundred court. It was the proper place to obtain the assurance of legal ownership that sworn witness could bestow. We have no direct evidence of this, but disputes about peasants' land and its ownership may have been settled there too. But while all the inhabitants of the hundred were required to be members of a tithing, by the early twelfth century it was becoming accepted that it is only the *meliores homines*, 'the better sort', who are to attend the hundred court.[7] By comparing the witnesses and jurors who played a part in settling land questions relating to Ely Abbey and its properties recorded in the *Libellus Æthelwoldi* with those recorded in Domesday Book, Robin Fleming has detected significant change over the intervening century: 'Supporters of litigants and members of local assemblies had ... shifted in some ways in the century. ... Individual witnesses and jurors identified in Domesday Book ... are almost always great lords speaking on behalf of their followers, men testifying on behalf of their lords, or officials giving evidence on behalf of their masters.'[8]

Geþyncðu provided a place in the moral order for a link between justice, land, and status: that link was the political responsibility brought by the ownership of land. That someone taking a political or legal role needed to have a certain amount of land, five hides or more, was so important to Wulfstan not because he was a snob. It was because owning land enmeshed people in the network of obligations which supported civil society. Hidated land was not simply land, but land that owed public service. While in less sophisticated days the hide had principally served as a unit for levying the supplies that went up to feed the king and his entourage, by Wulfstan's time it was part of a highly organised tax regime in which hides and their counterparts and subdivisions were the basis of assessment. Hides were also a unit for assessing military service, although whether having five hides was ever systematically used as the basis on which men were actually armed and sent into battle is another matter: what is involved here is less to do with military arrangements than with Wulfstan's view that the public obligations inherent in the right order of society had been abandoned.[9] The tone throughout *Geþyncðu* is of regret. The text begins *hwilum wæs*, 'it once was', that these principles governed behaviour, with the implication that is no longer the case. And what that could lead to was an old story: the downfall of Britain.

'There was a historian in the time of the Britons called Gildas who wrote about their misdeeds, how with their sins they angered God so grievously that finally he allowed the army of the English to conquer their land and destroy the host of the Britons entirely'. Wulfstan wrote in the shadow of current invasion, but his concerns about the 'defence of the realm', and the proper provision for this, have a long pedigree and one that he was well aware of.[10] The spectre of invasion loomed large in

English accounts of their past and one account above all, perhaps made all the more effective because of its melodramatic tone, was that given by Gildas. His 'On the Downfall of Britain', recounting the collapse of the British in the face of Germanic raiders, was probably written in the mid-sixth century and Bede, writing in the eighth, although he gave a much more scholarly account of the settlement period, knew Gildas' work. Bede's concerns about the state of England were expressed in a letter written late in his life to Ecgbert, bishop of York, and Bede's letter to Ecgbert was, in its turn, influential, quoted by Alcuin, director of the cathedral school at York from 767. It was probably through reading Alcuin that Wulfstan, another archbishop of York, knew it too, and in Alcuin's letters there was also one following another disastrous attack: the sack of Lindisfarne.[11] Bede's concern was over what we would call 'national security'. Aristocrats were profiting from the security of land granted by charter and originally intended to establish monasteries by setting up establishments that were anything but monastic. As well as being shocked by the distinctly irreligious standards that prevailed in these so-called monasteries he was worried that such grants had resulted in land which should have supported a military class falling into the hands of the wrong people. Instead of being owned by *milites sive comites secularium potestatum*, 'warriors or commanders of the secular powers to defend our people from the barbarians ... many places are, as people say "no use to God or man"'. He invokes the spectre of invasion in recommending that Ecgbert should 'annul the irreligious and unjust acts of our predecessors, and provide for those things which may be useful to our province whether in matters of church or state (*sive secundum Deum sive secundum sint utilia, prospicere*), lest in our times by the ceasing of religion, love and fear of him who sees into the heart be abandoned, or else, by the dwindling of the supply of secular troops, there arise a lack of men to defend our territories from barbarian invasion'.[12]

Bede had foreseen another problem, one which preoccupied Wulfstan too: well-born and testosterone-fuelled young men on the loose. 'For, what indeed is disgraceful to tell, those who are totally ignorant of the monastic life have received under their control so many places in the name of monasteries ... that there is a complete lack of places where the sons of nobles or of veteran thegns (*militum*) might acquire possession and thus, unoccupied and unmarried, though the time of puberty is over, they persist in no idea of continence, and on this account they either leave the country for which they ought to fight and go across the sea, or else, with greater guilt and shamelessness devote themselves to loose living and fornication, seeing they have no idea of chastity, and do not even abstain from virgins consecrated to God.' Landless and underemployed young men, keen to prove themselves in combat or simply disorder, were a constant threat to the social order in medieval Europe. In Wulfstan's England, as in Bede's, a landless young man with flashy weapons could make fighting a career. Another text associated with Wulfstan, originally applying to 'the northern people', the Northumbrians, raises the same concern as had *Geþyncðu*: 'If a *ceorl* prospers so that he has a helm and a byrnie and a gold-patterned sword' if he has not got five hides for the king's service he is still a *ceorl* 'although when his grandson acquires the land he will acquire a higher wergild as a *gesith*.' King Alfred, who had probably spent a good deal more time in the company of fighting men than either Bede or Wulfstan and was more tolerant of their ways, had himself written of the proper career of a thegn. After the end of a typical aristocratic youth spent in field sports and fishing on land lent him by his lord, the beginning of his maturity came when he was granted land in bookright, which would be passed on to his descendants. This meant that he could retire from a career as a freelance warrior, but he was still an armed man, and one who could be called up to military service for the king as a member of 'a *fyrd* manned by landholders'.[13] These were not simply ideals of behaviour: the link between land and fighting men was well rooted in pre-Conquest society and the five-hide unit was the backbone of this system. Five hides are a size of landholding which frequently occurs in Domesday Book, and gives several 'Fifields' their name: this may be because this was the amount of land considered in Domesday Book essential to support the proper provision of military obligations.[14] Wulfstan's concern that five hides should underpin the standing of those active in public life was thus no private obsession with the past but part of a moral order in which, for young nobles and peasant boys alike, acquiring land was the gateway to marriage and the establishment of a family and should mark the beginning of a man's life as a responsible *and armed* member of society.[15]

Many of Wulfstan's more immediate concerns were about the turbulent present in which he lived. In 'The Sermon of the Wolf to the English' he found this under threat from the social and moral breakdown he saw all around.[16] Again conventionally enough, he takes the English to task for their sinful behaviour: the English have, by their sins, brought trouble down on their own heads. But his fundamental concern is with the collapse of the moral order. Proper legal procedure is not observed. Wulfstan contrasts the behaviour of heathens, who are more correct in their observance of their own religion and respectful of its servants, than Christians are of theirs. 'There has been little loyalty among men. People have not pursued remedies as zealously as they should and lawless acts have taken place.' This is conventional enough, but Wulfstan knew a good deal about harsh realities of social breakdown, and the 'Sermon' then addresses two abuses which have disquieting echoes for a modern reader. One is sex-trafficking. The other is rape as an act of war. 'And it is shameful to speak of what has happened too widely, and it is terrible to know what many do too often, who commit that miserable deed that they contribute together and buy a woman between them as a joint purchase, and practice foul sin with that one woman, one after another, just like dogs who do not care about filth; then sell for a price out of the land into the power of strangers God's creatures and his own purchase that he dearly bought.' Trafficking and procurement imply collusion: if a woman had been bought, someone must have sold her and the people most likely to have had control over a free woman (Wulfstan does not imply that she is a slave) are members of her family. Earlier he has deplored the lack of family loyalty: 'Now too often a kinsman does not protect a kinsman any more than a stranger.' Women appear as temptresses and whores in many medieval texts, but the tone of this passage is a long way from traditional excoriations of licentiousness. Its particularity gives it an air of authenticity: Wulfstan may have known cases or reports of sex trafficking. His is a political stance, consonant with his preoccupation with the decay of the proper order of past times. What he has to say about multiple rape as a means of conquest and expression of dominance illustrates this: pirates 'ten or a dozen, one after another, insult disgracefully the thegn's wife, sometimes his daughter or near kinswoman, whilst he looks on, who considers himself brave and mighty and stout enough before that happened.' The rape of the thegn's wife is not just about rape. It is about the unmanning of the thegn so that he cannot enact his proper role: to protect her. Whether in peace or war, down on the estate or in the courts, the relations between people are never simply personal, in Wulfstan's view: they are part of the wider moral order.

Wulfstan's work may in turn have become a way of regarding Anglo-Saxon England from a Norman perspective. The following passage in William of Malmesbury's *Gesta regum Anglorum* seems to have echoes of the 'Sermon' of the Wolf: 'in process of time the desire after religion and literature had decayed for several years before the arrival of the Normans ... the commonalty left unprotected (by the nobility) became a prey to the most powerful, who amassed fortunes, either by seizing on their property or selling their persons into foreign countries ... selling their female servants when pregnant by them and after they had satisfied their lust, either to public prostitution or to foreign slavery.[17] It is that post-Conquest perspective that we turn to next.

Notes

1 Liebermann, *Gesetze*, i. 456–9. Translated in Rabin, *Political Writings*, 65–71. One version (CCC 201) gives it the title *be wergildum und be geþncdum*, 'of wergilds and rank', the other (Textus Roffensis f.93) *be leode geþincdum und lage*, 'of people's rank and law'. Rabin, *Political Writings*, 68 gives 'Concerning the ranks of people and law'.

2 Cited in this context by Runciman, 'Accelerating social mobility'; Wormald, *Making of English Law*, 393–4, 457–8, 461–5.

3 Bosworth and Toller, *Dictionary* and Toller, *Supplement*, s.v. *geþincdu*.

4 Thacker, 'Some terms for noblemen'.

5 Liebermann, *Gesetze*, i. 456.

6 Molyneux, *Formation of the English Kingdom*, 157–64.

7 Goebel, *Felony and Misdemeanor*, 391–9 with reference to *Leges Henrici Primi*; *Cartularium Monasterii de Rameseia*, 274–5 (Stukely, Hunts.); Maitland's eagle eye spotted in Domesday other distinctions: on a royal Norfolk manor, the earl had had jurisdiction over those farmers whose sheep had to be folded and their beneficial manure deposited on his land, not their own: Maitland, *Domesday Book*, 122. Bruce O'Brien has suggested that the association of being in frankpledge with personal freedom was increasingly being undermined by personal surety given by lords to members of their household and that by the mid-twelfth century 'only "villeins" needed to be in frankpledge'. O'Brien, *God's Peace and the King's Peace*, 86. I am not sure that this is consonant with the evidence of the frankpledge enrolments recorded on the court rolls of the thirteenth and fourteenth centuries, generally on the same occasion as the manorial court was held. Schofield, 'Late medieval view of frankpledge' and the studies cited there show that free tenants played an important part.

8 Fleming, *Domesday Book and the Law*, 38.

9 Harvey, *Domesday*, 228–9; Abels, *Lordship and Military Obligation*, 108–10.

10 Whitelock, *Sermo Lupi ad Anglos*.

11 Wormald, 'Archbishop Wulfstan and the holiness of society', 245.

12 Plummer, *Venerabilis Baedae Opera*, 405–23; translated in Whitelock, *English Historical Documents*, i. 735–46.

13 Keynes and Lapidge, *Alfred the Great*, 139.

14 *Norðleoda Laga*: Liebermann, *Gesetze*, i. 458–61. Harvey, *Domesday*, 227–32, 228. For similarities between the *fyrd* and the Norman *arrière-ban*, and Henry II's Assize of Arms: Haskins, *Norman Institutions*, 23.

15 There seems to have been a short-lived scheme to require two mounted men to be supplied from every ploughteam, possibly taken as the equivalent of the hide: II Æthelstan 16. Attenborough, *Laws*, i. 136–7, Liebermann, *Gesetze*, i. 158–9.

16 Whitelock, *English Historical Documents*, no. 240, 854–9; *Sermo Lupi ad Anglos*.

17 William of Malmesbury, *Gesta regum anglorum*, 279. Coven, '*Byrstas* and *bysmeras*'.

Part V

The Aftermath of Conquest

11   New Words in the Countryside

Wulfstan 'the Wolf' had been disturbed by the changes that he saw taking place in his time in the nature of power, from legitimate rule to naked force. These were undermining the traditional moral economy so that there were now pressures on 'free men' and their ability to 'go where they will and do what they will with what is their own'. This chapter, and the two that follow, look at the aftermath of the Conquest and explore the possibility that this too was a time when not only did power change hands but the nature of power changed too. It is not a topic that has a commentator like Wulfstan. Contemporary and near-contemporary accounts of the Conquest were intended as political narratives of how power changed hands at the highest level, not how it affected ordinary free men and their ability to 'go where they will'. The different versions of the Anglo-Saxon Chronicle are narratives of military campaigns and resistance and although the description by the Anglo-Norman historian Orderic Vitalis of the harrying of the North shows compassion for its victims, his main concern was with the process by which William 'divided up the chief provinces of England among his followers, and made the humblest of the Normans men of wealth, with civil and military authority.'[1] That 1066 brought change in the composition of the landed elite after 1066 is a topic well studied and documented, but the impact of the Conquest on the rural population at large has largely been a matter for conjecture. It is from the following century that evidence comes of what that impact was thought to have been, and some twelfth-century viewpoints will be the subject of the next chapter. However, although we may not have narratives for the eleventh century, we do have a rich seam of evidence to mine: words and their meanings, old and new. The Conquest did not only establish a foreign elite in England, speaking a foreign language: even in the common language of Latin several words were now used in a new way and new words came into use.

Most of our information about rural England in the eleventh century comes from the records created by two great administrative enterprises, the levying of the geld and the Domesday enquiry, one in Old English, one in Latin. Each had its own terminology. This chapter explores the possibility that the terminology of Domesday Book can be seen as itself an agent of change. The Inquest itself, the process of gathering information from the localities in response to the questions that the articles of enquiry had laid down, involved multiple episodes of translation. It is worth bearing in mind what this involved. When, the shire court having been assembled, the French-speaking commissioners arrived to hear the responses to the articles of enquiry they brought translators with them, some English, some French, but all bilingual in both languages. The six *villani*, priest, and reeve from each place who were to be chosen to give evidence but were probably in reality a much less tidy group, gave their evidence in English, that is to say in the Old English of the West Saxons, Old West Saxon.[2] By the time that it had been entered in the breve, the booklet recording the holdings of each landholder and then conveyed onto the folios of Domesday (and later of the book itself), each piece of information had been translated into Latin and abbreviated. If the Old English of the verbal evidence had been translated directly into Latin, then we would expect Domesday's terminology to consist of Latin terms which were already in use in England as translations of Old English words. While it is commonly assumed, this does not seem to have been the case. From the point of view of two scholars of place and personal names, Domesday Book was linguistically speaking 'an Anglo-Norman record. ... the Latin usages represented were ... in the main not those of pre-Conquest Anglo-Latin records but normally the Continental ones favoured by the Anglo-Norman administration. ... the aim of those responsible for the Domesday text was not to observe vernacular traditions of any sort, English or Norman, but to Latinize as thoroughly as possible every item that could be Latinized.' A handful of Old English words unfamiliar to Norman ears *were* simply Latinized by adding a suffix to produce *sochemanni*, *taini*, *cotarii*, and *hida* for 'sokemen' and 'thegns', 'cottagers' and 'hide'.[3] And of course many Domesday terms were everyday Latin for English words that were easy to translate, from 'mills' and 'woods' and so on (although plain English horses are on occasion gentrified as *palfridi*, 'palfreys') down to the pigs that William was notorious for having had counted. But 'French scribes played a dominant but not exclusive role in the production of the circuit returns', when the information was still in its raw state, and some of the Latin terms which are most crucial to the way that historians have interpreted Domesday Book do not appear in any English text before the Conquest, although they were current in eleventh-century Normandy and must have had their equivalents in spoken Norman French.[4] This chapter explores the possibility that in Domesday Book we are not only reading rural England from a Norman point of view, but reading it in Norman Latin. And it asks: Did Norman Latin bring into England some Norman ideas about land and people?

What strikes us first about Domesday, just as it struck people at the time, is its capaciousness, its thoroughness, and its detail. But if any late Anglo-Saxon king had wanted to lay his hands, for some reason, on much of the information contained there, even the number of pigs, local sources would have been perfectly capable of providing it. Lords with estates knew what land they had, and we saw in a previous chapter that a landowner of a great ecclesiastical estate, such as Wulfstan or Ælfric, knew a good deal about its management. Their reeves were people whose business it was to be 'canny', *gesceadwisc*, about it on their behalf and if pigs were to be counted could have come up with the appropriate tallies. Estates were not managed without written records, although few have survived, and the few that have survived were those that were thought important enough at the time to be carefully written out and kept in monastic archives.[5] The people in charge of the monastic estates knew what *feorm* was due from each property, and it was the business of the reeves running their estates on the ground to make sure it was delivered on time: a note on alterations to the *feorm* survives from the abbey of Bury St Edmunds: a sole relic of what may have been corpus of such records. Workers were valuable enough assets to need recording and we still have the names of *gebyrde*, 'native-born' individuals who had left the land of Ely in the eleventh century.[6] The records of the *micel weorc*, 'heavy labour', recorded as due on the inlands of the estates of properties of Bath Abbey and Winchester have become the basis of what several historians have written about pre-Conquest peasant obligations. When land changed hands in Anglo-Saxon England among the upper echelons of society, it was a major public occasion, the great were the witness of the donation itself, the people of the neighbourhood the witness of its boundaries. The resulting documentation has survived in the form of the charters, wills, and leases preserved in monastic archives, these being the safest place to deposit them. But memory and written record did not embody different attitudes to the importance of record itself. A possibly huge amount of no less important information was unwritten, or at least has not survived beyond the documentary tradition of the religious, but was preserved in memory, and handed-down memory, imprinted by occasions which were designed to achieve this. An earlier chapter has described the ceremonial aspect of important land transfers, but a plethora of small-scale property transactions took place in the local courts, where attendance was an obligation on free men. The transactions that took place as part of bishop Æthelwold's restoration of the fortunes of Ely

by dealing with local people literally filled a book, the *Libellus Æthelwoldi*.
People were used to providing information on a range of public matters
in the courts of shire and hundred. The vernacular laws emphasise the
importance of witness to cattle sales and purchases of even a single
animal: local memories preserved this information and it is likely,
although hard to prove, that land transactions took place there too. There
was also the criminal business of the public courts: very few crimes were
'reserved' to the king in the sense of being judged and punished at his
court, but were common knowledge.[7] Each place entered in Domesday
is accompanied by its rating in hides, the basis of the geld assessment,
and so many obligations had long been assessed in terms of the hide and
its fractions that these were terms which were familiar to everyone. Who
was commended to whom was the stuff of local politics, and this too was
common knowledge in the localities and found its way into the Domesday returns. In short, England was already awash with information,
although that information was not always written down.[8] When it came
to be written down, whose words were used?

Domesday Vocabulary: *Manerium*

> It seemeth unto me that this name mannor began with the Normans,
> and that it was not here before thare Arrivall, for I finde noe suche name
> with the Saxones.[9]

Let us try to get an idea of the problems involved in this enormous work
of data collection by looking at how the results were recorded. The
process brought new words to England. Any Norman granted land in
England, whether on a huge scale as one of William's 'chief men', on a
small scale as a minor official, or a sub-tenant somewhere in between,
would have come into possession of a very mixed package of resources.
People and livestock, arable land, meadows and woodland, mills and
fisheries, quarries, mines, and markets were now in the hands of new
lords and England's diversity, making recording this information thus a
formidable job. The principal collection of documents available to the
Domesday commissioners, the geld lists, were arranged to administer
divisions of the countryside which were totally alien to them.[10] Moreover, Normans and English did not see eye to eye about what lordship
entailed. In England commendation to a more powerful man, that essential insurance policy, still cut across any ties implied in ownership of land,
but 'it was difficult for men used to the continental practice, in which
land and personal homage were much more closely linked, to appreciate
the distinction'.[11] Across England there were differences in settlement

patterns, social structure, husbandry practices, and local custom. Some of the rural population were smallholders virtually tied to the economy of a substantial farmer or a great estate, some were entirely independent farmers, so a Norman granted land in one part of England would find that he now held packages of farms, farmers, and natural resources that might be very different from those of the land he now held in another part. The commissioners needed a single term for these packages and the word they chose was *manerium* or occasionally *mansio*. Orderic Vitalis explains that the bishop of Coutances was given *octogintas villas quas a manendo manerios vulgo vocamus*, 'eighty townships which we colloquially call manors, from dwelling'. C. P. Lewis' analysis of all the ways in which the term is used in Domesday Book has transformed our understanding of the subject: his analysis illuminates the concept at the heart of the 'manor'.[12] There was no OE equivalent: 'manor' was a word which the Domesday enquiry itself made necessary.

In one, restricted, sense the manor was nothing new. In France *manoir* had, and retains, the meaning of 'residence' for what the Anglo-Saxons knew as a 'hall': a principal residence, a dwelling of some distinction such as a landowner of any scale would be expected to have.[13] A hall, a substantial residence, perhaps several, had long been one of the assets of the Anglo-Saxon landowning class, its markers perhaps *Geþyncðu*'s 'enclosure-gate, bell-house and kitchen'. Domesday, although it is hard to see this as a consistent practice, sometimes records that there 'there is an *aula*' (sometimes *haulla*) or that one is shared, or that there is more than one. The archaeology of such buildings has recently been greatly advanced by the work of John Blair, who signals the mid-tenth century as the point after which the domestic sites of Normandy before 1066'.17 It is the phrase X *tenet* the elite 'assume a seigneurial aspect' with the re-emergence of the hall, now with associated provision for servants. What was new, in his view, was the association of landholding and homestead: 'Until the 1040s Old English legal vocabulary for landholdings ... showed no interest in defining them by reference to central homesteads.' A hall, however, does not seem to have played the same part in Anglo-Saxon 'performance' of lordship as it did in Normandy. William of Malmesbury saw it as a defining cultural difference between Normans and the English that the hard-drinking and hard-partying English 'consumed their whole substance in mean and despicable houses unlike the Normans and French who, in noble and splendid mansions, lived with frugality.'[14] Moreover, as Lewis has established, Domesday's *mansio* and *manerium* meant more than simply a prestigious house.

In response to the articles set out in the instructions to the commissioners, a binary division is literally written into Domesday Book. The first question to answer about the assets of a manor is the extent of the arable land in terms of the teams needed to plough it (and occasionally the meadow which would feed those teams). It runs 'how many ploughteams are there, both *in dominio* and *villanorum?*' The phrase *in dominio* is generally understood as meaning 'in lordship' and it is likely that it represented what Anglo-Saxons called 'inland', land cultivated for the lord's support. The counterpart of inland was 'warland', the land, and by extension the people, that bore the public burdens. It is unlikely that this was what the commissioners had in mind when they asked, 'How many teams do the *villani* have?', for Norman thinking did not work with these concepts. Lewis introduces the term *in servitio*, which comes from the language of feudal tenure, to translate it, and it was a term used in the description of the Domesday process by a contemporary, Robert of Hereford.[15] The concept of part of the manor being 'in service' to the dwelling at its centre goes to the heart of the matter: the term 'manor' marked a relationship between a principal dwelling and all the land and people now associated with it. The concept was stretched to its limits: some places which were probably at the time simply prosperous farms are recorded as manors. At the other end of the scale, a vast area of Kent, held together over centuries by the customary practices of the 'shire', became after 1066 the endowment of Battle Abbey, newly founded as penitence for the Conquest itself. J. E. A. Jolliffe's survey led him to conclude that what was called thenceforth 'The Manor of Wye' was 'irreconcilable with any one development such as implied in the word 'manor.'[16] If it was important to impose the manor as a way of describing property, it was equally important to impose the manor as an idea. What exactly it would mean to a place and its people that they were now part of a manor was to be worked out over many generations. It called for new words.

Domesday Vocabulary: *Tenet*

Debates about the meaning of particular words in Domesday Book matter because they are at heart debates about the nature of eleventh-century society, and of all words that matter, *tenere*, 'to hold', matters most and has been most strenuously debated. 'Who held it, at the time of King Edward, and now?' is second only to 'What is the name of this place?' in the list of questions that the jurors must answer and the phrases *tenet, tenebat, tenet de, tenet sub*, he/she 'holds', 'used to hold', 'holds from', 'holds under' occur throughout. Translating these questions is not itself the problem. Susan Reynolds has shown that *tenir* in twelfth-century France meant simply to have land and Stephen Baxter that OE *healdan* , 'to hold', 'frequently occurs in connection with land in the Old English corpus ... *teneo* in many charters issued in both England and Normandy before 1066'.[17] It is the phrase X *tenet de* Y, literally 'X holds *from* Y', that is at the heart of the debate. Reynolds has suggested a way of understanding this phrase in a different way. In her view, tenure cannot be deduced from Domesday. X *tenet de* Y does not mean 'X is the tenant of Y'. Rather, 'In the Latin of Domesday *de* surely meant "from": the land concerned had come to its holder, whether from the king or someone else, as one may say that one has something from someone, whether by gift of purchase.' This would certainly not be an adequate description of what went on between William and his chief barons. Their loyalty and the fact that they held their land from him were firmly entrenched by the Salisbury Oath. Baxter has recently argued that William had tenure written into the very structure of Domesday Book where, with an eye to the future benefits to be gained from their falling into his hands, the lands of his tenants-in-chief, both church and lay, head the county entries.[18] But not all tenures may have been settled so firmly in the twenty years since the Conquest. With lesser lords and their acquisitions, the idea that Domesday's 'he holds from' simply recorded known transfers from known people has the credibility of being in tune with some of the information contained in the survey itself. It seems very much in the spirit of the evidence collected by Robin Fleming from the *clamores*, the unsettled land disputes recorded in Domesday Book. It is in the nature of her evidence that these involved transfers of land, some very small in scale, some large, which were contested: the land had been 'seized', 'stolen' 'annexed', and so on and so may have been exceptional in the amount of detail which they contain. Nevertheless, what is striking is the detail in which the past history of the disputes had been remembered, with particular emphasis on the actual moment and method of transfers of land. Fleming remarks on the fact that that unlettered jurors 'were able to make the distinction between legal seisin and possession outside the law'. Some disputes went back well before the Conquest, some involving protracted court hearings and compli- cated witness statements. Particular attention was paid to the means by which land had been conveyed, and there was often a good deal of performance involved. Such was the power of this local witness that Domesday Book sometimes provides more evidence about the past land transactions of religious houses than they could find in their own arch- ives. Both memory and written record were valued in pursuit of evidence of title.[19] While jurors evidently knew a good deal about the 'when' and 'how' and 'from whom' those who had land in 1086 had acquired it, from whom they held and on what conditions could well have been new questions. What immediately mattered was, 'Who had this land and who has it now?'

Whatever view we take of the meaning of *tenere* in Domesday Book itself needs to take into account the fact that tenure in the sense of holding land 'from' another itself may have been a Norman idea imported in Norman heads.[20] The work of Emily Tabuteau has established that tenure in eleventh-century Normandy had come to express a relationship in which one person with land is dependent on another with regard to that land. Tenure had not evolved, but had been imposed from above: 'Ducal grants created tenure not ownership and grants further down the social scale did the same. … In Normandy a society in which substantial amounts of land were owned was, in the course of less than a century, transformed into one in which the only demonstrable type of lay possession was tenure.'[21] If this was their background, it is no wonder that 'the Domesday commissioners found it difficult to conceive of lordship which was not tenurial and tenure which was not dependent.' It has not only been the commissioners who have found it difficult: the extent to which land in pre-Conquest England was 'held' by one person 'from' another has been debated by English historians for many years. Jolliffe's position, that no one in pre-Conquest England 'held' as opposed to simply owning, has been revived by the work of George Garnett. He has bound the introduction of tenure into his description of the Conquest itself, in which, William having inherited not usurped the Crown, all rights in land derived from the Conquest and his grant. From this standpoint, Domesday Book is 'legitimating theory' made record. It was permeated, in Edward Miller's phrase, with 'Norman preconceptions about what Old English facts should have been. … Our perception of lord's rights and men's rights in land may be governed more than it ought to be by the change the Normans made in this society by turning all social relationships into tenure.' Domesday Book itself, in Miller's view, 'emphasizes (even where it does not invent) a territorial basis for social relationships' and for John Hudson 'the Domesday record introduces an element of tenure into the holding of bookland that does not appear in the Anglo-Saxon evidence'.[22]

There was nothing specifically Norman about linking land with service. *Healdan* was applied to office: kings 'held' kingdoms, bishops bishoprics, *ealdormen ealdormannries*. But *ealdormen*'s land, as has recently been shown by Stephen Baxter and John Blair, is likely to have been only theirs while in office and a bishop's diocese was not his property.[23] Rather, to hold office entailed service and those who rendered service were supported by grants of land (or, more accurately, by the labour of those who worked on that land): that was how those who served the state and the church were maintained throughout the middle ages. In this sense land was a kind of salary: to lose a role as a royal clerk would mean losing the income from the estate that supported it; to lose his 'living' meant the parson was out of a job. Thegns, whose name derives from 'servant', were defined by the level of service they owed. Wulfstan's *Geþyncðu* lists some of the duties of the two highest ranks: 'a thegn (who) prospered so that he attended upon the king and rode on his business in his retinue, if he had a thegn who followed him who had five hides for the king's service, and had attended his lord in the king's hall and had gone on his business three times to the king' can rise in rank. But these thriving thegns are not granted the land in return for service: they must already have the land because, in a symbiosis which we have encountered so often, it is the hides themselves that owe it, that are 'for the king's service'.[24]

If people on both sides of the Channel were accustomed to 'holding' land in this way, was the introduction of the language of 'tenure' of any real significance? Could it be understood as simply part of the 'legitimising rhetoric' intended to justify the dispositions made under a new regime? Politics made it matter and it was because it mattered that lawyers refined it. It came to matter at all levels of society. Tenure was central to the concept of *feudum*, 'fee', in lawyers' terms 'heritable land held in return for service', the word which would later give 'feudalism' its name'.[25] The introduction of the idea of tenure represented an important shift in the moral economy: what had happened to the English landowning class would have an equal, and similar, impact on peasant lives. Like lords, the land they had once 'had', they now 'held from'. But before pursuing the effects of this transformative change, we need to investigate what kind of people Normans thought English peasants were.

Domesday Vocabulary: People

For its new Norman lord, probably the most confusing aspect of his newly acquired estate was its people.[26] For the purposes of the Domesday enquiry the commissioners were to ask, 'How many *villani, cotarii, cothcethles* and *servi* , how many *liberi homines* and *sochemanni* and how much had or has each freeman or sokeman?' at each manor or named place.[27] The categories of people that were to be counted: *cotarii, servi, liberi homines,* and *sochemanni* are listed in a single description of the articles of enquiry and are generally supposed to be Latinized English words. Another possibility is that some of them had come to England in Norman heads. The historian of medieval Normandy, Lucien Musset, principally from the evidence of charters, looked at the terms for people which were current there in the ducal era. He found that at this time 'the vocabulary of social categories lost its ancient complexity', and by the twelfth century rural Normandy was inhabited by people variously described in the Latin sources as *milites*, *vavassores*, *franci homines*, and *villani*. While there were differences of rank among them, *franci homines* sometimes being contrasted with *villani* and associated instead with those with military association like *milites*, 'all were 'incontrovertibly taken as free'. Others – *bordarii*, *vernaculi*, *hospites* – were part of 'a vast and very varied group of rural tenants', people whose lower status was linked either to their having been housed by an employer or to their being 'natives' born to their very constricted condition. When it came to the vocabulary of Anglo-Norman England, Musset thought, the process of categorising the English population for the purpose of enumerating them for the Domesday returns had entailed 'manhandling' this vocabulary, whose 'unsuitability to national realities is almost shocking. *Villanus* is a foreign word introduced by the official Latin of the functionaries of the Exchequer to designate a class more or less artificially assigned to the inferior classes, *bordarius*, also imported, will not succeed in naturalizing itself.'[28]

Villani

Villani formed the largest group recorded. Maitland's approach to Domesday Book was to see 'beyond' it into Anglo-Saxon England. There he found the *tunesmanna*, the members of the township. Domesday's *villani* in his view were these 'people of the vill', or *tunesmanna*, 'townshipmen', who were collectively responsible for paying the share of the geld owed by the whole township. This interpretation would correspond with what we know about the geld assessment. Generally speaking, each county's overall obligation having been divided among its constituent hundreds and the hundred's obligation among its constituent townships, 'townshipmen', the members of the township, Latinized as *villani*, the members of the vill, were the geld payers.[29] Thus when an entry refers to *terra villanorum*, 'the land of the *villani*', what is at stake is sometimes geld liability. This could be a contentious issue. It was 'unjust' that the half-hide which had been 'quit of all service' when it belonged to the Church of St Constantine in Cornwall had 'paid geld unjustly as *terra villanorum*, the land of the *villani*, after Count Robert had taken it'.[30] Their numbers had been important for at least a century for the purpose of collecting and assessing taxation: the geld or land-tax. Geld was a progressive tax: those with more land paid more. True witness to the facts about a neighbour could be a matter of hard cash, so arriving at a fair assessment of each taxpayer's liability was essential. In parts of the country with many small settlements, sometimes single farms dispersed across a small area with no known boundary, like parts of Suffolk, the township was much harder to identify and a different unit, the lete, became responsible for its collection. As *villani*, the majority of the population, were the principal source of the geld, it mattered who exactly the *villani* were.[31] Some land was exempt, so assessing it fairly, or at least in such a way that it stood a reasonable chance of being collected, was a complicated job which would certainly have needed accurate local knowledge of who was liable to pay for what land. That is why it was 'unjust' that the half-hide which had been 'quit of all service', to the Church of St Constantine in Cornwall had paid geld.

Thus, as far as the operation of the geld system went, Maitland's interpretation of *villani* as the geld-paying *tunesmanna* has stood the test of time. What the Domesday commissioners meant by *villani* is another matter. Other than as a deprecatory term meaning something like 'rustic', and that itself is rare, the word does not appear in any pre-Conquest Latin text in England before 1086. In Normandy *villani* were members of a large, undifferentiated class of free peasants and Harvey's choice of 'husbandmen' for *villani* exactly conveys the essence of a farmer with his own property.[32] Domesday Book is not going to help us much further than that. William intended to secure the loyalty of all the *land-sittene* men, the chief men who held from him, and the men who held from them. This excluded a great many people, we do not know how many, below these ranks. Many English 'held from' a Norman newcomer after the Conquest the land they had owned before it, but at no level of society does Domesday Book record *all* those in this situation. With independent peasant farmers the situation is even more obscure, although local studies which give a picture of the kinds of farms which were characteristic of particular regions are doing much to make it clearer. Topography had a good deal to do with this. Remote farms are more likely to be recorded separately than those in more concentrated settlement. On the fringes of Dartmoor they may have their own Domesday entry, recording in the prescribed way the owner's name, their hidage, their draught stock, their *villani*, and occasionally their boarders, their farm workers and slaves, and their value. There are separate entries for dispersed farms in woodland areas like parts of Essex, for similar reasons, and the same is true of the open land of the Lincolnshire Wolds. But we do not know how many owners of other substantial farms will have been reckoned among the *villani* of the most substantial place of the neighbourhood.[33]

Bringing such a range of different kinds of people into association with a new entity, the manor, made possible the changes to be described in the following chapters, which reconfigured social relations in the English countryside.[34] The process began with language. In the new context of the Domesday manor, *villanus* was now someone who belonged to that manor and whose land was part of that manor: *terra villanorum* seems to have meant simply 'the peasants' land' as opposed to the lord's land *in dominio*. Some lords treated it as if it was at their disposal; this could cause enough resistance for the matter to be noted and this may mean that it had been a matter for legal dispute. Probably many more transfers of land in and out of manors took place over the heads, as it were, of the people using it to support themselves: 'land which he has given away to support one of his knights, to add to his manor, because it was a valuable pig-denn in Kent'. 'Reeve-land', the land assigned to support a reeve, could have been a useful tied tenancy to secure reliable supervisory staff: a reeve who held two hides from the monks of Winchester *quasi villanus* 'could not go where he wished'. That a *villanus* family and their land were an acquisition worth having appears in references to *villani* having been 'taken away' from manors by lords: to take away a *villanus* was to appropriate a farming family and its land and the obligations attached to both people and land, into another manor. Whether this was for their potential as workers or rent-payers is never clear: at the royal manor of North Benfleet in Essex the free man in this manor 'who has been made one of the *villani*' was a man with half a hide: a considerable amount of land for Essex. On another Essex manor where this happened, one *villanus* had had half a hide which 'paid customs', one had a single acre, and a woman, Beorhtgifu, had eighteen acres for which she paid the equivalent of two Danish *ora*, thirty-two pence, to the manor each year.[35] Those thirty-two pence may be another reason that *villani* were worth having, or appropriating: they yielded hard cash, although not necessarily in the form of, or the language of, what we would call 'rent'. A term commonly found for obligations due from the user of land to its owner is *gafol*. *Gafol* was more akin to tax than to rent.[36] If *villani* were counted and entered in Domesday as an asset of a manor it could well be that the *gafol* due from their land was indeed an asset worth having. The commissioners did not need any prior knowledge of their exact status, or their geld obligation, to lump peasants together as *villani*: what mattered more was what they could yield.

Every stage of the Domesday project involved linguistic issues: the initial gathering of verbal information in Old English, its translation, via Norman French, into Latin, its recording in the returns, its reduction to standard abbreviations, and the copying of the information in the returns into the final text. Not all the information came from the same kind of informants. While the articles of the enquiry ruled that information should be provided by the local community, and to this end six *villani*, the reeve and the priest from each place were to be sworn to give evidence, it is thought that it was often the agents of lords who provided the information about their estates and it was from this estate-based information that many Domesday entries were compiled. Some of the information about people, therefore, may have been made from their viewpoint, or that of their (probably initially French-speaking) managers, rather than from that of the representatives of the vill.[37] But however precisely the English would have described themselves and their neighbours, when the Domesday commissioners were instructed to count the *villani*, *cottarii*, *servi*, free men, and sokemen, the intention was to give the king an idea of the size of the rural population at each place, not to make hard-and-fast distinctions between them. For Domesday's purposes, as long as the overall numbers were about right, rough equivalents were probably all that were needed. When Robert, bishop of Hereford, an eyewitness of the Domesday process, said that William had had recorded both 'those living in cottages and those possessing houses and fields', this sounds very likely the way in which both Norman and English aristocrats would have summed up the rural population.[38] It may not be so far from the way in which a major landowner in any period might describe the people on his estate: so many farmers, or in earlier times, 'husbandmen', so many labourers and people with cottages. Even if *villani* were enumerated as tax payers from one point of view, and as 'people with fields and houses' from another, putting into Latin a familiar Norman French term for a familiar English kind of person would do.

Domesday Vocabulary: *Sochemanni et Liberi Homines*

There is nothing Norman about the term *sochemanni*, 'sokemen'. They are very unevenly distributed in Domesday Book, with a markedly higher proportion of the recorded population in the eastern counties, as is the case with 'free men.' 'Free men', when they can be categorised at all, cannot be summed up in any way yet discernible to Domesday scholars, although David Roffe has pointed out that they were hardly ever found in the same county as sokemen.[39] It is worth bearing in mind that no original copy of the articles of enquiry survives, and the information we have about what it contained comes from the archive of Ely Abbey, Cambridgeshire, and that questions about how many people there were in each category may have been answered differently between, even within, circuits. Ely was in one of the circuits, that for East Anglia, whose returns record sokemen, the others being those of the East Midlands and the north. That sokemen were recorded with particular care in some counties and not at all in others may have less to do with their actual numbers on the ground in those counties and more to do with the form and the amount of detail in which information was presented. Vital as they were to the families concerned, the fine detail of their distinctive status and freedoms 'in the time of King Edward' while not of any particular interest to the Domesday commissioners may have been recorded simply because they served to identify, in a still unfamiliar countryside, which particular fields, people, and houses were meant when they had been granted to new owners 'in the time of King William'.

The jurors had been instructed to count, in addition to the numbers of free men and sokemen, 'how much each sokeman or free man had or has there'. They did not consistently do this, but the fact that the information was sought could be significant. Possibly what made *sochemanni* distinctive in Norman eyes was their relationship to the ruler. 'Sokemen' and 'soke' were Old English terms entangled in Old English political arrangements. Whatever their economic position, which varied hugely, sokemen typically owed nothing but the usual public dues.[40] This could have been something that newcomers could recognise: sokemen may not have been unlike the kind of people whom Peter Coss has noted were occasionally recorded in Domesday Book as, in the Norman French term, *vavassores* and whom he describes as 'free men holding directly under the Crown' with 'modest estates'.[41] In a way, sokemen were small-scale tenants-in-chief: a category of people always of interest to the King. Their exact status must have been extremely important to sokemen themselves and well known locally. Ann Williams shows the complex arrangements at the manor of Abington Piggotts in Cambridgeshire. It made up quite a small area over four different vills, none more than a mile of two from another, but Little Domesday Book records that before the Conquest, apart from the main manorial centre, there had been seven distinct properties there in four different vills. Three of their owners were simply 'sokeman', two were named, all were commended to powerful men and free to find another lord should they wish. The findings of the jurors in 1086, when asked about Abington Piggotts, thus had a dense and detailed and carefully preserved body of local knowledge to draw on, built up from the experience of some seven family histories. None had ended well: by 1086 all the properties were in the hands of major Norman landowners or their subtenants and, while the identity of each property and its location were preserved, nothing more is heard of the sokemen's freedom and their commendation.[42] As with the *villani*, whatever the exact nature of their obligations, status, and entitlements, these people 'on the ground', for the purposes of the Inquiry, seemed much like the *liberi homines* or *vavassores* they knew.[43] We need to remind ourselves once again that Domesday Book, after all, was written for the Normans, not the English.[44] Approaching words from Domesday's terminology as essentially Norman enables us to approach the text from another perspective, that of the categories of people who do *not* seem to be there. Where are the thegns? They were an important element in England on the eve of the Conquest, but they do not appear among the articles of enquiry. In the text itself, thegns of important people or the king appear as named individuals and lesser administrators and are sometimes listed together at the end of a county. There are thegns in most counties while being much more heavily represented in some. The same patchy distribution is true of 'thaneland'. Again, there are very few reeves in Domesday Book, but there must have been very large numbers of men working as 'reeves', agents, for landowners. While there must have been such people in Normandy, Norman terminology may not have been so particular as to provide them with a description which indicated their occupation or role. *Liberi homines*, the 'free men' who in Normandy were sometimes contrasted with *villani* and associated instead with those with military association like *milites*, was a catch-all category broad enough to have included them.[45] In short, when English heads were counted for the purposes of the Domesday enquiry they were counted in terms which had arrived in Norman heads, and by and large these did well enough for William's purposes. Much as medieval historians would like it to have been the case, the Domesday commissioners were probably not particularly concerned with recording any degree of finesse the social composition of the English population, still less the relationships among them. William was interested in the statistics, quite literally in the 'bottom line', which in a typical manorial entry included the term *valet*, 'it is worth'. The last articles of the enquiry had instructed that it should be enquired, '*et si potest plus haberi quam habeatur*'. Frank Thorn has recently suggested that, given the classical Latin preferred throughout the Domesday text, this final phrase should be translated 'if more can be reckoned there than may (currently) be reckoned' but the more general interpretation, from which a great many deductions have been drawn, has been more literal: 'if more can be had than was had before.'[46] As to this, Domesday Book delivered William some vital statistics: what his new acquisition, England, was worth and how that worth could be increased, what property his 'chief men' had, what it was worth, what more profit it might yield, and whether the country was delivering the amount of tax that was due and who was evading it. In whatever language, money talked.

Nevertheless, the fact that Domesday terminology involved putting English people into Norman categories did matter. In the language in which the answers to these questions was recorded, the way in which that information was re-organised, and in the ideas around which that reorganisation was itself recorded, new and powerful messages were being conveyed. We could look at this in terms of changing attitudes to people and of attitudes to land. It was nothing new to think of land as property: powerful lords had probably always thought in such terms about their lordships, which might cover square miles, and so too had ordinary peasant farmers about their properties. It was nothing new for peasant households to feel the demands of lordly ones. Many peasant lives had long been constrained by the fact that they were tied into the economic regime of lords' inlands: when Domesday Book recorded the land, people, and livestock *in dominio* before the Conquest it may often have been recording what were essentially late Saxon inlands. The mutual obligations of many people to help another out at haymaking and harvest and so on had no doubt become fixed obligations to work at the 'boons' on a lord's home farm. Many *villani* may have owed regular labour in the form of week-work, but even roughly how many, or how much, is something we will never be able to discover from Domesday Book. But many other peasant lives can have had only the loosest connection with lords who were powerful remote figures who figured in their lives only, if then, in connection with matters of justice and peace-keeping. Common sense suggests that the fact that so many pre-Conquest people were living on farms which were many miles from anything that might be called an estate centre would itself mean that they were likely to have had very tenuous ties, perhaps no ties at all, with that centre, although they would all have turned up at markets and hundred courts – often the same occasion. Whether people like this are either exceptionally well recorded in parts of England or, alternatively, really were confined to those areas is still not determined. The manor brought all these disparate peasant lives together in a new social form, set over them a new kind of lordship and a new kind of lord: the 'lord of the manor'. Domesday Book's terminology had an important part to play in this. Barbara Harvey has drawn attention to the way that a new word could bring new ways of thinking: using the manor for ordering the survey rather than the vills or hamlets in which people actually lived 'helped on' the process of manorialisation.[47] The manor as a form of property, as a form of property which was 'held', a form of property whose total resources could be counted both in terms of its arable capacity and in terms of its people and their arable capacity, all these were new.

Domesday Vocabulary: Measuring Land

Domesday reveals that attitudes to measuring land were to change too. It reflects an emphasis on reckoning land in terms of its capacity to produce cereal crops: 'from the government's point of view the recognized normal holding was arable-based'.[48] This meant that particular attention was to be paid to the means of production, and in all medieval Europe that meant the oxen that pulled the plough. The numbers were required for how many working ploughteams there were *in dominio* and how many *hominum*, 'of the men'. These are questions which could well have been of interest to authorities well before the Conquest: ownership of a ploughteam had in the past been used for official purposes, both military and ecclesiastical.[49] Assessing land in terms of how many teams would be needed to keep it in cultivation was common sense: Anglo-Saxon farmers had been doing so for centuries: 'An *æcer* or more' is the amount of land Ælfric's ploughman had to plough each day and the acre was a widely used unit of land. On lands of the archbishop of York the term 'manslot', from ON *manshlutr*, 'a man's share', was described as 'every third acre' and so on: clearly this was arable land of some kind. Landowners on a large scale before and after the Conquest, particularly any who were producing grain for the market, could well have found the number of teams at work on their estates a handy guide to their arable assets. S. P. J. Harvey has demonstrated how useful a guide to estate policy is the ratio of teams *in dominio*, in lordship, to those of the peasants, *villanorum*.[50] This was a common way of measuring arable land in Normandy and came to be used in Norman charters conveying land in England so when the Commissioners came to the Danelaw counties, they would have found a familiar feature of measurement already in place.[51] Throughout Domesday Book land is measured in terms derived from words for ploughs: *carucata*, *carrucata*, carucate from Latin *caruca*, and in Kent sulungs, from OE *sulh*, which modern translations render as 'ploughlands'.

A new kind of information appears to have been of interest too: 'How many ploughteams is there land for?', 'How many are there?', 'How many could there be?' do not appear in the list of questions to be asked listed in *Inquisitio Eliensis*. This kind of information is sometimes supplied, and where it is supplied the Domesday returns could have given a useful pointer to manors where the last question it lists is: 'Can more can be had than is had?'

What does seem to have been an innovation are the linear measurements in leagues and furlongs that appear in some Domesday entries in eastern England and which may have been township boundaries.[52]

Measuring a large area of land in leagues was to do it by the *mensura Normannica*, the 'Norman measure': this is how Battle Abbey's inland, the 'league surrounding the church of Battle', which came to be called its *leuga*, was laid out.[53] Dudo of St Quentin, writing in the early eleventh century, while his object was to provide the Normans with a prestigious origin myth, described in prosaic terms the Vikings' partitioning of Norman estates by 'dividing them up by the rope': a practice which is common in the Danish law-codes.[54] His observation has been dismissed as merely a biblical reference, but a recent commentator commends Dudo for the care he took to provide accurate information about practical matters. In this respect he could well have been drawing on what he knew from his own observation: measuring land *funiculo hoc est corda*, 'that is, by a rope', occurs in a Norman charter of the early eleventh century, where it was specifically open land, not woodland, that was to be measured. The practice was brought to England: Ranulf Flambard, chief financial officer to William Rufus, may have been behind the wording of a writ ordering Thorney Abbey's lands to be measured in this way, *praecipio ut..admensuratis funiculo mensus est*: 'I order it to be measured by the rope'. When Orderic Vitalis castigated him as the *exactor*, 'the enforcer', of the spoliation of England by both kings, the accusation that Flambard 'measured and recorded all the ploughlands which the English call hides' was part of his indictment. Accurate linear measurements of all England's land, if not on the scale of the Ordnance Survey but on similar principles, would have been modernisation indeed and as Orderic noted, it was something more: a deliberate break with English practice.[55]

How Many Hides?

Domesday's numbers of ploughteams and ploughlands brought together information about land, capital equipment, and labour inputs: all factors that are still relevant to farming today. Taken together, the result would be a fair approximation of a manor's real arable productive capacity. This was not something that could be measured by counting hides. Nonetheless, it is with hides that every Domesday entry begins. When land was granted before the Conquest hides were still being used as a rough guide to its value and area. In many cases they must have been a very rough guide indeed, but they retained their place in the way that people thought about land for a great many more reasons than their accuracy. They were the taxable unit: raising the geld would have been impossible without hidages. In England the numbers of taxpayers had been important for at least a century for the purpose of collecting and assessing the geld or land-tax. Although Domesday Book was not intended as a 'geld book', it incorporated a great deal of information which was already to hand in the geld records: every entry begins with an assessment of the place in hides, the unit on which geld liability was calculated. Generally speaking, each county's overall obligation was divided among its constituent hundreds or their equivalents, the hundred's obligation then being divided among its constituent elements: most often these were the townships and in all these contexts members of the township whose land was hidated were the geld payers. Broadly speaking, only hidated land was liable to geld and land not assessed in hides was exempt, or to put this in human terms, it was the farmers who paid the bulk of England's taxes. The hide as the 'land of one family' which bound farms and households together was also the basis on which liability to public burdens, and thus membership of free society, had long been based: geld was yet another such burden. Hides have appeared throughout the earlier parts of this book, embedding social meaning of many kinds: the basis of the family farm and of independent status in peasant society as well as of the public obligations of the thegn. Domesday's recording of England's hidation thus inscribed into the record not only the tax system of an older society but also its categories of land and people. In David Roffe's words, 'Ultimately geld defined the freedom of the free man.'[56] Ploughlands and ploughteams came from a different mind-set altogether in which the freedom of the free man was neither here nor there: what mattered was productivity, and from productivity, if 'more could be had than is had', would come profitability.[57]

The people whose situation would be most profoundly changed by the new ways of thinking about land in terms of tenure and the manor were the *villani* or peasant farmers, the 'people with houses and fields'. Essentially what was at stake was the question of who had rights over their labour. Words would play an important part in this too. Our sources will only allow us to see indirectly, but they do allow us a glimpse of two situations in which lords' demands came face-to-face with peasant resistance. One took the form of legally recognised episodes of negotiation. The other was the law court. The next chapter follows some peasants and their landlords into court. And we hear more about negotiation.

Notes

1 *The Ecclesiastical History of Orderic Vitalis*, ii. 219.
2 Interpreters: Tsurashima, 'Domesday interpreters'. For the primary collection of information: Fleming, *Domesday Book*, chapter 1: 'Oral testimony and the Domesday Inquest'; Baxter, Crick, Lewis, and Thorn, *Making Domesday*; Fleming, *Domesday Book*, 13–14 for the size and composition of the juries.

3 Clark, 'Domesday Book – a great red herring', 158–9 citing von Feilitzen at 157; Clanchy, 'Latin and the language of Domesday Book' in *From Memory to Written Record*, 35–8; Thorn, '*Non Pascua sed pastura*' emphasizes the classicising tendency of the choice of Latin terms in the Domesday text.

4 Baxter, 'The making of Domesday Book', 290.

5 Tallies, notched sticks, could well have been used, but have only the slenderest chance of survival: Clanchy, *From Memory to Written Record*, 125–6.

6 Pelteret, 'Two Old English lists of serfs'.

7 Lambert, *Law and Order*, chapter 7, 'Rights and revenues' arguing that not until the eleventh century was there a change towards more legal rights and the ensuing revenues, being formally reserved to the king, fundamentally challenges the view of Campbell and Wormald.

8 Clanchy, *From Memory to Written Record*, 30–5.

9 Hone and Green, *A Mannor and Court Baron*, 11.

10 *Domesday Book: Lincolnshire*, 8.

11 Williams, *English and the Norman Conquest*, chapter 4, 'Survivors' traces the situation in terms of individuals and their land over three counties, quotation at 71.

12 Lewis, 'Invention of the manor'. Loyn, *Anglo-Saxon England and the Norman Conquest*, 347–56 is a clear setting-out of regional differences in the way that land was recorded in Domesday Book; Harvey, 'The life of the manor'; *The Ecclesiastical History of Orderic Vitalis*, ii. 223; entries of 'land' rather than 'manor' being grouped manorially: Palmer, 'The Domesday manor', 147–52.

13 For the English evidence for seigneurial residences see now Blair, *Building Anglo-Saxon England*, chapters 10 and 11. Gardiner, 'Origins of manorial buildings'.

14 Blair, *Building Anglo-Saxon England*, 400; William of Malmesbury, 274. I shall always be grateful to Henry Mayr-Harting who first brought this key passage to my attention.

15 Stevenson, 'A contemporary description of the Domesday Survey'.

16 Jolliffe, *Pre-Feudal England*, 4–5.

17 Baxter, 'Making of Domesday Book', citing ASC 1085, ms. E.

18 Baxter, 'The profits of royal lordship'. Reynolds, 'Tenure and property in medieval England' at p. 565.

19 Fleming, *Domesday Book*, chapters 3 and 4, quotations at 69, 63.

20 DMLBS, *s.v. tenere* (11) misleadingly dates the first use of the Latin word *tenere* in English sources, in the sense of tenure of land, by citing it from King Alfred's will, composed in the ninth century and written in OE, of which the earliest Latin translation is of the fourteenth or early fifteenth century: Whitelock, *English Historical Documents*, 492, AND, *s.v. tenure* show it established in English legal sources by the thirteenth century. Forthcoming work on Exon Domesday will show examples of *tenet* being substituted for *habet* in the process of reorganising the returns: I am grateful to Chris Lewis for this information.

21 Tabuteau, *Transfers of Property*, 103–4.

22 Jolliffe, 'Alod and fee'; Garnett, *Conquered England*, 28. The English evidence is reviewed in an essay by John Hudson, 'Imposing feudalism on

Anglo-Saxon England' in a collection on the ongoing debate on feudalism, quotation at 131. Miller, *The Abbey and Bishopric of Ely*, quotation at 50. Abrams, *Anglo-Saxon Glastonbury* usefully assembles the representation of Glastonbury's estates in Domesday and only adopts the term 'tenant' with caution. Reynolds, 'Bookland, folkland and fiefs' argues strongly against there having been tenure before the Conquest. Against this viewpoint, a strong articulation of the importance of 'dependent tenure' before the Conquest was by T. H. Aston, whose posthumously published article on the 'Ancestry of English feudalism' took the Domesday vocabulary of tenure to reflect pre-Conquest conditions, particularly on ecclesiastical estates. He was careful to distinguish this from the military obligation to provide a quota of knights, which had long been considered an essential element in 'feudal' tenure.

23 For *ealdormannic* estates, Baxter and Blair, 'Land tenure and royal patronage'.

24 *Gebyncðu* 3: Leibermann, *Gesetze*, i. 456. Five hides, thought by Wulfstan to have been the essential landed basis for the supply of armed men, was a fairly common size of landholding in Domesday Book, and was by then well-established to have given rise to place-names such as Fifield. Arguments for there having been a pre-Conquest military 'quota' system based on a five-hide unit are effectively critiqued by Abels, *Lordship and Military Obligation*, 108–15

25 For the fee in England as a Norman innovation: Jolliffe, 'Allod and fee'. On the fee and the 'knight's fee': Hyams, 'Notes on the transformation of the fief'. For the fee in *Mirror of Justices* see Chapter 12. 'Fee', 'feudal', and related words are an essential part of the vocabulary commonly used by historians to describe social relationships at a higher social level than that of the peasantry. Bloch, *Feudal Society*, 166–8 extended it by defining the fief as 'a property granted against an obligation ... to do something', and describes it as 'an institution, originally very comprehensive, which was transformed into one pertaining to a particular social class', with French peasants with specialised obligations having a 'fief' in the sense of remuneration, or as we would say, a 'fee'. Reynolds, *Fiefs and Vassals* argues that the term is anachronistic, 'feudalism' having been a coinage of the seventeenth century. Peasants holding by feudal tenure are suggested in Chapter 14, 'Thinking feudally'.

26 I owe this acute observation to David Pelteret.

27 The instructions to the commissioners were recorded in *Inquisitio Eliensis*, Ely Abbey's copy of the list of questions. It is generally assumed that they were identical for all circuits. A full description of them is Darby, *Domesday England*, 4–5, although for the procedures of collecting, translating, abbreviating, and recording see now Baxter, Crick, Lewis, and Thorn, *Making Domesday*.

28 Musset, 'Les domaines de l'époque franc', 68. Musset's idea of 'ancient complexity' may have been based on his belief that a domainal system along the lines of those in the *polyptyques* had prevailed in pre-Viking Normandy. For the *bordarii* see Chapter 6.

29 Maitland, *Domesday Book*, 82–9. Some modern translations of Domesday Book, such as the Alecto and Penguin editions, have tried to avoid the anachronism of 'villein' or 'villager' by opting for 'villan'.

30 Fleming, *Domesday Book and the Law*, no. 313. For current thinking on geld exemption see Pratt, 'Demesne exemption', Harvey, *Domesday*, 219–22.

31 This may be the reason why, on some of the abbot of Bury's Suffolk manors, Domesday Book gives linear measurements of an area: possibly the geld was assessed on this area and collected from the people who lived within these bounds.

32 Musset, 'Les domaines de l'époque franc'; DMLBS, *s.v. villanus* 1, 3, and 4. Harvey, 'Domesday England', 50–8.

33 Maitland illustrated this essential difference, beginning *Domesday Book and Beyond* with two Ordnance Survey maps and a discussion of the 'land of villages' and 'the land of hamlets'. Banham and Faith, *Anglo-Saxon Farms and Farming*, chapters 8, 10, and 11 for individual farm studies. Walkhampton, Devon, is an example of a (royal) manor, whose entry includes six *villani*. These can be shown to be the owners of large 'worthy' farms strung out between the Walkham valley and the edge of Dartmoor, while the inland was a 'magnate farm' enclosed by a substantial bank: Faith, 'Some Devon farms'; Faith and Fleming, 'Walkhampton enclosure'.

34 Aston, 'Origins of the manor', 8.

35 Fleming, *Domesday Book and the Law*, nos. 92 (reeveland, *terra villanorum*, and land paying the *feorm* put into Henry de Ferrers' manor), 313 ('after Count Robert took it' previously exempt land paid geld as *terra villanorum*), 1654 ('Andsgot holds one and a half hides: *propria*, it is rightly, *terra villanorum*'), 1660 (*terra libera vel villana*), 604 (reeveland), 1795 (free man *effectus est unus de villanis*), 1807 (Beorhtgifu paying geld), 1967 (Raymond Gerald took away a *villanus* of whom Robert Gernon was seised), 2160 ('fourteen freemen and twelve *villani* whom Ralph Baynard now holds have been taken away from this manor').

36 Vinogradoff, *English Society*, 210–11; Neilson, 'Customary Rents', *s.v. gafol*. The *gafol* owed to lords in return for a 'yard' of land in Ine 67 is discussed in Chapter 9. Land and people owing *gafol* are miscellaneous, but when the amounts owed are given they look too uniform to have been related to the value of the land concerned, or to the status of those who paid it: in *Rectitudines singularum personarum* both the independent *geneat* who does responsible jobs around the estate and the *gebur* who is essentially a serf owe *gafol*.

37 For information provided by estate administrators: Thomas, *The English and the Normans*, chapter 11, gives a rounded picture of the mix of English and French at the level of society from which manorial and estate administrators might be drawn.

38 Stevenson, 'A contemporary description of the Domesday Survey'.

39 Roffe, *Decoding Domesday*, table 7 on p. 222. Darby, *Domesday England*, 61–4.

40 For soke and sokemen: Maitland, *Domesday Book*, essay 1, chapters 4 and 5. Goebel, *Felony and Misdemeanor*, 336; Purkiss, 'Early royal rights in the Liberty of St. Edmund'.

41 Coss, 'Literature and social terminology', 117; Musset, 'Les domains de l'époque franc', 68.

42 Williams, 'Hunting the Snark'. Maitland, *Domesday Book*, 90–3 for examples of explicit re-categorising of sokemen as *villani*.

43 Maitland, *Domesday Book*, 95–8, 120–1, 136–7; Darby, *Domesday England*, 61–3.

44 Not every entry in Domesday Book is from a Norman perspective. The rights that the heads of some extremely well-endowed religious houses claimed had been given them by the king over the people on their land might be attributed a much longer ancestry than they were strictly entitled to. The 'ancient liberty' of Oswaldslaw in Domesday Book has been shown by Patrick Wormald to have been 'created' by the monks of Worcester to be entered as theirs in Domesday Book. The rights of Bury St Edmunds to 'customs', 'services', and to the 'soke' and commendation of so many on the abbey's estates is another case in point: Wormald, 'Oswaldslow'; Purkiss, 'Early royal rights in the Liberty of St. Edmund'.

45 For overall numbers of thegns by county: Darby, *Domesday England*, 343; thegnland (*tainlanda*) e.g. *Domesday Book: Somerset*, 1.21, 8.16. Finn, *Eastern Counties*, 124–6.

46 Thorn, '*Non Pascua sed pastura*', 112–13.

47 Harvey, 'The life of the manor'.

48 Harvey, 'Domesday England', 51. Harvey's chapter remains the most knowledgeable and authoritative survey of the agrarian economy in 1086 known to me. Duby, *Rural Economy*, 111, notes that in thirteenth-century Normandy all valuations at inquests were made in terms of bovine animals.

49 The ploughteam is the basis of an obligation to provide military service in the form of one horse to be supplied from each in II Æthelstan 16: Attenborough, *Laws*, 136–7, Liebermann, *Gesetze*, i. 158–9. Hart, *Early Charters of Northern England*, 14–15 for carucation as part of military organisation.

50 Darby, *Domesday England*, chapter 4 gives the formulae used in each circuit. A rough count showed that measurements in ploughlands are about as common as measurements in hides in charters relating to English lands in Bates, *Regesta*, *Index verborum*. Harvey, 'Domesday England' uses the ratio of ploughteams on inland ('demesne') to those on peasant land as a guide to estate policy.

51 I am concerned here simply with terminology, and am grateful to respondents to an email enquiry on this subject: Lesley Abrams, Stephen Baxter, John Blair, Sally Harvey, Richard Purkiss, and David Roffe. For the intricacies of how the ploughland was calculated and its real and fiscal nature: Darby, *Domesday England*, 5, 6, 7, 121–35; Roffe, *Decoding Domesday*, 203–10. For the ploughland in Normandy: Fauroux and Musset, *Receuil des Actes*, nos. 122, 140, 224, 139, 202, 214; in Norman charters for lands in England: Bates, *Regesta*, nos. 9, 47, 59, 62, 92, 116, 117. Although farmers on both sides of the Channel must have used teams of varying size and composition, it is possible that Domesday brought in a new unit of assessment: the standard team. The Domesday ploughteam is generally supposed to have consisted of eight oxen but references to the size of teams in Norman charters indicate much smaller teams, of three or four oxen: anything larger seems to have been a *carruca fortissima* and it is not clear why the Domesday unit was calculated on the basis of an eight-ox team. For the four-ox ploughteam in Normandy: Fauroux and Musset, nos. 139, 202, 214. Possibly the Domesday unit was

calculated on a similar basis, *pace* Finberg, 'The Domesday plough-team', followed by Harvey, 'Domesday England', and Lennard, 'The composition of the Domesday *caruca*', followed by Langdon, *Horses, Oxen*, 62–74. For ploughs and ploughing and their Old English terminology: Banham and Faith, *Anglo-Saxon Farms and Farming*, 50–74. There is a possibility that the Normans also brought in a new kind of bread wheat, rivet wheat (*Triticum turgidum*), which was suitable for heavy clay land. John Letts has suggested that 'a genetically diverse population of rivet wheat was introduced to Britain soon after the Norman conquest': Letts, *Smoke Blackened Thatch*, 18.

52 These are also used in some circuits to give the dimensions of woodland. The linear measurements in leagues and furlongs that appear in some Domesday entries in eastern England may have been township boundaries: Banham and Faith, *Anglo-Saxon Farms and Farming*, 285–6 and references thereto work suggesting they delineated the limits of common fields. I am grateful to Richard Purkiss for sharing his work on a Suffolk example. Measurement by the rope in Dudo of St Quentin: Musset, 'Les domaines de l'époque franc', 55; Faroux and Musset, *Receuil*, no. 46, p. 153. I am extremely grateful to Lesley Abrams who supplied me with this reference. For *Mensura Normannica*: Bates: *Regesta regum Anglo-Normannorum*, nos. 159, 25.

53 DMLBS, s.v. *funiculus*.

54 I am grateful for this information from Prof. Helle Vogt.

55 Orderic Vitalis: *The Historia Ecclesiastica*, x. 8: *omnes carrucatas quas Anglice hidas vocant mensus est et descripsit.* Harvey, 'Anglo-Norman governance'. Writ of William Rufus to Justiciars: Bates: *Regesta Regum Anglo-Normannorum*, i. 422 and L. xii. Clarke, 'Condensing and abbreviating the data', 259–62, considers that what Orderic was referring to here was not a new kind of assessment contemplated by Rannulf for the purposes of the Domesday inquiry but for a later scheme that came to nothing.

56 Roffe, *Decoding Domesday*, 196.

57 The Domesday mind-set led to some misunderstandings of, or perhaps merely indifference to, English farming systems. Entries in the Devonshire folios which record that there were an insufficient number of teams on a manor may simply not have understood the local practice of convertible husbandry: Banham and Faith, *Anglo-Saxon Farms and Farming*, 252–3.

12   Narrating the New Social Order

Wulfstan's picture of the social order and what held it together had been imbued with his veneration of the idea of reciprocity, of what was rightly due to, and rightly due from, the various ranks in society, and it was through this framework of what should be, or rather of what 'once was', that he observed social change. The views of the social order in the aftermath of the Conquest which are found in the texts considered here are different altogether. In place of the language of 'what should be' they are descriptions of historical process and explanations of power relationships.[1] In place of the language of entitlement and obligation they use the language of rights and contracts, negotiation and legality. One such perspective comes from the late twelfth century, in the words of Richard Fitznigel, Treasurer of England and bishop of London, who ascribes William's aim in having Domesday Book drawn up to be 'that every man should have his own rights and not encroach unpunished on those of others'.[2] The question of rights, and the foundation of rights, in the new regime may go some way to explain the interest that Norman legal writers took in English law. It is important to remember that while militarily the Conquest was a forceful takeover, in Anglo-Norman political culture it was justified and presented in terms of continuity, based on William's claim to be the legitimate successor of Edward the Confessor. (Harold, crowned in 1066, was written out of the picture.)[3] Claiming continuity with Old English legal tradition was part of this position and several collections were made containing versions of what was known, or purported to be known, of the vernacular law codes.[4] One of these, written in the first decades of the twelfth century, claimed to be 'The laws and customs which King William granted to the people of England after the conquest of the land, the same which King Edward his cousin held before him', and became known as the *Leis Willelme*, 'The Law of William'. It is the first work we know of that was written in French: a Latin version was included in the same manuscript as the legal compilation known as the *Quadripartitus*.[5] Most of its fifty-two chapters are based on the English laws, principally those of Cnut. A few are taken from Roman law, by this time known on the Continent although not in England and it is possibly for this reason that experts on legal history have claimed it for the legal curriculum and played down its relevance to actual conditions. If the entire work had simply consisted of recording the vernacular law codes and splicing in some Roman law to make up for their deficiencies, that would make it a fairly standard kind of academic compilation for its time.[6] Nicholas Karn has suggested that although there was as yet 'no scope for professional advocates', there was a kind of 'textual community' in early twelfth-century England, in which the legal literature played an important part in acquainting Normans with English law. Bruce O'Brien considers Leis Willelme to have been something rather more practical than that: 'the intended purpose may have been to teach law', possibly for Norman agents who had business in the local courts.[7] Something more practical still may have been at issue. Four clauses were derived neither from Roman nor from Old English law. Their importance lies in the fact that they can provide us with a Norman view of the deficiencies of Old English law when it came to disciplining the peasantry. These deficiencies can easily be summarised: there was no Old English law when it came to disciplining the peasantry. Later chapters will look at the consequences of this disjuncture, which would give learned lawyers the task of producing an entirely new body of law: the 'law of villeinage'.[8] The more immediate problems arose from practice in the public courts. This is where French lawyers had to struggle with the everyday problems of getting Norman ideas into English heads. The first of these would be to bring English legal practice into line with the Norman concept of tenure.[9]

Changes On the Estate

Birth mattered at every level of medieval society and in a 'mixed race' society such as Anglo-Norman England, it could be particularly important when it had a bearing on status. Norman lords would expect their peasant tenants to be English. Writing in the 1170s, Fitznigel described the situation in his day when English and Normans at the higher level of society have so intermarried that 'it can scarcely be decided who is of English birth and who Norman'. But this is only, he says, in the case of the free: 'except of course those *ascriptitii qui villani dicuntur quibus non est liberum obstantibus dominis suis a sui status condicione discedere*, those *ascripticii* who are called *villani* for whom it is not allowed to depart from their condition if their lords object.' *A(d)scripticii* was a Roman legal term for peasants who had been registered at, 'ascribed to', an estate'.[10] When it came to people like this, English and Norman landlord attitudes were at one, for a permanent skilled labour force was essential to an estate of any size. Throughout earlier chapters small peasants with some land of their own but with heavy labour obligations have surfaced occasionally in the written sources, taking on land, dwelling, and equipment in return for labour rent in Ine's law of the eighth century, owing labour and crops as *geburas* in the *Rectitudines*, as 'loaf-eaters' getting their bread as 'hinds' in farmers' households. Such people in England were *gebyrde*, 'born into', their condition and their obligations. Known as *neifs* in Normandy, from Latin *nativi*, 'born', 'native', they were similarly named from having been 'born into' theirs. If such people on either side of the Channel wanted to better their lot they would have had no recourse but flight to look for a better deal elsewhere.[11] If they tried their luck on another estate, it is unlikely that solidarity among the landowning class would have been strong where acquiring such a valuable labour supply was concerned, and 'poaching' as well as purchasing worker-tenants was an option.[12] Yet Old English law does not seem to have provided any reliable method, other than force, of bringing them back. *Leis Willelme* appears to be the beginnings of a body of law, or perhaps a body of practice, to rectify this situation by enforcing lords' control of their tenants in the courts and ensuring that other lords would be part of the process. Clause 30.1 deals with 'natives' who are flouting the lords' arrangements and looking for a better life elsewhere. *Li naifs qui depart de sa terre dunt il est nez e vent a autri terre nuls nel retenge ne li ne ses chatels enz le facet venir arere a faire son servise tel cum a li apend.* 'A native-born who leaves the estate of which/where he is born and goes to another estate no-one shall retain either him or his possessions (but) shall make him return ( ) to do his service such as belongs to him.' Now the law will come to the aid of estate owners who have lost labour in this way: *Si les seigneurages ne facent altri gainurs venir a lour terre la justice le facet.* 'If the lords do not make other people's cultivators return to their estate, justice will do it'.[13]

This is the kind of law most land-lords would favour and it was being conveyed in new terms which themselves carried weight. *Seigneurages* was one. That lords had more in common with each other than they had with the people working for them would have surprised nobody in pre-Conquest England, yet there seems not to have been any Old English equivalent of *seigneurage*. OE *hlaford-scipe*, 'lord-ship', was an abstract term which meant 'dominion', not an analogy with *tūn-scipe*, a group of people with something in common. New too, as we have seen, was the manor. A wide variety of people of very different wealth and status, owing very different kinds of obligation, were now to be considered to 'belong' to a manor and to 'hold' their land from a manorial lord. This brought issues of tenure to the fore. *Leis Willelme* shows us people who had been looking for certainty of their terms of tenure and had been looking for legal evidence to support them. Among those who took the legal route were some who had the least real independence: those 'born onto' the inland of an estate and were tied to the obligations of their tenure. Clause 30 rules that *Les naifs ki departe(n)t de la terre ne deivent cartre faire n'avurie quere que il ne facent leur dreit service que append a lour terre.* 'Native-born who leave their land must not make a charter nor seek avowry that they do not owe the due service which belongs to their land.'[14] These 'native-born' have not just resorted to flight but have been challenging the very terms on which they had their land. The new emphasis on the terms of tenure did not only work against the least powerful: *Leis Willelme* has an eye to abuses by lords and by the same token, the right of a tenant who provided due service not to be evicted. *Cil qui cu(l) ti(v)ent la terrre ne deit l'um travailer se de leur droite cense noun; ne leist a seigneurage departir les cultiveurs de lur terre pur tant cum il pussent le dreit seirvise faire.* 'No-one may harass the cultivators of the land but for their due rent: nor is it permitted to lords to part the cultivators from their land *as long as they can do their due service*'. That the *Leis* was not intended simply as an academic exercise but was of practical use in court appears from the fact that an expression in the Latin version of this entry, *coloni et terrarum exercitores non vexentur ultra debitum et statutum*, is echoed in the wording of the writ *ne vexes* which tenants could bring against a lord who oppressively harassed them.[15] There was coming into being something new: legal rules to govern a lord's relations with people who owed him work.

Changes in the Courts

Procedures in court were changing too. The evidence of *Leis Willelme* suggests that it was still common, even routine, to take the traditional route and 'seek avowry', choosing pledges to stand surety for the truth of his claim. Now there are to be constraints on this. *Si hom volt derehdner cuvenant de terre ver sun seineur par ses pers de la tenure meismes qu'il apelerad a testimonie lui estuverad derehdner.* 'If a man wishes to deraign (produce in court) a covenant of land towards his lord he should call witness by his peers of the same tenure which is the proper deraignment.'[16] The law in *Leis Willelme* will insist that a man must call on his 'peers', people who are tenants holding land on the same terms as he does: *ses pers de la tenure meismes.* They are the proper deraignment for him, 'because he cannot deraign by strangers', *kar par estrange nel purrad pas derehdner.* 'Strangers' are likely in this context to have been used in the countryman's usage of 'foreigners', people from outside the immediate vicinity, anyone 'not from round here'. This prompts the speculation that the principle that 'each person is to be judged by men of equal status and from the same district as himself', a principle which underlies the composition of the public courts before the Conquest, was now proving insufficient to discipline tenants.[17] Implicit in privileging the testimony of fellow-tenants in this way did not only signal a new emphasis on tenure. If this clause had become adopted as law, it would have undermined a basic element in Anglo-Saxon justice. Standing surety, responding to a call to support someone in court, had long been part of the way that disputes were settled and there were rules about whom an accused man could call as 'pledges', who would warrant him, swear to his trustworthiness. The early law codes had restricted these to people with personal knowledge of the accused, who could bear witness on his behalf and these must often have been members of his kindred, but by the eleventh century sureties might be drawn from a wider group. The connections formed from family relationships, trading, and a web of other links now invisible to us meant that country people were always part of networks much wider than the bounds of where they lived and worked: we know much more about such networks at the level of the aristocracy, like that of the Mercian earls studied by Stephen Baxter, but lesser people had them too. Susan Kelly has looked into the background of the pledges given in lawsuits whose records came into the archive of Peterborough Abbey: these *festermen* were 'local people who were recruited or came forward to vouch for the good faith of the vendor' and would stand as warranty for him. Many of the properties involved were quite small, some appear to have been single farms, and while many of the *festermen* were drawn from the neighbouring peasantry, others were from further afield. These suits would have been a very public affair, held in the hundred court, itself becoming a more formally organised forum, in which local witness was vital. It was precisely because these courts relied on the long-embedded values of local witness and reputation that they retained a strong hold on public esteem: James Holt found that in 'Conquered England', in spite of the evolution of new systems of justice and new means of proof, 'some chose wager of law (as finding pledges was called) preferring oath-helpers to a jury'. Compurgation was not finally abolished until 1833.[18] The author of *Leis Willelme* seems to have had an altogether different view of what should constitute witness: a man bringing a suit in any other court than the king's need only choose one man to vouch for the truth of what he has said in court, as long as he is a 'trustworthy, *entendable*, man who has seen and heard all the suit'. If it represented actual practice this would surely have been a far cry from the old-fashioned wager of law. We have no means of knowing whether or not it did, but it would not have been altogether unlikely.[19] After a long history as mainly a group of local people responsible for local policing, particularly with regard to cattle, during the eleventh century the tithing was becoming to be seen as a useful means of promulgating official policy in the localities. Under Æthelred the heads of tithings were to be responsible for making sure that fasts and almsgiving were carried out and Cnut had found it necessary to rule that 'every man must in a tithing' to ensure that the system was firmly in place. The tithing system was coming to be known as 'frankpledge' (the early twelfth-century 'Laws of Henry the First' seems to have taken it for granted that tithing and pledging group were much the same thing).[20] At the same time pledging was becoming socially restricted: lords were expected to stand surety for their own households and followers, while *villani* remained in the traditional pledging system. In the words of *Leis Willelme*: *E puis seient tuz les vilains en franc plege* must be in 'let all *villani* be in frankpledge' and 'everyone who wishes to be in benefit of the law must be in frankpledge'. (This appears to be the first use of the term in a text written in England.)[21] The *Leis Willelme* author was well acquainted with the traditional kind of pledging and must have known that it would be a break with traditional practice to restrict the pool of pledges to 'those of the same tenure', rather than the wide choice of friends, family, or neighbours such as the Peterborough *festermen*. To restrict their pool of witnesses or sureties to 'those of the same tenure' would put any peasants who were in dispute with lords at a great disadvantage when it was precisely their liability to the conditions attached to this 'tenure' that was in dispute. A wider conflict is implicit in these developments: for witness to remain in the hands of the locality might well undermine the ability of lords to assert their right to the *dreit service que append a lour terre*, 'the due service which belongs to their land'. We do not know whether or not these additions to the old English laws became practice, but if they had they would have served lords well.

But the new situation was not only a matter of enforcing a new economic regime. These conflicts are signs of a wider tension between people's traditional ways of thinking about their status and the new ways which the law was attempting to impose. While the law as recounted in *Leis Willelme* recorded people as bound to the soil as 'natives', this is not the behaviour of people who saw themselves in that light. Another clause smacks of individual negotiations: *nullui ne toile a soun seinour sun dreit servise pur nul relais que il li a fait en arere*, 'no-one shall withdraw from his lord his due service by any remission he has granted him in the past'.[22] Evidently not everything, legally speaking, was going in the way that the *seigneurage* would have wished, and some peasants were able to negotiate their way in the new legal climate. Obtained by someone 'native-born', a document, *cartre*, relating to his obligations which amounted to a written formal agreement with his lord, a 'covenant', settling what is due, *debitum et statutum* in the Latin translation, looks very like evidence which might be called on as proof in a court of law.[23] Enough proceedings of this kind have evidently been brought for a rule to be introduced which attempted to limit their scope. Some tenants evidently wanted to negotiate terms, and secure them by a written agreement, and do this by legal process, and considered that they had thereby been granted some kind of legally enforceable contract with their lords. Far from simple resistance to the demands of a landlord, this seems to stem from their belief in legal process and their capacity to negotiate. If so, they were in touch with the changing times, for *Leis Willelme* was at odds with some deeply embedded elements in the traditional moral economy. At the root of the surety system had been reputation and reciprocity: the tithings were groups of people who knew one another's worth, or lack of it. Now to be 'of the same tenure' was to be the deciding factor. To have a charter drawn up, to summon witnesses against one's lord in a court of law, to call on one's lord to uphold a formal commitment, amount to something markedly different. They amounted to a recognition that matters which had once been questions of reputation were becoming matters of contract. From the point of view of lords, while there was not yet in place a legal doctrine of 'villeinage', in the sense of unfreedom recognised as such by the law, *Leis Willelme* would have provided the legal reinforcement that the new manorial regime required. Used to guide Norman lawyers through the English courts, its practical rules mark the beginning of the legal thinking which would lead thirteenth-century lawyers to construct the legal status which was neither slavery nor freedom: villeinage.[24]

Narrating the New Order

As well in its laws, Norman administrators were interested in England's machinery of government. This was the concern of the authors of two texts in particular: *Leges Henrici Primi* from early in the twelfth century and Richard Fitznigel's 'Dialogue of the Exchequer' from the late 1170s. His book takes the form of a dialogue between the Master and his Scholar, during which the scholar learns, in great detail, not only how the Exchequer works, but because so much of pre-Conquest administration and law was still in place, he also learns a good deal about matters such as tithings and hundreds. Chroniclers and commentators did not generally concern themselves with the plight of the peasantry as a distinct group but what had happened to the landlord class and the relationship between the two deeply interested both these men and both drew on the witness of the countryside. *Rustici hoc norunt*, says one when it comes to describing local conditions, 'countrypeople know about this'. One of the matters which interested Richard Fitznigel was the fate of the English population and he recounts what he had been told by the 'natives' about what happened shortly after the Conquest.[25] The Master, instructing the Scholar about this, tells him how the *murdrum* fine originated in those troubled times. 'In the period immediately following the Conquest what were left of the conquered English lay in ambush for the suspected and hated Normans and murdered them secretly in woods and unfrequented places as opportunity offered. ... [I]t was finally decided that the hundred in which a Norman was found killed without his slayer being known ... should be mulcted in a large sum of assayed silver.' The Scholar asks whether this should apply in the case of a murdered Englishman and the Master replies: 'It did not do so originally ... but nowadays, when English and Normans live close together and give in marriage to each other, the nations are so mixed that it can scarcely be decided (I mean in the case of free men) who is of English birth and who of Norman: except of course the *adscripticii* who cannot alter their condition without the leave of their masters.' For that reason, for whoever is found slain nowadays the murder-fine is exacted, except where there is definite proof of the servile condition of the victim.[26] This leads the Scholar to enquire further into the immediate aftermath of the Conquest and the Master tells him 'what I have been told by native-born English'. His account of how the indigenous English eventually came to hold their land under Norman incomers stresses orderly transfer: 'whatever they had been able to obtain from their lords by due renders and by a lawful agreement having taken place, should be granted to them in inviolable right'.[27] This could be read simply as a handy 'legitimising theory' which would justify the status quo in much the same way that Domesday Book had justified all tenure as stemming from William's coronation. John Hudson has argued that the 'Dialogue's view of the past was to become part of "lawyers" time' and would become 'the collective memory of Henry II's administrators' and the later part of this chapter will illustrate the important place it would come to have in English political thought.[28] But Fitznigel's account of the immediately post-Conquest period, although it is hard to link to specific events, does sound like something more than rhetoric. This is what he had been told: all those who had fought the invaders and survived (these must be those who fought at Hastings and immediately afterwards) and the heirs of those who had fallen were 'deprived of all hope of recovering their former lands, farms and rents, for they counted it real gain to be allowed to live in subjection to their enemies'.

Fitznigel continues the story like this. 'Over time those who had not fought ... acquired the goodwill of their lords by devoted service and began to hold tenancies at the will of their lords, for themselves alone, however, without hope of succession. But as time went on, when they were everywhere thrown out of their holdings because *odiosi* to their lords, and nor was there anyone who would restore what had been taken away.'[29] We are in the dark, as we are with much of his text, as to what Fitznigel meant by 'when they had become *odiosi* to their lords'. There are plenty of circumstances in which landowners could have found the arrangements they had made in the disrupted times immediately following the Conquest no longer met their needs and wanted their tenants out. For their part, tenants wanted security and heritability and were evidently prepared to pay to secure them: 'at last it was decreed that whatever they had been able to obtain from their lords by due renders and by a lawful agreement having taken place, should be granted to them in inviolable right. They might claim nothing in the name of succession to other property from the time of the conquered people. ... From then on they were obliged to purchase the goodwill of their lords by devoted service. Thus whoever of the conquered people possesses landed property ... not what he considered due to him by right of succession but only what he has earned by due demands or by some agreement having taken place.'[30] It is not clear whether Fitznigel thought that those English who held their land 'by agreement' were in the same position as those he refers to in a brief passage about Domesday Book, drawn up, in his view, 'that every man may be content with his own right and not encroach unpunished on the rights of others', but both passages in this very obscure work do convey that a new proprietorial order had been established and that it was legitimised not simply by force of conquest, but by negotiation.[31]

Historians have not been inclined to take seriously what the Dialogue has to say about the unsettled times immediately following the Conquest. For its most recent editor, 'his description of the settlement ... can hardly be regarded as history but cannot safely be neglected as evidence'. George Garnett's careful assessment, however, is more respectful of Richard's judgement. Having dismissed possible written sources the author may have used, he concludes that Richard himself is responsible for this account which recognizes, more readily than the legal compilations and in much more explicit analytical detail than the histories, that the Conquest had transformed the terms on which English tenants held.[32] Fitznigel's account shows one aspect of this transformation which Domesday Book seems to confirm: the relationships of the pre-Conquest past had no longer any force: 'They (...) might claim nothing in the name

of succession to other property from the time of the conquered people. ...
whoever of the conquered people possesses landed property ... not what
he considered due to him by right of succession but only what he has
earned by due demands or by some agreement having taken place.'
Domesday Book carried this message too. When new lords took over
the estates of those who had them before 1066, referred to as their
'antecessors', this was not by right of succession: new rights came by
new grants.

The Dialogue did not distinguish lords from peasants among the
'conquered people' and its reference to those who, dispossessed, 'would
be forced to take service abroad' is more redolent of fighting men than of
farmers. Nor does Fitznigel seem to have thought that the negotiations he
described were at the root of the condition of those at the very bottom of
rural society: his word for these is *ascriticii*: the *neifs* of the *Leis Willelme*.
A broad section of English landholders must have been trying to recover
'their former lands, farms and rents'. Nevertheless, a concept links
Fitznigel's 'agreements' arrived at after 'due demands' and the 'covenant
of land towards his lord' of *Leis Willelme*. That concept is negotiation.[33]
That belief that the status and obligations of peasants had been settled by
negotiation also figures in two later texts. Both have echoes of Fitznigel's
account, which presumably means that it was considered at least plausible, possibly had become the received wisdom of the post-Conquest
situation. The *De legibus et consuetudinibus angliae*, 'On the laws and
customs of England', attributed to judge Bracton, is a revision, made
sometime after 1250, of a lost collection on legal procedure which had
been compiled in the 1230s. The parts of the work which deal with
villeinage have been assembled and analysed by Paul Hyams, who has
distinguished the influences on the author both of the 'learned law' of
Roman and canon law, and of decisions made in recorded cases involving villeins and villeinage.[34] However there is a passage in *De legibus* on
the origins of villein tenure which seems to derive from neither of these
sources but which recalls the language of the Dialogue: 'free men who
held their holdings by free services or free customs ... when they were
thrown out by more powerful people, on returning afterwards took the
same holdings up again to hold in villeinage, doing work for them which
was servile but set and specified'.[35] The second account comes in *The
Mirror of Justices*, a work written early in the fourteenth century.
The Mirror of Justices is generally associated with Andrew Horn, London
fishmonger and antiquarian with responsible office in the City.[36] Introduced by the heading 'And note that tenants who are free and quit of all
services become enserfed by contracts made between lords and tenants',
his narrative of a 'new deal' resembles that given by Fitznigel in the

Dialogue. The author uses the language of feudal law, of the *feudum*, the 'fee' to describe the post-Conquest settlement: 'contracts were made by our first conquerors when the counts were enfeoffed of counties, ... the knights of knights of knights' fees, the villeins of villeinages ... some received fees ... to hold by villein custom to plough, lead loads, drive droves, weed, reap, mow stack and thresh ... and sometimes without receiving food for this. ... And whereof various fines have been levied which may be found in the treasury, and which make mention of such services and vile customs, as well as of more courteous services.'[37] Horn adds an interesting comment of his own about obligations, which seems to go beyond legal arrangements to address some important and worrying changes in the moral economy. Addressing the topic of contract as the basis of all legal obligation, he considered that the model form of contract had been that of espousal, made without documents, which had been the kind of arrangement 'made by our first conquerors'. Written contracts were a falling-off from this ideal state of affairs and represented a worse deal for the peasantry: 'Tenants who are free and quit of all services become enserfed by contracts made between lords and tenants ... these contracts ... are made by writings, charters and muniments ... which used to be made without muniments with solemn testimony.' Horn's belief in the strength of the unwritten arrangements of the immediate post-Conquest settlements led him to the opinion that, even without 'muniments' or written proof, tenants who were ejected were entitled to sue 'providing that they know exactly what services their ancestors had owed, their ancestors before them having been *astriers* (houeseowners) for a long time.' He was concerned here with obligations which had been added 'in excess of these right customs' and records that 'Saint Edward' 'had busied himself in his day in this matter by making inquest into all the grievances that were done to cultivators in excess of their right customs'. There is a good deal of Wulfstan's '*hwilom wæs*' about this: the good old days when a man's word was as good as his bond had given way to a world of formal contract.

For Patrick Wormald, *The Mirror of Justices* was 'a tendentious tract', and Maitland's introduction to the *Mirror* comprehensively rubbished Horn as a legist: 'He is borrowing from Bracton and enforcing the loan by romance.' However, Maitland respected him as an antiquarian and Jeremy Catto has established him as a knowledgeable Londoner with a strongly held belief that 'London's and England's liberties were not the creation of Magna Carta but ascended to remote antiquity.' Like other Londoners in his day he was interested in the Anglo-Saxons and their origins and owned a collection of the laws of England from Ine to Henry II, the *Leges Anglorum*.[38] As Chamberlain of the City of London from

1308 until his death in 1328, Horn had had manuscripts transcribed for him for occasions when the justices sat at the Tower and he had to prepare materials to defend the City's rights in court. One set of records that he might have seen, although no manuscript survives which might be connected with him, are the returns to two enquiries initiated by Edward I. The first are to an enquiry of 1274–5 into abuses by the king's officials. The second are the Hundred Rolls of 1279, which comprise the replies to an enquiry into what property was held by virtually the entire population (although the returns from only five counties survive), and on what terms.[39] Horn's notion of contracts by which 'counts were enfeoffed of counties ... knights of knights' fees, villeins of villeinages' corresponds very well to the material in the Hundred Rolls of 1279.[40] These covered not only the holdings and term of tenure of the major landholders, but also 'the size of holding of every free man, villain, serf or cottar, and its terms ... from who held and by what services or dues'. Although his reference to 'Saint' Edward remains a mystery, when Horn, concerned with historical origins notes that 'Saint Edward' 'had busied himself in his day in this matter by making inquest into all the grievances that were done to cultivators in excess of their right customs', he may have had these documents in mind.[41]

Thus two Norman writers in the twelfth century, the author of *Leis Willelme* in its first quarter, Fitznigel in its last, had presented rather similar narratives of challenge, negotiation, and settlements between tenants and lords which had resulted in binding agreements on the part of tenants to perform agreed services. The most respected legal work of the thirteenth century, 'Bracton', had formalised these into an account of a change from unwritten agreements to formal contracts and detailed lists of services. At the turn of the fourteenth century, a Londoner who believed that 'London's and England's liberties ... ascended to remote antiquity' also believed that villeinage tenure had been introduced by feudal contract. Educated opinion was that the Conquest had brought fundamental change to the relationship between lords and their peasant tenants. It is time to consider how far this represented a shift away from what earlier chapters have proposed as elements of the 'moral economy' in pre-Conquest England.

From Commendation to Tenure

For better or worse there had always been a personal element in pre-Conquest lordship. This was looking increasingly frail in the new legal climate. Connection with an important patron is vital in many peasant societies, especially when courts of any kind are involved, and what the powerless needed in early medieval England was powerful friends who would 'swear for' them. *Mannraedenn,* the act which established commendation, was symbolic of submission: the man bows before the lord and swears an oath of allegiance and in return the lord could be called upon to protect his commended man, who in turn and owed him 'service'.[42] Commendation was thus nominally a reciprocal process and although reciprocity in these relationships between powerful and much less powerful individuals must always in fact have been minimal, it seems to have mattered nonetheless. As was suggested in the previous chapter, when Wulfstan lamented that in his day *Frige men ne motan waldan heora sylfra, ne faran ða hi willað, ne ateon heora agen swa swa hi willað,* 'Free men are not allowed to keep their independence, nor go where they wish, nor to deal with their own property as they wish', one possibility is that he thought that people who considered themselves free were losing their capacity to 'commend themselves' to the protection of a lord of their choice. Commendation may never have delivered the 'protection' claimed for it, or had only delivered it at a price, but it had been valued nonetheless. In some Domesday circuits, commendation was carefully recorded and the fact that some people could no longer 'seek a new lord' as they once had been able to do is recorded too.[43] If to be commended could be a form of protection, to have as many people as possible commended to one was a form of power. The entries for the abbot of Bury take care to note that he had the commendation of the people on all the abbey's properties as well as the *soc,* their right to have them sue in his courts. But commendation to a powerful institution such as Bury could prove to be a slippery slope, at the bottom of which was tenure. One of Ely's historians has shown that the abbey was extending its protection to people who were thereby becoming its tenants. He describes this as 'the development of tenurial relationships ... from the small man's need for protection and the church's need for service'.[44] This makes Domesday Book's entries for the East Anglian counties particularly informative, enabling us to see the tangle of personal networks that lay across tenurial ones, in fact very often running counter to tenurial ones, as if people in need of protection were taking care not to be dependent for it on the person from whom they held their land. Ann Williams has disentangled some of these networks of commendation recorded in Domesday Book, often cutting across family ties, that had woven a safety-net for 'lesser men' who now 'had to accept new customs (a closer link, perhaps, between landholding and lordship) and new social *mores.*' Peter Coss has summed up the change like this: 'In the form of homage, commendation ceased to be personal: it became both personal and tenurial. No longer could a free man commend himself with his land to whom he would. The tenurial relationship arising from the Conquest trumped all.'[45] This change would, over time, affect the moral economy of the countryside as a whole, but it would not affect its people equally. Many would survive and adapt, many would thrive: for peasants the change would be fundamental. As 'immemorial custom' is so often thought to have governed their lives as manorial tenants, it is time to investigate when exactly it was invented.

Notes

1 For historical writing proper: Campbell, 'Some twelfth-century views of the Anglo-Saxon past'.
2 Johnson, *Dialogue of the Exchequer*, 63.
3 Garnett, *Conquered England*, chapter 1.
4 Williams, *English and the Norman Conquest*, chapter 7, 'Remembering the past', surveys the whole field of attitudes to the pre-Conquest past, specifically to the law at 155–64.
5 LEIS WILLELME Prologue, clauses 1–52.2.
   Manuscripts
   Two mss survive in French, both including the Prologue and clauses 1–28.2. These are
   1. London, BL ms Add. 49366 ff 141r–144v formerly Holkham ms 228 (H in Liebermann, *Gesetze*) where *Leis Willelme* is added to the legal collection *Quadripartitus* compiled in the last quarter of the twelfth century (Wormald, *Making of English Law*, 236–44, 407).
   2. Los Angeles UCLA Research Library Δ 170/159 ff.188–92, dated to the first half of the twelfth century in Otaka, 'Sur la langue des *Leis Willelme*'.
   A further French original must have been the source for the entire text, the second part of which contains the clauses 28.2 to 52 which are absent from both mss of the existing French text and was used by the *Quadripartitus* author. It may also have been the one seen by the author of *Historia monasterii Croylandensis* compiled 1135–1212, who claims, 'I brought with me from London ... the laws of the most just king Edward ... which William had proclaimed in the same language in which they were originally published.' The author was known as 'Pseudo-Ingulf' (I in Liebermann, *Gesetze*) and his work is full of claims for Croyland based on fabricated charters but he shows a genuine interest in language and handwriting and it is hard to believe that he would have faked the entire *Leis Willelme* in French. Sargent, 'Laws of William the Conqueror', 4 considers that 'none of the surviving manuscripts or printed sources ... is a translation of copy of one of the others.'
   Printed editions: Liebermann, *Gesetze*, i. 492–520, Robertson, *Laws*, 253–75 prints clauses 1–52 with his English translation, as 'The (so-called) Laws of William I'. Prologue and clauses 1–52.2 are printed in *Ingulf's Chronicle of the Abbey of Croyland: with the continuations by Peter of Blois and anonymous writers* edited by Thomas Riley from the Holkham ms with the editor's translation. A Latin version added to *Quadripartitus* is the source for Liebermann's Latin version, L. Hence the Latin translation is possibly fifty years later than the

French original. A new edition and translation of the short version by Bruce O'Brien, Ian Short, Paul Brand, and Yorio Otaka is www.earlyenglishlaws .ac.uk/laws/texts/leis-W11 and http://www.earlyenglishlaws.ac.uk./laws/ texts/leis-W12

Commentaries: Richardson and Sayles, Law and Legislation, 123–5, 141–2, 166–7, Wormald, Making of English Law, 407–9, whose revised view of the dating is at 408n.665. For Sargent it represents 'a private work ... not related to any law of William's' and he cites Liebermann's opinion that this was 'Norman land law': Sargent, 'An examination of the Laws of William the Conqueror', 80. O'Brien, God's Peace and King's Peace, 29 considers that 'the intended purpose may have been to teach law', Wormald, Making of English Law, 409 that 'For all that it was written in French, it is an intellectual's exercise.' For Goebel, Felony and Misdemeanor, 380: 'The Leis Willelme with its free use of French legal jargon suggests a wholesale effacement of ancient meanings.' This is in line with his interpretation of post-Conquest England as a time when 'changes in tenure, importation of foreign status concepts and current feudal ideas of courtkeeping shifted the whole societal structure.' Richardson and Sayles, Law and Legislation, 123–5, 141–2, assuming from its use of Roman law that it dated from the time of Henry II that it was 'an independent statement of the law relating to villeinage written ... in the first half of Henry II's reign'. Sargent, 'Laws of William the Conqueror', 41: Leis Willelme was 'a private work', 'not related to any law of William's', 138, 136.

6 In Maitland's view, it seemed 'destined to define the position of the English peasants as being similar to that of the Roman coloni': Pollock and Maitland, History of English Law, 102 i. n.1. Maitland also said of this text: 'There are certain clauses which would be of great importance could we suppose that they had an authoritative origin and which in any case are remarkable enough.' Domesday Book and Beyond, 78. I am grateful to the members of a symposium arranged by Professor John Hudson for their advice on Leis Willelme.

7 O'Brien, God's Peace and the King's Peace, 35; Karn, 'Quadripartitus', 151–2; Hyams, Kings, Lords and Peasants, 263–4. These were perhaps the same kind of users that Hyams has suggested were the intended audience for the OE text known as Lad on how to conduct suits between French and English disputants: Hyams, 'The common law and the French connection', 78, Liebermann, Gesetze, i. 487; Robertson, Laws, 239–43c.6.

8 Principally Chapter 14, 'Thinking feudally'.

9 I am grateful to Jane Bliss and Paul Hyams for their help with this text.

10 Johnson, Dialogue of the Exchequer, 53 where Johnson's equivalence of these with 'villeins' rather confuses his interpretation of this passage.

11 They are discussed in Chapter 7. It is not until 1086 that we get any idea of their numbers, when these bordarii, 'boarders', number c.81, 000 to the c.109, 000 of the villani: Darby, Domesday England, appendix 3.

12 Bloch, 'Personal liberty and servitude', 83; Musset, 'Les domaines de l'époque franc', 72 for vernaculi who work on the demesne but are not housed, which strengthens the similarity with the OE gebur. On the Glastonbury estates the Latin nati had become nethi and in thirteenth-century England nativus would be synonymous with 'serf'.

13 *Leis Willelme*, 30.1, 31: Liebermann, *Gesetze*, i. 512–13, Robertson, *Laws*, 268–9. 'His' may refer to the lord's possessions. Robertson's note to clause 30 points out that it repeats the gist of II Edw.7; III Æthelstan.4 and II Cnut 28 but these do not appear to me to have the implication that the person who has left a lord's service was anything that could be described as a *cultor*, which is how the compiler of the *Quadripartitus* translated *gaineur*. Robertson, *Laws*, 370.

14 *Leis Willelme*, 23: Liebermann, *Gesetze*, i. 510–11, Robertson, *Laws*, 266–7. My translation departs from Liebermann and Robertson in translating *na [vu]rie quere* (I) as 'seek avowry'. For that I follow AND, s.v. *avouerie*. The Latin version gives *nec querant ingenium*, 'nor seek a device'. Robertson, following this, gives 'excuse': both seem to me to miss the meaning of the original, in fact to be somewhat tendentious. For warranty: Hyams, 'Warranty and good lordship'.

15 *Leis Willelme*, 29.1, Liebermann, *Gesetze*, i. 512, Robertson, *Laws*, 369 gives *gafol* for *cense* in this passage and equates the *dreit seirvise* with the labour obligations of *Rectitudines*. Orderic Vitalis uses *colonus* as a general term for 'husbandman' in *Ecclesiastical History*.

16 13 *Leis Willelme*, 23: Robertson, *Laws*, 266–7; Liebermann, *Gesetze*, i. 510–11.

17 *Leges Henrici Primi*, 31.7, 134–5: *Unusqisque per pares suos iudicandus est et eiusdem provinciae*.

18 Baxter, *Earls of Mercia*; Kelly, *Peterborough Abbey*, 331–46, quotation at 335; Holt, *Colonial England*, 19.

19 *Leis Willelme*, 24: Liebermann, *Gesetze*, i. 510–11, Robertson, *Laws*, 266–7. The Latin of *Quadripartitus* has 'two men'. Robertson, *Laws*, 369 cites a twelfth-century use of similar phrasing.

20 II Canute, 20: Liebermann, *Gesetze*, i. 322–3, Robertson, *Laws*, 184–5; *Leges Henrici Primi*, 8.2, 103–4.

21 *Leis Willelme*, 25 (for which Liebermann and Robertson give only the Latin version), supplied here from *Ingulf's Chronicle*, 20.30a. Also 'Ten Articles of William I', 8: Liebermann, *Gesetze*, i. 488–9, Robertson, *Laws*, 240–1 and note.

22 *Leis Willelme*, 32: Liebermann, *Gesetze*, i. 514, Robertson, *Laws*, 268–9.

23 Chibnall, *Anglo-Norman England*, 174 for the implication of these terms.

24 Richardson and Sayles, *Law and Legislation*, 141–2, ascribing the *Leis Willelme* to the reign of Henry II, summarises the clauses discussed here as 'an independent statement of the law relating to villeinage'.

25 Raftis, *Estates of Ramsey Abbey* discusses these passages at 44–6; Faith, *English Peasantry* at 219–21, 247–9. Clanchy, *From Memory to Written Record*, discussing 'the formation of a Norman official memory' at 26–30, cites Fitzni-gel's account of William, having critically examined the Old English codes, bringing England 'under the rule of written law'.

26 Johnson, *Dialogue of the Exchequer*, 52–3 Johnson's translation of *adscripticius* as 'villein' is not followed here. For the *murdrum* fine see Lambert, *Law and Order*, 361 as a feature of 'the rise of collective punishment ... in post-Conquest evidence'.

27 Bloch, *Feudal Society*, 171 argued that 'while the two great property rights were finally drawn, villein tenants holding by custom, allods (which included peasant allods ...) which remained completely independent' he saw peasant obligations having originated in a process very similar to the one described here: in the context of surrenders of land from the less to the more powerful, peasant lands were returned charged with rents in money and kind and with agricultural labour services. Tabuteau considers that peasant allod-holders, despite their superior resources and wealth, were becoming tenants in the eleventh century: *Transfers of Property*, 103–4.

28 Hudson, 'Administration, family and perceptions of the past', 87–8.

29 Johnson, *Dialogue of the Exchequer*, xx, 54.

30 Johnson, *Dialogue of the Exchequer*, 54.

31 For the importance of this in the ideology of the Norman Conquest: Garnett, *Conquered England*, 24–33. Raftis, *Estates of Ramsey Abbey*, at 47 notes that 'over the mid-12th (*sic*) century large amounts of land were lost from the villeinage on Ramsey estates by being 'freed' for money rents or court services, when the abbot ... began to attempt a recovery of such lands ... villeins as well as freemen were found to have purchased charters for non-free lands.' Susan Reynolds, 'Tenure and property', has proposed that tenure is not recorded in Domesday Book but was the result of subsequent negotiation: 'What was ... peculiar to England was that until 1290 anyone who acquired land through gift or purchase apparently owed services and "incidents" to the person from whom they had acquired it.'

32 Amt and Church, *Dialogus*, xx; Garnett, *A Broken Chain*, i. ch. 2. Raftis, *Estates of Ramsey Abbey*, 44–7 devotes several pages to a careful consideration of this passage with reference to the Ramsey Abbey evidence and see also Faith, *English Peasantry*, 219–21.

33 *Leis Willelme*, 30: Robertson, *Laws*, 268–9, Liebermann, *Gesetze*, i. 513.

34 Hyams, *Kings, Lords and Peasants*, which incorporates the dating of *De legibus* by S. E. Thorne.

35 *Bracton, De legibus*, II.fo. 7 at p. 37.

36 *The Mirror of Justices*, introduction. Catto, 'Andrew Horn: law and history'. Catto's dismissal of Horn as author of the *Mirror of Justices* results in his underestimating the part it played in his interest in the pre-Conquest English past as evidenced by his possession of the legal collection *Leges Anglorum* and his use of *Quadripartitus*: Wormald, *Making of English Law*, 237n.304.

37 *Mirror of Justices*, 80.

38 Catto, 'Andrew Horn: law and history', 382. Horn could have benefitted from the fact that London and Southwark were centres of historical writing at the time. He had read Arnold of Themar's *Liber de antiquis legibus* which contained a good deal of William of Malmesbury's *Gesta regum anglorum*: Stone, 'Connections and collaborations', 209.

39 Raban, *A Second Domesday?*.

40 *Mirror of Justices*, 144.

41 *Mirror of Justices*, 77, 80. Horn must have known that the Hundred Rolls had been compiled during the reign of Edward I; was he perhaps evoking here a

tradition that the Confessor had been a reformer? His reference to 'our first conquerors' is equally mysterious.

42 *Swerian*: Liebermann, *Gesetze*, i. 96–9; Wormald, *Making of English Law*, 383–4. For the role and importance of commendation: Baxter, *Earls of Mercia*, 219–25.

43 Whitelock, *English Historical Documents*, 856n.4 and *Sermo Lupi ad Anglos*.

44 Miller, *Abbey and Bishopric of Ely*, 52.

45 Williams, *English and the Norman Conquest*, 96; Coss, *Aristocracy in England and Tuscany*, 314–15.

Part VI

In the World of the Manor

13 Establishing Custom

Language mattered, but the post-Conquest settlement was achieved by force, not words. William's 'harrying of the North' in 1069 was a policy of 'shock and awe' intended to crush resistance. 'Wasting', destroying the rural economy by burning crops and houses and driving off cattle, was a deliberate tactic to subjugate the countryside by starving its people. David Bates' heartfelt account shows how far this went beyond the tactics of a routine military campaign into those of ethnic cleansing.[1] Contemporary accounts of such violence may be one reason that modern historians have, almost without exception, dismissed or ignored Fitznigel's narrative of agreements arrived at through negotiation. Scholarly scepticism is understandable. His description of the effects of the Conquest was written long after these violent transformations, and was very likely based on what he could learn from informants in the south of England, which had been spared the extreme measures meted out to the North. It is difficult to get much of an idea of chronology from his account of ad hoc arrangements made in the aftermath of 1066 breaking down and being superseded by permanent 'lawful agreements'. It would be reasonable to suspect that when he wrote in the 'Dialogue' that the English had come to formal agreements which had bound them into contractual relationships with lords that he was simply concerned with justifying the social relationships of his time. How likely is it that 'whoever of the conquered people possesses landed property not what he considered due to him by right of succession but only what he has earned by due demands or by some agreements having taken place'? And how likely is it that this could have been the case for peasants as well as for people with landed property? Are local bargains and negotiations really a plausible explanation for the situation of peasants vis-à-vis their lords? This chapter begins by looking at estate policies as a way of investigating these questions.

As their new acquisitions of land and people were in a country whose language, customs, and law were all unfamiliar, the first generation to profit from the Conquest may most often have done so by ad hoc

171

measures. S. P. J. Harvey places her discussion of landlord policies in the aftermath of 1066 in the context of the political takeover of landholding by a group of 'foreign lords ... who used their English lands to fund Continental adventures' and whose main concern was with obtaining cash. The policy many adopted was probably to put their new possessions out 'at farm' (the origin of the term is probably OE *feorm*), renting them out for a term of years, often to their former owners.[2] 'Farming' was a well-established form of managing land, and ecclesiastical landlords had long adopted this option of a fixed rental income either in cash or in kind. Bearing in mind that he wrote from the perspective of more than a century later, could this be the situation which Fitznigel described when he wrote, 'Over time those who had not fought ... acquired the goodwill of their lords by devoted service and began to hold tenancies at the will of their lords, for themselves alone, however, without hope of succession'? In the last quarter of the twelfth century, in what has been described as 'the resumption of demesne farming', many lords took their manors back 'in hand' and put in agents to manage them. Economic historians can explain this change of policy by the fact that in an increasingly commercialised society, cash was in short supply and the fixed returns from 'farming out' manors had not kept up with the rise in prices and a growth in the market for agricultural produce.[3] Direct management would give lords the opportunity to profit from these new conditions, but its success would depend on their capacity to command from the people on their estates a secure supply of labour. However, describing post-Conquest estate policies in purely managerial terms may be to miss an important dimension: the new attitudes to land and people which had come in with the Conquest and which would give landlords a new kind of authority, should they have thought in these terms, to carry out new policies on their estates.

Estate Policy

For lords who wanted to take their property back 'in hand', one of the most important matters was what they could lawfully demand from the people on their estates. Historians seem to agree that a new Norman lord would expect to get what his antecessor had, if he could find out what it was. Some common-sense assumptions may be allowed about what this is likely to have included. The few surviving records, described in Chapter 9, dating from before the Conquest of peasant obligations – the Hurstbourne document, the Tidenham survey, and *Rectitudines singularum personarum*, which all refer to ecclesiastical estates – show that there was a well-established and organised labour supply on the inlands of the church. Lay landowners too are likely to have been able to rely on a permanent labour supply to cultivate their 'inlands', the core of the property which provided the food and drink for the seigneurial household. When the original author of the *Rectitudines singularum personarum* distinguished the labour obligations of different categories of people he used very common terms for them – *gebur, kotsetla,* and so on – and presented the information as if these were likely to have been employed at the centre of any large estate. Ælfric took the work of the estate ploughman and shepherd and so on as models from which to teach his students Latin. S. P. J. Harvey's work on the policies of major lay landlords in the twenty years between the Conquest and Domesday Book showed that a Norman incomer who took over an estate which already had a considerable workforce *in dominio* would be likely to continue the arrangement.[4] Thus on the eve of the Conquest, there were already a large number of people whose livelihood depended on their working for a landowner and whose forebears and descendants were similarly dependent.

Notwithstanding the flood of information brought in by the Domesday survey, it is not very much easier to get an idea of what labour was owed to lords in the eleventh century from the rest of the peasantry than it was in the tenth: the *villani*, the people 'with houses and fields', the largest group in the enumerated Domesday population and who are found in every county that the survey covered, off manors and on, at large places and small. Geographical conditions alone must have been an important factor in determining the amount of labour which a lord might be able to demand from the people on his manors. When it is possible to identify individual pre-Conquest farms 'on the ground', some are still what we think of as a farm today, a farmstead with its land around it, others were clustered with neighbours amid their minuscule amounts of shared land, yet Domesday Book records all these very different kinds of peasant farmers simply as *villani*.[5] Regular labour rent, vital though it would have been both to the landowners who demanded it and to the people who did the work, was not a topic which concerned the commissioners and Domesday contains virtually no reference to it. When it is noted that *villani* 'owed customs' or 'served as *villani* do', their 'service' and 'customs' turn out to be not necessarily agricultural nor, although onerous, particularly servile. In fact they seem rather the reverse. The thegns of West Derby, 'as if they were *villani*', have duties not of ploughing or reaping, but of building hunting lodges for the royal hunt.[6] The 'service' and 'customs', religiously recorded on the abbot of Bury St Edmunds' land, are the days of harvest boon-works which had their origins in local custom: they were owed, and highly resented, by respected townsmen as well as by peasants. Norman clerks may have recognised something familiar in these examples, for *villani* in Normandy might owe similar obligations.[7] Although Domesday's broad categories obscure social differences which may have been of great importance locally, they are sometimes revealed by chance references to substantial farmers who were nevertheless bound by regular obligations. These are sometimes people with a service tenancy, land granted to an estate official, like the reeve at Chilbolton in Hampshire who had more than four hides before the Conquest but 'could not go where he wished', and held two of his hides 'like a *villanus*'. Churches, even parish churches, may have been able to command service from their tenants, like 'the men of the church serving as *villani*' who had five hides and a half of land at Chalke in Wiltshire.[8] For people like this, locally recognised as 'of the better sort', to be explicitly recorded as holding land 'as *villani*' and to be under the same obligations as the other 'men of the township', suggests that negotiations had taken place in which the reeve of Chilbolton and the men of Chalke had come off the worse. We cannot generally know what 'serving as *villani*' entailed in 1086, but it was evidently understood what it meant at Chilbolton and Chalke, just as it was at West Derby, although at each place it meant something different. And at each place, such was the Domesday process for obtaining information by the testimony of a body of local jurors, what was recorded was what had been sworn to.[9]

At all levels of society marking individual responsibility for service by an agreement sealed by an oath may have been becoming more formally signalled by the carefully preserved written word. Some of the Bury services were recorded, and re-recorded, in a highly prized manuscript book, a Benedictional. Rory Naismith remarks of the monks of Ely that 'their conception of moralized land management in the early eleventh century seems to have revolved around individuals ... what mattered were the names and details. Entering these into a holy book brought the current seigneurial position into the direct sight of God and St Æthelfryth and placed both the information and those who offered it under divine scrutiny.'[10] Although we cannot tell from an entry in a twelfth-century survey that 'X holds land for which she/he owes Y in rent and service' implies individual oath-taking, surveys were frequently headed by the names of jurors who had sworn to their veracity, expressing the idea of formal negotiations and fixed agreements of the 'Dialogue of the Exchequer' and *Leis Willelme*. Possibly some agreements over services were the result of transactions between individuals of the kind referred to in *Leis Willelme*: *Si hom volt derehdner covenant de terre ver sun seineur*: 'if a man wishes to deraign (produce in court) a covenant of land towards his lord'.[11] That the initial arrangements did not guarantee stability, still less heritability, to the lessee, according to Fitznigel was the reason that more formal arrangements ensued: 'at last it was decreed that whatever they had been able to obtain from their lords by due renders and by a lawful agreement having taken place, should be granted to them in inviolable right. They might claim nothing in the name of succession to other property from the time of the conquered people. ... from then on they were obliged to purchase the goodwill of their lords by devoted service. Thus whoever of the conquered people possesses landed property ... not what he considered due to him by right of succession but only what he has earned by due demands or by some agreement having taken place.'[12] However, the evidence of both *Leis Willelme* and the account given by Fitznigel suggests that opportunities for such individual bargains and ad hoc agreements were becoming constrained. For someone 'native-born' to obtain a document, a *cartre*, recording his obligations or a 'covenant' with his lord settling what was due, *debitum et statutum*, and could be called on as proof in a court of law could well have represented a threat to lords.[13] Enough cases of individuals taking their disputes over service to court had evidently been brought for a rule to be introduced which attempted to limit their scope: henceforth only fellow-tenants, holding their land by 'the same tenure' should be called to witness such agreements. Moreover, legally enforceable agreements with individual tenants were unlikely to have ensured landlords a reliable and sufficient supply of peasant labour and resources. What would in time be the 'custom of the manor' was to provide this, but took many decades to establish.

Custom

Cash rents may have seemed the best option for many new lords: after all, one of the Conqueror's first acts had been to levy a heavy geld. To obtain regular supplies from a property demanded organised labour, routinely performed and stabilised as 'custom'. Several estate owners expected to receive both. We think today of 'custom' as 'what has always been done', and this has been a long-standing attitude in rural societies to what, although not actually recorded, is locally believed to be the case. Two studies of the documents in which peasant obligations were recorded as 'custom', the Frankish polyptyques and English custumals, have re-examined this assumption. Two of their conclusions are particularly relevant here. The first is that the point at which peasant obligations were recorded as 'custom' was often in fact the point at which innovations were being established. The second is that custom was essentially not simply what has been remembered but what has been sworn to.[14]

These are useful perspectives from which to view the English evidence. The explosive growth in the keeping of written records in the twelfth century extended to the running of estates, and surveys of the lands and people of a handful of ecclesiastical landowners survive.[15] These record tenant obligations in a significantly different way from pre-Conquest examples. While those had simply recorded what was owed by each category of peasant tenant, the *ceorlas* at Hurstbourne or the *geburas* at Tidenham and the various categories of people in the *Rectitudines*, landowners began to require a record of what they could expect from named individuals. A glimpse of these changes in approach is provided by those surveys which relate to earlier circumstances. In 1181 Ralph de Diceto, the dean of the bishopric of London, Wulfstan's old see, set up an enquiry into the peasants on the canons' property to find out *qui gravarenter operibus qui colonorum libertate gauderent quive qui censuales quive cottarii*, 'which of the peasants enjoy freedom and which are burdened with works, which are rent-payers and which cottagers?'[16] The single fragment of the result of this enquiry which survives relates to the canons' manor of Belchamp St Paul in Essex. The first section, headed *isti tenent de dominio*, 'these hold from the demesne', seems to be looking back over a miscellaneous collection of arrangements: exchanges, a mass of acquisitions by tenants from the manorial inland, many of tiny amounts of land a few acres added to a holding here and there, all for cash rents. Then, headed 'These are free tenants' (or strictly, 'these are holding freely') is a list of named people with very varied amounts of land for cash rents, but all of whom 'plough and reap at the lord's boons', *ad cibum eius*, with food provided by him. The next section is headed *isti tenent terras operarias*, 'these hold worklands': three of these paid a substantial rent in cash. As only this fragment survives we will never know what work these seven tenants of half-yardlands and a single yardlander were obliged to do, or how many other such tenants there were on the manor in 1181. From the perspective of 1181 it looks very much as if over the preceding years, and there is no way of determining how many, there had been a mass of individual negotiations and adjustments between the canons and the peasants and others on their lands. The only obligations that look well-established enough as to need no detailed description were the lord's 'boons'.

Political circumstances in the wider world affected estate policy towards peasant obligations and their recording. Many of the bishops and abbots of the major sees and abbeys in the late twelfth century came from the Anglo-Norman elite, the same milieu as had Fitznigel, whose father had been bishop of Ely and treasurer to Henry I, and the higher echelons of government have been described as 'a sort of family party'.[17]

Some of these powerful landowners took a retrospective look at what had been happening to their possessions, in both land and people, in the chaotic political conditions of the mid-twelfth century. That so many estate surveys date from these years may reflect an effort to recoup assets, services, and renders which had slipped away, or simply not been rendered or performed, during the unsettled times which followed the death of Henry I in 1135 and in the civil wars which followed. The extents compiled on the estates of Ramsey Abbey look back from the time of Henry II (1154–89) to that of Henry I (1100–35) not only with regard to what its 'freely enfeoffed' tenants had then owed but also what the labour obligations of its peasant tenants had been and how they had changed. Several of the 'custumals' and surveys drawn up in the 1180s and 1190s came out of a deliberate policy of reviewing and revising tenant obligations established earlier in the century: the surveys made at Ramsey, Worcester, and Glastonbury all refer to early twelfth-century conditions. Now there was to be more precision about tenant obligations. A survey drawn up in 1189 at Glastonbury Abbey was to enquire into 'who holds freely and in what manner and by what service and by what warranty and from what time ... if any land was free in the time of bishop Henry of Blois (1129–91) or after which should work, by what warranty this was done and how much was free. ... If the demesne was occupied or put out *in libertate* or *in vilenagio*, and if it was more useful to the lord thus or revoked.' Not simply are the peasants' obligations now to be systematically recorded, which they duly were, but estate policy itself is now to be under review. Part of that review is to find out whether peasants had been getting away with negotiations which had freed them from labour rent. The very detailed survey drawn up on the instructions of the new abbot Henry de Sully does exactly that at Glastonbury. At Bury, we learn from his biographer, as part of the vigorous campaign of setting the abbey's finances in better order, abbot Samson soon after his election 'caused an enquiry to be held as to the annual rents due from the free men in each manor and as to the names of the peasants and their holdings and the services due from each, and he had them all set down in writing'.[18]

This kind of improved record-keeping made it easier to achieve the situation in *Leis Willelme* of a group holding 'by the same tenure'. Surveys from late in the twelfth century and later, which are much more plentiful and systematic than earlier surviving examples, frequently group tenants with holdings of similar size together and the obligations are the same for each member of the group. To return to St Pauls: in 1222, forty years after Ralph de Diceto's attempt, another enquiry was set in train into conditions on the canons' manors, and this time the results have survived. A massive new survey was compiled for the entirety of the estate, listing in extreme detail the different categories of tenants and their obligations: not for nothing did it become known as the 'Domesday' of St Paul's. It throws light on a deepening division within peasant society: while many more free tenants are listed than had been forty years before, now many more Belchamp tenants were leasing parts of the demesne land in return for heavy labour rent. Under the heading 'these hold worklands', fifteen tenants with yardlands and half-yardlands are listed and their obligations recorded: they are identical for each size of holding, harshly administered and extremely heavy. Yardlanders owed three days' work a week, set acreages of ploughing, renders of seedcorn, chicken at Christmas, and eggs at Easter.[19] The canons had made a thoroughgoing reform in that most basic element of administration, data. They now knew, as did all their tenants, exactly what was owed for a 'workland' and who owed it. The uniformity of conditions strongly suggests that this situation had come about on a once-and-for-all basis. What part negotiation had played in that process we shall never know, but Fitznigel's account of a shift from ad hoc arrangements with individuals to standardised and permanent conditions imposed on a group would be a good summary of what, broadly speaking, seems to have been going on. On St Pauls' lands after 1222 the expression 'those of the same tenure' would now have had a real meaning it might have lacked forty years before.

Norman Monasteries and their English Lands

If there was now more systematic pressure on the populations of monastic estates, this was part of an important cultural change. The first generation of Normans granted English properties tended to give to religious houses in what they still regarded as their homeland. A change began early in the twelfth century, with subsequent generations who identified their interests with their English properties and made gifts to English monasteries. But whether English or Norman foundations were concerned, the aim was to benefit Normandy, not England. John Le Patourel made no bones about describing the result of 1066 as 'the colonization of England'.[20] Donald Matthew's study of the Norman monasteries and their English possessions revealed an economic relationship which might be characterised in other historical contexts as that between metropolis and colony: the economy of the colony being subordinated to the demands of supplying the centre. In his words, the French monks who came to run them 'came to reap the benefits for their monasteries and cathedral chapters in Normandy ... English manors were intended to be profitable'.[21] Such transfers of goods and cash, later known as 'apports', and the business of producing and transferring them, made efficient record-keeping essential. The best information we have comes from the Norman monastery of Bec-Hellouin and the nunnery of La Trinité, Caen. Both had extensive lands in the West Country. One of Bec's manors was Ogbourne St Andrew in the Wiltshire valley of the Ogbourne, north of Marlborough. In the tenth century it had been part of the huge 'empire' of *ealdorman* Æthelwold which he left in his will to his brother.[22] With land in three counties, Æthelwold may not himself have seen Ogbourne as a place to settle, even visit, but even in his time it was not simply an area of Wiltshire valley and downland but a place with a distinct identity and a resident lord of some kind. It was already a desirable asset. Before 1066 Ogbourne had been Harold Godwinson's land and like other of his properties it had and retained a substantial inland. In 1086 three of its ploughteams and four slaves were at work on six of its ten hides there while the fifteen *villani* had the same number of teams. The mill, which produced 30 shillings a year in tolls, speaks of what was already a valuable corn-producing area.[23] This could well have been why it became such an asset to the monks of Bec, whose prior organised production there not in the traditional sense with the aim of supporting a resident manorial lord, but to produce a surplus of corn and wool for export. We cannot know how, and when, the successors to the fifteen *villani* and *bordarii* who were there in 1086 became liable for the heavy labour rent described in custumals on the abbey's English lands, as these survive only from the mid-thirteenth century. But it is clear that conditions of tenure had been worsening in the twelfth century: alterations made to the custumals record exactly that: three people named at Ogbourne St Andrew had their obligations increased. The administrative resources a large estate owner could provide may have made a difference: all three of Bec's Wiltshire manors were run on similar lines with heavy weekwork imposed on uniform terms to maximise production for the market.[24]

Negotiations and Agreements

Estate surveys give, by their very nature, a 'top-down' view, recording what landowners wanted to have recorded. There are few peasant voices here. Nevertheless, negotiation and agreement may lie behind the details. While peasant obligations were becoming much more standardised, in the sense that there are many examples of groups of tenants in a manor all holding 'by the same tenure', they were at the same time becoming very particular and local: they differed, if only in their details, from manor to manor. When the canons travelled around St Paul's' estates, for instance, they had to make extremely detailed records of the services owed by the tenants on each manor, even on those which were quite near one another, there was so much variety in the nature and extent of the tenants' transport obligations. As none of the pre-Conquest charters recording donations to St Pauls survives in the original, we cannot be entirely sure how long the dean and chapter had owned most of the properties recorded as theirs in Domesday Book and it is possible that the peasants on these were already burdened with labour service when acquired. However, on nearly all their manors there are many obligations which are so specific that they can only have been agreed on by negotiation on the spot, word for word, with the canons. While some work was owed on the manors themselves, other work involved a trip or trips to London to deliver the 'farm', the deliveries of corn and malt to the canons' bakery and brewery in London: this called for precision. Corn from Barling went by water, the tenants taking it to the boat and the canons' providing the boat and the skipper. But nineteen tenants from another Essex coastal manor, Tillingham, threshed the grain for four farms and took it to London 'at their own cost and their own risk' with a servant of the *curia* whose food was paid for by the canons. Navestock, Essex, owed only three farms, but could call on forty tenants, free men as well as serfs, for a total of three hundred carrying services to 'St Pauls granary'.[25] These details may seem trivial to us, but they were important to the people concerned and there is something about the minute detail in which tenant obligations are recorded in some twelfth-century custumals that suggests years of wrangling. We know, from a period when this kind of information becomes plentiful, that such negotiations continued well into the later middle ages, with agreements with the lord, as well as tenant obligations, being carefully recorded.[26] It is the detail and the minute differences between different places, perhaps more than anything else, that show that the commentators were right: 'services' and 'customs' were the result of private bargains made between local people and lords. In spite of its name, 'custom' was not what had been the case 'from time immemorial', but what had been negotiated and agreed to be owed from what was now a 'tenement'. For large numbers of peasants on these large church estates, in southern England at least, 'holding by the same tenure', in the words of *Leis Willelme*, was becoming a reality.

Almost all our information about peasant obligations comes from the documentation produced for estates like these which were run to support an ecclesiastical community, whether in England or Normandy, whether conventual or collegiate, of ancient or post-Conquest foundation, whether or not they were supplying the market. This support came principally in the form of grain for bread and brewing and, cereal production being by far the most labour-intensive operation in agriculture, labour obligations had always had ploughing at their core. Many smaller estates, and the properties of lay people, while they had lesser demands for labour, may not have been essentially different in this respect.[27] Ploughing services were a vital element in peasant obligations for a very simple reason: they gave lords access not only to peasant labour but to peasant capital in the shape of their ploughbeasts. A well-trained team, fit for the work, represented years of knowledgeable investment in its rearing, feeding, and training.[28] Ploughing was a long, drawn-out business and to ensure that reliable numbers of peasant ploughteams turned out where and when they were needed demanded a high degree of organisation. This is what the large, well-staffed estates could provide, and these are the ones whose documentation has survived. We know much less about parts of the country where arable farming was much less prominent in the economy (although of course there was arable everywhere) such as woodland and upland regions, and until later in the middle ages we generally know much less about small estates. We also know little about the circumstances which led to some tenants being recorded as 'free'. Sometimes a former small landowner is recognisable, sometimes someone farming a long way from any manorial centre, sometimes a prominent farmer who was able to come to a private arrangement with the estate administrators.[29] Nor do we have any firm idea of how widespread labour rent was at any time. Even when, in 1279, tenant obligations were recorded in detail for the purposes of a royal enquiry, the resulting Hundred Rolls survive only for a few counties in southern England. It can only be an impression, then, that when peasant obligations began to be systematically recorded, the primary impetus for this was the drive for grain production.

Language once again reveals new attitudes. The hide has already appeared so often at intervals throughout this book that readers may well be thinking about it by this point as 'that dreary old question' Maitland sometimes felt it had become. It was its very familiarity in rural life that gave it a new role as the basis of assessing tenant obligations. What had been the units on which to levy the geld now became the units on which to levy service and rent. The surveys record peasant holdings in terms of 'yardlands', *virgarii* and *virgatarii*, equivalent to a quarter of a hide, 'half-yardlands', and even smaller fractions.[30] This prosaic fact reflects a momentous change. In the first part of this book the families with hidated and geld-paying land had public obligations which were at the very root of their free and independent status. Yet it was on these people that the labour obligations which appear in the twelfth-century surveys were now being imposed. Language set the situation in stone: the peasant rent obligations that were recorded in the surveys came to be called the *redditus assisae*, 'the renders of the assize', from the French term *assise* used in twelfth-century England for a formal 'settling' or 'establishment'.[31] Such stability may have proved a double-edged sword for landlords, for while assized rents assured them a cash income of striking stability, over time this very stability could prove a disadvantage in times of inflation. Yet they seemed curiously difficult to increase.[32] The term *redditus assisae* became standard in later manorial records for what rent was owed from customary tenancies. It was a term which expressed an important element in descriptions of the post-Conquest land settlement: obligations and land should be formally bound together on terms that had been formally settled, 'assized'. In Bracton's words, 'free men who held their holdings by free services or free customs ... when they were thrown out by more powerful people, on returning afterwards took the same holdings up again to hold in villeinage, doing work for them which was servile but set and specified'.[33] This idea is followed further in the next chapter, into another aspect of the power of language: feudal thinking.

Notes

1 Bates, *William the Conqueror*, 313–21 and 527–8.
2 Harvey, 'Domesday England' and 'The extent and profitability of demesne agriculture' quotation at p. 70, Lennard, *Rural England*, chapters 5–7.
3 Miller and Hatcher, *Medieval England*, chapter 8.
4 Harvey, 'Domesday England', 115–21.
5 The economy and nature of the pre-Conquest farm, with many examples of individual farms, is the subject of Banham and Faith, *Anglo-Saxon Farms and Farming*.
6 *Domesday Book Cheshire*: 'Between Ribble and Mersey'; Fleming, *Domesday Book and the Law*, no. 1288.
7 Bury St Edmunds: Robertson, *Anglo-Saxon Charters*, 119, 220–21; Tabuteau, *Transfers of Property*, 103.
8 Fleming, *Domesday Book and the Law*, nos. 604, 1611.
9 Harvey, *Domesday*, 273–5 for the importance of the oath.
10 Bury: see Sarah Foot's forthcoming edition of the Bury charters for the British Academy. Naismith, 'The Ely memoranda', 375. Birrell, 'Manorial custumals' for the importance attached to negotiations and formal agreements regarding peasant obligations in the twelfth and thirteenth centuries.
11 *Leis Willelme*, 30: Robertson, *Laws*, 268–9, Liebermann, *Gesetze*, i. 513.
12 Johnson, *Dialogue of the Exchequer*, xx, 54.
13 Chibnall, *Anglo-Norman England*, 174 for the implication of these terms.
14 Morimoto, 'Trois notes'; Birrell, 'Manorial custumals', 10–13.
15 Harvey, *Manorial Records*, 15–24. Hilton, 'Freedom and villeinage' draws on a wider range of this material than I do here. Miller and Hatcher, *Medieval*

England, 221–2 link these trends with a new attitude to peasant population on these estates which were experiencing this managerial revolution involving a closer definition of villeinage and the obligations it entailed. An example of early post-Conquest practice, recording simply geld obligations, is Abingdon Abbey's survey of the 1140–1150s: *Historia ecclesie Abbendonensis*, i. App. III.

16 Hale, *Domesday of St Paul's*, 114–7.
17 Johnson, *Dialogue of the Exchequer*, introduction, xiv. The quotation cited there is from Stubbs.
18 Ramsey: *Chron. Ramesei*, iii. 241–314; Raftis, *Estates of Ramsey Abbey*, appendix A305–8. Glastonbury: Stacy, *Survey*, 103; Bury St Edmunds: Butler, ed., *Chronicle of Jocelin of Brakelond*, 28; St Pauls: Faith, 'Demesne resources'.
19 Hale, *Domesday of St Pauls*, 32–3.
20 Le Patourel, *The Norman Empire*.
21 Matthew, *Norman Monasteries*, 43.
22 Sawyer, *Anglo-Saxon Charters*, 1504.
23 By 1086 Ogbourne was held by Miles Crispin and it was through his family that it became part of the estate of the Norman abbey of Bec.
24 Morgan, *Bec*, 81–4.
25 Hale, *Domesday of St Pauls*, 67, 64, 74.
26 Birrell, 'Manorial custumals' and 'Peasants eating and drinking'.
27 This is not to deny the role of livestock as a peasant asset which could be exploited. An important contribution to the productivity of an estate such as Bury was their tenants' obligation to graze their sheep on the abbey's fallows, known as 'fold-soke'.
28 Banham and Faith, *Anglo-Saxon Farms and Farming*, 84–91.
29 Miller and Hatcher, *Medieval England*, chapter 5 surveys the variations in peasant status and conditions of tenure.
30 These derive from *virgata*, the measuring rod. Stacy, *Survey*, 28 states that 'an effort seems to have been made to keep the number of customary tenants in line with the geldable *terra villanorum* of Domesday Book'. My interpretation of the association of the geldable land with peasant tenancies differs from Dr Stacy's only in this: he understands it as a result of Glastonbury Abbey's policy of allotting hidated land, owned by the abbey, to peasants, whereas I see the hidated land as that previously owned and farmed by largely free and geld-paying peasants who were now brought into tenancy.
31 AND, s.v. *asseer* 7 and 9. For this term in English texts: Neilson, *Customary rents*.
32 Lords had other options for increasing or maintaining their cash income: much higher rents were charged for assart land, for lettings made 'by convention', and so on. Many of the obligations listed in Neilson, *Customary rents* may well have been imposed specifically for the purpose of commutation.
33 *Bracton, De legibus*, II.fo. 7 at p. 37.

14   Thinking Feudally

While in their dealings with the English in English courts Normans had to negotiate with English ideas, to their dealings with one another 'the Norman nobility brought their own law.'[1] Norman property law was feudal law, the law of fees. A fee in land (there were other kinds) was not property in the sense that Anglo-Saxon *land* or *irfe* were land (simply, land, inherited land). A fee was land which was part of a relationship to which tenure was central. In lawyers' language land in 'fee simple' was 'land held hereditarily, by service'. Holding land 'in fee' was an idea central to the Normans. It applied even at the very highest level, for the implication of 1066 was that 'victory has been given to our race by the Most High as it were in fee'. At the other end of society, peasants too came to hold their land 'in fee', for 'Norman law did not distinguish between noble and peasant custom'.[2] This may have been because the idea of tenure was becoming embedded in Norman society, and for Norman lords peasants were a kind of tenant.[3] Tenure was new to England and it was new at all levels of society. This chapter looks at how these feudal ideas played out in the English countryside.

Swearing fealty to a feudal lord was of the essence of feudalism but loyalty to a lord was nothing new in England: personal commendation has featured in earlier chapters as a bond by which a lord's support could be assured, possibly signified by the lesser man 'bowing' to the greater.[4] The work of Emily Tabuteau has already been cited as demonstrating that by the mid-eleventh century Norman grants of land gave tenure, not ownership. What may have been a new usage in Norman England was a link being established between tenure and doing 'homage'. Alice Taylor, looking at the way homage was represented by four Norman chroniclers, finds that this association was not being made until late in the twelfth century. Before that, something more like English commendation seems to have been the way that the link between a man and his lord was expressed: in the description by Dudo of St Quentin (c.1015), he 'bowed his head' and committed his hand into another's hand'. 'Fealty', not homage, was William of Jumiege's term in the latter part of the eleventh century. The Norman chroniclers did not use the term *hominium*, 'homage', for a performance which linked loyalty, obligation to holding land from another, until the late twelfth century.[5] By that time, the link had been made in spectacular fashion across the Channel when 'all the landholding men there were of any account over England, no matter whose men they were' came before William at Salisbury in 1086 and 'bowed to him and became his men, and swore an oath of loyalty to him against all other men'. Anglo-Saxon Chronicle uses the language of personal loyalty: they swore *holdaðas*, 'hold oaths'.[6] There is an ongoing, or recurring, debate over whether or not this episode involved the chief landholding men doing homage *for their lands*. This became an important topic for eighteenth-century lawyers. One of these, Martin Wright, expressly connected it with the introduction of tenures and with Domesday Book.[7] For modern historians, too, the importance of the Salisbury Oath lay in its connection with the completed Domesday survey. For Sally Harvey, 'William's position was undoubtedly strengthened by ... the acquisition of the Domesday data in some form.' For George Garnett, Domesday entrenched the message that all tenure ultimately depended on the king: 'The oaths taken at Salisbury were undoubtedly intended to affect the understood ties between the king and his tenants-in-chief and major subtenants.'[8] As far as William's relationship with his 'chief landholding men' was concerned, not only those who were later called 'tenants-in-chief' but their men too, the personal bond of commendation had now become a tenurial one.

However, each entry for these *landsittende* men Domesday Book also records, although it seldom names, a great many more people of various kinds, perhaps representing three to four million of them, most of them peasants. As Norman law did not distinguish between noble and peasant custom, did all these peasants become feudal tenants, holding their lands in return for service? Taking seriously what Fitznigel had to say about the aftermath of 1066 has suggested that the establishment of tenures in the aftermath of the Conquest was a long, drawn-out series of negotiations and agreements between Norman *landsittende* men and the English. An earlier chapter has noted that for peasant tenants 'the establishment of custom' was a protracted and negotiated process towards the final settlements of their obligations recorded in the late twelfth-century surveys. To enquire into how peasant tenures became 'feudalised' will need us to look first at *where* that may have happened.

Courts

Calling ancient ideas of heroic loyalty to mind, as was done at Salisbury, reveals the importance, in all business to do with the transfer of land, of solemnity. Anglo-Saxon and Anglo-Norman England had this in common. When land changed hands this called for a special occasion, and the occasion needed witness to inscribe the occasion in people's minds. An assembly of the people around an important man, where status mattered, where a ceremonial meal might well be eaten, which might be dignified by the prayers of senior clerics, where decisions were witnessed by the most important people and carefully recorded in prestigious documents which were carefully archived, such an occasion was a *curia*, a court.[9] For their equivalents in Normandy a court in the legal sense is exactly what it meant. They would expect to have 'private' jurisdiction, even 'blood justice' over their own vassals.[10] So although, as we saw in an earlier chapter, writers of the twelfth century studied and respected Anglo-Saxon laws and the Anglo-Saxon system of public courts at an intellectual level, nevertheless for Norman lords taking over English lands jurisdiction over one's 'men' was a valuable part of what lordship entailed. The baron of an 'honour', the totality of his holdings, could hold a court for all the free tenants of that honour, of whatever rank. Very little evidence of such courts seems to have survived and it could be that they were often purely verbal proceedings of the baron's dealings with his men, which were not recorded if land did not change hands and perhaps not even if it did. Lords of lesser status, who wished to instil into the people on their land the same respect for the idea of tenure which they now owed to their superiors, would need a court too: that is why it is taken for granted by the author of *Leges Henrici Primi* that where there is a lord there will be a 'court of the lord', *curia domini*.[11] If we think of courts, however, not only as occasions where justice was done but as occasions where transactions of importance took place, then the contrast between high and low may be less stark.

The Hallmoot and the Manor Court

The more important difference was between public and private justice. Before the Conquest people always remained clear that the local public courts, those of the hundred and the shire, were the proper forum in which to settle disputes.[12] People who appeared there did so as subjects of the king, taking the oath of loyalty to him *in pleno folkesmot* but they were not the king's courts either.[13] Nor were they the courts of lords. However powerfully they may have made their presence known there, pre-Conquest lords were not entitled to exercise private justice. But 1066 brought Norman lords to England who felt themselves traditionally entitled to hold their own *curia*, a court which all 'their men' who held land within their honour had the obligation to attend and which dealt with the disputes, principally over land, that arose between them.[14] An honour, comprising the entire holdings of a single tenant in chief, could be vast, and summoning even those of his tenants who had horses must have posed a baron with many problems, so some held one court for their knights, the *curia militum*, and another, the *curia intrinseca*, at the estate centre. We do not know where, or when, the court for lesser tenants originated that would evolve into the manorial court, but a likely origin is in something similarly territorial: a court for the tenants of each manor within the honour.[15] Perhaps concerned that the proliferation of such private courts should not lead to judicial 'no-go' areas in which important criminal cases remained unjudged and profits lost to the Crown, both Williams and Henry I supported the old public courts, Henry ruling that 'all men should go to the shires and hundreds.'[16] It is in these courts that the possible readers of *Leis Willelme* would have been practising, and where they would have found not only that Anglo-Saxon law was singularly lacking any viable means of disciplining the peasantry, but that Anglo-Saxon courts had an obstinate preference for traditional methods of procedure. There was bound to be conflict between two such different conceptions of dispute settlement, each derived from very different ideas of authority. What came to be called the 'court of the manor' bore the marks of this very mixed inheritance. The local courts served two purposes: they were the place for settling disputes and managing other business among members of a community, but they were increasingly useful to the authorities as a policing measure. Hence it was incumbent on those in charge, the 'moot-reeves', to make sure that 'the tithings were full' and that every adult male was properly sworn in as a member of a group of ten.[17] Once again words mattered and some twelfth-century legal scholars were aware of the implications of English terminology. The compiler of the collection of laws he called, although it was nothing of the sort, the 'Laws of Edward the Confessor', explained the OE term 'moot', the hundred meeting, in a passage on the *mot-bell*, the moot-bell, rung 'to gather together all who in English are called the *folc-gemote*'.[18] Moots were held at traditional assembly places, but well before the Conquest these meetings were beginning to come indoors from the rigours and inconvenience of the open air: one landmark in an eleventh-century Hampshire charter boundary was the 'moot-house'.[19] Others entered the essentially private space of the largest lay building, the lord's hall. 'The hall-moot' occasionally appears in Domesday Book: at Acton in

Cheshire, it records, 'this manor has its pleas (*placita*) in the hall of the lord'.[20] A fourteenth-century compilation of documents relating to Stoneleigh Abbey, Warwickshire, records how this change was remembered there. Attendance at the outdoor public courts was strongly associated with freedom in the collective memory at Stoneleigh where, unusually for the county, there was a large body of sokemen, a category unusual, although not unknown, outside the Danelaw. 'The court of Stoneleigh, to which the sokemen used to owe suit, from antiquity used to be held on the hill next to the vill of Stoneleigh called Motstowehul, so called because they pleaded there. But after the abbots of Stoneleigh had that court and liberty they made a court house in the middle of the vill for the convenience (*pro aysiamento*) of the tenants and suitors, to which all the sokemen of the manor come and do suit every three weeks.'[21] Now the moot was his hall-moot, his *halimote*. The change from public outdoor spaces, some, as the Stoneleigh reference points out, of great antiquity (Motstow Hill has an impressive collection of barrows), may in itself have given the moot proceedings an air of private justice and by early in the twelfth century this was becoming more of a reality. A donation to Abingdon Abbey by Edward the Confessor of an entire hundred stipulated that 'no shire-reeve or moot-reeve may have any soke or moot there except at the abbot's own behest and permission'.[22]

However, the hallmoot's distinct identity as the meeting of the people of a district endured, and when the copious records of the proceedings of manor courts survive, from the mid-thirteenth century on, their titles show how much they retained of these earlier origins. Their equivalent was sometimes known in the later middle ages as the 'wapentake court' or the 'sokemoot court' and, mainly in East Anglia, the 'leet court': these were all territorial, not tenurial, units.[23] (Indeed, at Laxton in Northamptonshire, where England's last surviving open-field cultivation is still practised, it is the Leet Court which deals with farming and minor legal matters.) Lords could profit from the fines levied there: the author of the *Leges Henrici Primi*, writing sometime between 1114 and 1118, who wrote knowledgeably about the courts of the county and the hundred, also discusses the *halimota*, the hall-moot, of lords who have soke, and thus rights to a share of the profits of justice and, more particularly, of *vavassores* who are entitled to receive the fine and wergeld of offenders caught in the act on their land, such fines to be assessed by representatives of the court.[24] When it comes to the kind of cases that the hall-moots were dealing with in the eleventh and twelfth centuries, the *Leges* author lists only criminal or civil matters that were justiciable in the public courts. The honour courts may have swept up a good deal of local moots and their business which then became part of the work of the 'manorial' courts. What came to be called 'manor courts' retained some of the essential characteristics of the traditional public courts: 'the entire corpus of court suitors fulfilled the rules of "fact-finder" and judgement-renderer' and the lord's steward presided over them as moderator rather than as judge.'[25] It is not the steward but 'afeerors' who set fines and the swearing of the men into tithings, strictly the business of a distinct 'View of frankpledge', is sometimes done on the same occasion as the holding of the manor court if the lord of the manor also had as his responsibility to hold the view.[26]

Feudal law had to be stretched to cover a great many situations which arose from what was essentially business arrangements. Lords must have had a great deal of purely estate business which needed immediate attention and the author of *Leges Henrici Primi* seems to have been familiar with such matters.[27] Leasing being a common form of estate management in the twelfth century, it gave rise to particular categories of dispute. If the manor was held from the lord by 'his man' who has done homage for it, then problems must be sorted out in the lord's own court where appeal could be made directly to him. Land was commonly leased 'at farm' to a lessee or 'fermor' fully stocked: when the lease was up and the stock returned, it was necessary to have some kind of audit. According to the *Leges* disputes about this, and they could well have been common, should be settled *in ipso manerio*, 'on the manor itself': the grain inspected in the barns, the herdsman questioned about the stock in the fields, all checked by tallies, and the payments due from their tenants. All these were matters of normal estate administration.[28] It seems that, while a great deal of the everyday business of running an estate must always have led to disputes which needed to be settled, early in the twelfth century, when the *Leges* author was writing, this was not yet done in a 'manor court'. Nevertheless there were ways in which justice was becoming increasingly 'privatised'. This was partly a matter of location. When hundreds became attached to particular manors, as was increasingly becoming the case, their courts came with them and were very likely held at the estate centre.[29] The membership of courts was changing too. Signs from the century before the Conquest have shown that fewer peasants could retain the status that participating in the law had once bestowed. Peasant elites had probably always dominated local justice informally, but now access to the local courts was becoming expressly confined to those seen to be more free or better endowed with land. Although the *Leges* author was knowledgeable about, and seemingly respectful of, the way that the courts of shire and hundred were tradition-ally run, his work is scattered with assumptions that they should not be open to all as judgement finders: *villani* and smallholders, *viles et inopes*, lowborn and poor people 'should not be judges of the laws' (and thus do not suffer, he adds, from liability to contributing to communal fines for misjudgements). It is all the *meliores homines*, 'the better sort', who are to attend the hundred court.[30] On one of the Ramsey manors it was considered important to note of a man 'freely enfeoffed in those days' (i.e. in Henry I's time), that he had 'attended the county and hundred and the abbot's pleas'.[31]

Tenure in the Manor Court

The introduction of the concept of 'tenure' represented a change in culture, not simply a shift in power and as such it was in conflict with a traditional and highly regarded principle of the moral economy: the inheritance of land. Inheritance had always been respected right across society and the Norman rulers were traditional in their views: the coronation oaths of both Williams and of Henry I pay respect to the principle that 'every man shall be his father's heir'. Yet if land is rightfully passed down from parent to child, what becomes of the link implied by the new idea of 'holding' it from a superior? The Anglo-Norman establishment appears to have negotiated this difficulty by the creation of what was essentially a performance in which both the lord's interest was preserved and the heir's rights were maintained. It was a performance involving a transaction which had the appeal of a whiff of the heroic past by invoking the loyalty of the warrior to his lord. At its centre was the payment of what became known as 'heriot' in Middle English. The term came from OE *heregeat*, literally 'army-gear': the equipment given to the young warrior by his lord/commander and returned to him at the end of his service. By the eleventh century this conception of warfare was to a large extent illusory, but its appeal had not yet faded (if it ever truly has). Cnut's laws list heriots 'fixed with due regard to the rank of the person for whom they are paid: 'For an earl eight horses ... four helmets and four byrnies and eight spears and as many shields and four swords and four mancuses of gold ... thegns a horse and its trappings and his weapons or his *healsfang* in Wessex and in Mercia £2 and in East Anglia £2, and those who have less wealth £2'. *Leis Willelme* repeats this more or less exactly, but the author's term for *heregeat* is 'relief', the term used in Normandy for the payment made by an heir in order to come into his inheritance.[32] And he makes a significant addition: the peasant tenant now owes heriot too, the 'best animal that he has, either a horse or an ox or a cow'.[33] The impressive and hugely valuable war gear of Cnut's law seems a world away from the family cow which the family of the *vilain* in *Leis Willelme* must hand over, but the language and the symbolism are exactly the same: inheritance is dependent on the tenant recognising his lord's rights in the tenement. The rules of tenure did not respect status, so we may expect that as, in the court of his 'honour', a Norman baron could 'put in' as his tenant an Englishman whose family may actually have had the land for generations, lesser men would 'put in' as their tenants peasant heirs who may have had the farm for generations too. If a baron charged his tenants heriots of warhorses and war gear, these men in turn can demand from their own tenants the peasant equivalent: 'his best beast, either horse, ox or cow'.[34] Marriage and property were never far apart in medieval society and peasant marriages, like those of the elite, may well have long been occasions for the involvement of a group of people beyond the immediate family. Now that tenure would mean that the group would include the couple's lord, whose permission must be sought.

From the later evidence of the records of manorial courts we learn that manorial lords regularly symbolised their interest in the transmission of their tenants' land between generations by the formula of 'surrender and admittance', the heir 'surrendering' the land to the lord who would allow him (or occasionally her) for a price, to acquire it. That price is the 'relief', the same term that is used in Henry I's coronation charter for what he will only 'justly' charge his tenants-in-chief. We do not know when the formal procedure of 'surrender and admission' became established in the courts which lords held for their manorial tenants, and we do not know how widespread such courts were before the date of the earliest reference to those on the estate of the bishops of Winchester in 1208–9. This reference is from one of the most document-minded estate administrations in England: earlier and less formal records from lay manors are an unknowable possibility. But if relief had become so well-established that the author of Leis Willelme knew what was due even from a peasant, it is quite possible that, within half a century of the Conquest, a Norman lord would expect to be an essential party to the formal transfer of land between the generations of the peasants on his manor, allowing heirs to succeed their fathers only after having 'surrendered' the family farm and paid heriot. That only by payment of 'relief' could they to get it back hammered home the new fact: on the manor as in the wider realm all land was now held from someone with a superior interest in it.[35] That could well be why Andrew Horn used the terminology of feudalism to describe peasant tenures: 'The counts were enfeoffed of counties ... the knights of knights of knights' fees, the villeins of villeinages.'

'Enfeoffing', putting a tenant into a fief, was a key moment. Accompanied by the performance of fealty, it initiated a tenure.[36] The link between the land and fealty was vital: swearing fidelity to a lord had long been part of the way that social relationships of many kinds had been expressed: the Chronicle could call on a traditional expression, *holdaþ*, 'hold-oath', to describe what had been given at Salisbury. Linking homage to tenure, as the author of 'Bracton' did, made it into 'a bargain about a tenement', in Maitland's phrase.[37] At the level of peasant–lord relationships it is not until the records of manorial courts become available, from the mid-thirteenth century, that we observe the villeins being 'enfeoffed of villeinages', but when we do that seems an apt description. It became entrenched in court procedure: a fourteenth-century treatise gives the oath the incoming tenant takes to his lord: 'I will be faithful and loyal, and faith to thee will bear *of the tenement that I hold of thee* in villeinage'[38] Important to feudal tenants was the principle that services once fixed, if performed permanently, ensured the tenant security of tenure. *Leis Willeleme: Cil qui cu(l) ti(v)ent la terre ne deit l'um travailer se de leur droite cense noun; ne leist a seigneurage departir les cultiveurs de lur terre pur tant cum il pussent le dreit seirvise faire*: 'No-one may harass the cultivators of the land but for their due rent: it is not permitted to lords to part the cultivators from their land *as long as they can do their due service*'. This would come to be a principle of enormous importance: we know from later evidence that lords, however powerful, would never find it easy, even possible, to evict their customary tenants. John Hatcher's view, from a study of manorial court rolls, was that 'eviction was rare and arbitrary eviction scarcely known'.[39] If the service is performed, the tenant cannot be ousted: it seems that this principle, the essence of feudal landholding, made no distinction between peasants and lords. One of the themes of this book has been that the values embedded in a moral economy can legitimise some very exploitative relationships. Occasionally, though, they can have unexpected consequences. This chapter has described some of the values embedded in feudal tenure which can be seen as conferring, in a very unequal society, albeit at a price, two important benefits to peasant tenants: the hereditability of their land and the security of their tenure.

The language of feudal tenure did not remain the preserve of lawyers and courts. It came to be routinely used for tenure at the peasant level. Estate administrators, and possibly peasants too, used it too: A handy way of referring to holdings which had been established by an earlier settlement grant was as the 'tenures of the old enfeoffment'.[40] An entry in the cartulary of Eynsham Abbey, Oxfordshire, is a telling example of the tenacity of 'thinking feudally'. Refounded early in the eleventh century, the abbey benefitted from donations from the Anglo-Norman gentry, made in terms such as 'a quarter of a knight's fee'. One donation was of 'a quarter of a knight's fee in the township of Finstock', which amounted to a few acres in what became the village's common field. In the sixteenth century, the monks themselves could benefit from the handy guide in the cartulary to converting real acres into feudal terms: '12 inches maketh a foot and sixteen foot and a half makyth a perch and 40 perches in length and three in breadth maketh an acre of land and four acres maketh a yard of land (presumably a yardland) and 5 yard maketh an hyde of land and eight hyd maketh a knight's fee'. The 'scutage', or payment made in lieu of knight service, owed from this perfectly ordinary scrap of land must have baffled local people almost as much as it baffles local historians today.[41]

By the late twelfth century, as a result of the new concept of tenure which now governed relationships at all levels of 'feudal' society, thousands of peasant families were becoming bound to their obligations as tenants holding land from lords in return for service on terms which were understood as, and increasingly recorded as, 'the custom of the manor'. If the ideas expressed in the *Leis Willelme* had become current practice, and we do not know whether or not that was the case, they were also becoming increasingly constrained in what they could achieve by going to court about their conditions. In the language of the new moral economy, that of 'feudalism', at all levels of society the English were now in much the same position as were their Norman counterparts: powerful and peasant held their 'fee' in return for service. In the words of Marc Bloch: 'The lands of the peasant were returned to him charged with rents in money or in kind and with agricultural labour services. The person of higher status and warlike habits, after having done homage, received back his former possessions as the honourable fief of a vassal.'[42]

Notes

1 Hyams, 'The common law and the French connection', 78; Le Patourel, *Norman Empire*, 353. In this important article Hyams showed the dependence of the early twelfth-century legal compilation 'Glanvill' on contemporary Norman and French *coutumiers*, records of custom. His account of the adoption of feudal tenure and its phraseology, therefore, does not claim to cover the situation in 1086.

2 Hyams, 'Common law and the French connection', 87.

3 Tabuteau, *Transfers of Property*, 103–4.

4 I am grateful to Hannah Boston and Richard Purkiss for their advice here, which does not in any way commit them to my view.

5 Taylor, 'Homage', 233ff.

6 *The Peterborough Chronicle 1070–1154, sub anno* 1085 (for 1086).

7 Holt, '1086', 42–3. Wright's view was that Domesday would have recorded quotas of knight service among tenurial conditions, which is no longer thought to have been the case.

8 Garnett, *Conquered England*, 83–96, at 87; Harvey, *Domesday*, 237. The topic, and its treatment by historians, is now comprehensively reviewed by Stephen Baxter in 'Title to property in the age of the Great Confiscation'.

9 Wormald, 'Charters, law, and the settlement of disputes', 215–19; Baxter, 'Lordship and justice'.

10 Haskins, *Norman Institutions*, 24–5.

11 *Leges Henrici Primi*, 57.2, 176–9.

12 The OE term *mot* is from the verb *motian*, to address an assembly, discuss, and in many contexts has a wider meaning than 'court' in the sense of a forum for the legal settlement of disputes. Lambert, *Law and Order* uses 'assembly' for this reason, and is more correct. I am using the narrower meaning here, in order to make the contrast between English and Norman expectations of what a court was.

13 *Leges Edwardi Confessoris*: Liebermann, *Gesetze*, i. 655, cited by Maddicott, 'Oath of Marlborough', 296.

14 For honorial courts: *Leges Henrici Primi*, 55, 55.1, 1a, 1b; 55.2; Hudson, *Formation of the English Common Law*, 40–3. For the absence of 'private' justice in England at this period and its importance in Normandy: Goebel, *Felony and Misdemeanor*, chapter 6. For courts other than these, such as those for settling disputes over drainage, boundaries, and ad hoc meetings, see Stenton, *English Justice*, appendix V; Banham and Faith, *Anglo-Saxon Farms and Farming*, 161.

15 Razi and Smith, *The Manor and the Manor Court*, 631.

16 Stenton, *English Justice*, 56–7; Garnett, *Conquered England*, 16–18 for a much more cynical approach.

17 *Leis Willeme*, 20.3a and 25: Robertson, *Laws*, 262–3, Liebermann, *Gesetze*, i. 506–7.

18 Bosworth and Toller, *An Anglo-Saxon Dictionary*, s.v *mot*. I have not been able to find the reference there to the *mot-bel* in *Leges Edwardi Confessoris'*. Razi and Smith, *Medieval Society and the Manor Court*, 613–15, 631–2. Harvey, 'The manorial reeve'. *The Order of Keeping a Court Leet and a Court Baron*, published in 1650, carefully distinguishes the differences between the two kinds of court (the court baron was for the free tenants of a manor) at every stage of the proceedings, even when they were held at the same place and entered on the same record.

19 Sawyer, *Anglo-Saxon Charters*, no. 360. This may have been where the Micheldever hundred met.

20 Fleming, *Domesday Book*, no. 284.

21 Hilton, *The Stoneleigh Leger Book*, 102.

22 Abingdon: Sawyer, *Anglo-Saxon Charters*; 1066: Harmer, *Anglo-Saxon Writs*, no. 5, 122–33. D. M. Stenton pointed to the parallel situation of the court held by that innovation of the early years of Henry I, the itinerant justiciar, which although it 'may have met where the shire court met, it was not the shire court. It was a royal court transacting the king's business.' Stenton, *English Justice*, 67.

23 Campbell, 'Hundreds and leets: a survey with suggestions'.

24 *Leges Henrici Primi*, c.9.4, c.27.1; pp. 319–20.

25 Razi and Smith, *Medieval Society*, 50.

26 Harvey, *Manorial Records*, 46–7.

27 *Leges Henrici Primi*, 56.1, *pace* Downer's translation which interpolates a redundant 'court' for the original's *in manerio*, 'on the manor'. For leasing, Lennard, *Rural England*, chapters 5–7; Goebel, *Felony and Misdemeanor*, chapter 6 for private justice in Normandy.

28 *Leges Henrici Primi*, 56.1-4. Downer has inserted a 'manor court' into his translations of these entries.

29 Cam, *Hundred and Hundred Rolls*.

30 *Leges Henrici Primi*, 29.1a; 7.8.

31 Goebel, *Felony and Misdemeanor*, 391–9 with reference to *Leges Henrici Primi*; *Cartularium Monasterii de Rameseia*, 274–5 (Stukely, Hunts.); Maitland's eagle eye spotted in Domesday other distinctions: on a royal Norfolk manor, the earl had had jurisdiction over farmers whose sheep had to be folded and their beneficial manure deposited on his land, not their own: Maitland, *Domesday Book*, 122. Bruce O'Brien has suggested that the association of being in frankpledge with personal freedom was increasingly being undermined by personal surety given by lords to members of their household and that by the mid-twelfth century 'only "villeins" needed to be in frankpledge'. O'Brien, *God's Peace and King's Peace*, 86. I am not sure that this is consonant with the evidence of the frankpledge enrolments recorded on the court rolls of the thirteenth and fourteenth centuries, generally on the same occasion as the manorial court was held. Schofield, 'Late medieval view of frankpledge and the tithing system' and the studies cited at Razi and Smith, *Medieval Society* show that free tenants played an important part.

32 Haskins, *Norman Institutions*, 22.

33 II Cnut 70, 71, 73.4, 78: Robertson, *Laws*, 208–11, Liebermann, *Gesetze*, i. 356–61. *Leis Willelme*, 20–1: Liebermann, *Gesetze*, i. 506–7, Robertson, *Laws*, 252–75. Bosworth and Toller, *Anglo-Saxon Dictionary*, s.v. *heregeat* for heriot in wills. Goebel, *Felony and Misdemeanor* discusses inheritance at 251–3. The new concept was driven home and reinforced under Henry II by the emphasis which the new possessory writs put on the lord 'putting in' tenants. Only this gave 'seisin': Milsom, *Legal Framework*, 39–40.

34 *Leis Willelme*, 20: Robertson, *Laws*, 262–3, Liebermann, *Gesetze*, i. 506–8.

35 Hudson, 'Anglo-Saxon land law and the origins of property' discusses the trend towards property from tenure at a higher level of society than is regarded here. The tenants he discusses were able to acquire something very like ownership as a result of the Angevin reforms. Homans, *English Villagers*, Book II, 'Families' gives a very full description of late medieval manorial court practice with regard to the transmission and inheritance of land. 'Surrender and admittance' is described at p. 255.

36 It seems to have been the case that only tenants-in-chief did homage for their land: all others did fealty: Maddicott, 'The Oath of Marlborough', 305: The Salisbury Oath was an exception in exceptional circumstances. Pollock and Maitland, *History of English Law*, i. 301; For peasants doing homage rather than fealty, for a tenement, which might imply their free status, 305. Hyams, *Kings, Lords and Peasants*, 13, for villeins doing fealty, 11–12.

37 Pollock and Maitland, *History of English Law*, i. 301.
38 Quoted in Homans, *English Villagers*, 255. My emphasis.
39 *Leis Willelme*, 29.1: Robertson, *Laws*, 268–9; Liebermann, *Gesetze*, i. 512. Hatcher, 'English villeinage and serfdom', 10. None is mentioned in Ralph Evans' meticulous analysis of lord–tenant relations in 'Whose was the manorial court?'.
40 Neilson, *Customary Rents*, s.v. *Antiqua tenure, assize*.
41 Salter, *The Eynsham Cartulary*, ii. 2 in 'a hand of c 1520', according to the editor. Grants of portions of knight's fee at e.g. i. 134, 146–7. This approach continued to have a valued place in English historiography. The early volumes of the *Victorian County History* identified the feudal structures of parishes, a practice now discontinued, and the notes in the Phillimore edition of Domesday Book follows Domesday holdings into their later manifestations as fees.
42 Bloch, *Feudal Society*, 171.

15　From Rank to Class

Medieval thinkers did not ignore the fact that they lived in a society supported by peasant labour. Some justified this as part of the moral economy: for king Alfred 'those who work' were the third leg of the stool of government, for abbot Ælfric 'the ploughman feeds us all'. When the twelfth-century philosopher John of Salisbury pictured society as a human body, peasants were the feet on which it stood. For Henry I, who had a nightmare about them, peasants were powerful enough to be a threat. However they were regarded, they were felt to be an important enough stratum of society for their role in that society to be awarded a rank, just as there was a Norman French *seigneurage* and an Italian *signoria* and there was coming into being an English 'gentry'. Ælfric referred to the *laboratores* 'who give us food' as an *ordo*, an 'order' of society, in much the same spirit as Alfred had referred to them as a *geferscipe*, a group of 'fellows' in the sense of people with a common interest.[1] Whether peasants in the year 1200 felt themselves to be a distinct rank in society is another matter. Throughout this book, the difference between inland and warland has been reflected in the different obligations that their inhabitants owed. The people of the inland, who had accepted tied tenancies in return for labour and rent, appeared in our earliest sources. They are there in Ine's laws, of the early eighth century, having been given an 'outfit' of stock, land, and housing, and they are there in *Rectitudines singularum personarum* in the late tenth or early eleventh, the *geburs* who owe heavy labour rent on very similar terms and under very similar restraints on their freedom. The situation of people on the warland cannot be summarised in this way in terms of what their obligations were. It was their land, and the obligations it owed, that set them apart. They were taxpayers obliged to attend the public courts. These were the people most likely to have felt the heavier demands of the changing political climate of post-Conquest England. The negotiations and agreements which lay behind the more organised obligations recorded in the twelfth-century surveys had left them with security of tenure but 'burdened with works'.

All studies of peasants emphasise their diversity, and when we are able to investigate actual farms, for after all, peasants were farmers, we find a wide variety, from substantial farms, some still functioning today, to tiny smallholdings. There were wide differences even in a small township, between the extent to which peasants were involved in public life and had public responsibilities. The older established farms, the 'old austers', seem to have had their own respected status. A peasant ploughing with his own team was surely very different from one using a scratch plough or even a spade. 'Houses' were nothing like the *tuguria*, 'cabins', of Robert of Hereford's description. Manorial populations must have had their own internal class structure. When the twelfth-century surveys make it possible to look more closely at them, they show a huge variety of people in various stages of negotiation with lords and owing an equal variety of obligations: some degrading, some less so. When we see peasants in the written sources it is through other people's eyes and those people generally had their own priorities: one was to simplify. In the vernacular laws, as we saw in the early chapters of this book, the important distinctions were those between noble and non-noble, between free and unfree. There was no term which would have distinguished peasants from others in the category of *ceorlas*, the free non-noble mass of the population. For those involved in the Domesday operation, the primary distinction was between assets *in dominio* and what was *in servicio*. Tasked with calculating total manorial populations in a very short time, they did this by sorting people into one or other of its categories: *bordarii* and *villani*, the 'people with cottages and the people with houses and fields', *sokemanni* and *franci homines*. It is not at all clear if *bordarii*, *villani*, and *franci homines* would have thought of themselves as all belonging to the same 'class' or 'rank' as 'peasants' with a common interest. *Leis Willelme* uses the term *nethi* for those 'born into' serfdom, who would have been instantly recognised before the Conquest, and the term *seigneurage* for lords as a body, but we cannot tell whether or not his third term for people, simply *hom*, 'man', had any particular connotation of rank. The author of the 'Dialogue of the Exchequer' does not distinguish peasants in his chronology of the relationship between lords and tenants of all kinds when 'over time those who had not fought … acquired the goodwill of their lords by devoted service and began to hold tenancies at the will of their lords, for themselves alone, however, without hope of succession'. Feudal tenure did not distinguish peasants from the rest of the free: it took the work of lawyers, case by case, to do that. Perhaps it was a sign that peasants were both seeing themselves, and being seen, as something like a distinct order in society that two literary accounts in the late twelfth century portray them armed with the tools of their trade. The farmers described in the 'Dialogue of the Exchequer' who gathered at the king's court, or, what seemed to him more serious, frequently mobbed the king himself, to protest about the burden of delivering the very considerable amounts of produce they were obliged to hand over as *feorm* did so *oblatis vomeribus*, by 'brandishing their ploughshares'. When the illustrator of the chronicle of John of Worcester, possibly the author himself, wished to illustrate the nightmare of Henry I, in which he was threatened by the three orders of society, the peasants are armed with scythes, the knights with swords, and the churchmen with crosses.[2] The rare recorded examples of protest were not made by peasants as a class but by groups of people with particular grievances, and were not against landowners as such but as usurpers of a community's resources, like the Fenland villagers assembling in defence of their commons encountered in an earlier chapter, or the peasants armed with scythes visiting the sleeping Henry I in a nightmare protesting against over-taxation.

If after 1200 the English peasantry did become a 'class for itself', and the history of concerted peasant resistance and rebellion in the following two centuries suggests that this is indeed what they then began to do, then the conditions concerning why that took so long to come about are worth investigating. There are some cogent reasons why collective action employed in resistance to landlord demands took a long time to build in England at a time when, in France and Catalonia, for instance, organised large-scale demonstrations and acts of resistance had become frequent. The first was Norman violence, or the threat of it. If news of the ferocity with which the authorities responded to resistance had crossed the Channel, the violent reputation of the Norman ruling class could well have acted as a deterrent: a rising in Normandy was put down by armed force by an 'army of knights', and the leaders' hands and feet cut off.[3] The *murdrum* fine brought in heavy communal penalties for killing a Frenchman. (In the 'Dialogue of the Exchequer' it is the explanation of this that leads the Master to explain to the Scholar the history of the Conquest.) The Harrying of the North was not forgotten or forgiven. However, the circumstances in which most English peasants experienced the change of regime were less likely to have included violent oppression, although it cannot be ruled out. The fractured chronology of the post-Conquest era in the 'Dialogue' seems to have described a real situation in which periods of disruption had been followed by tenant obligations becoming fixed by negotiated settlements. Pressure on peasants after the Conquest could well have taken some time to build up, as new lords themselves took time to consolidate, let alone increase, what they expected their tenants to provide. When Domesday Book records that the value of a manor had increased in the twenty years since the

Conquest, we cannot assume that this was always the result of increased pressure on the peasantry. As S. P. J. Harvey has shown, there were other, more immediate options, and many received much the same 'value' from their manors as Domesday Book recorded that their antecessors had done, or more.[4] Pressure on tenants may have been mediated by leasing. As was described in the previous chapter, many new lords put their properties out 'at farm' to lessees who were less able to ensure labour discipline and some even rented their manors out to the peasants themselves. In this period of both a high demand for and a shortage of currency, many lords preferred to commute tenants' services for cash, and inventing 'traditional' obligations which could then be commuted was probably not out of the question.[5] Simply getting together and recording tenant obligations must have taken time, patience, and expertise. The evidence of surveys made in the late twelfth century suggests that, at least on the large ecclesiastical estates, tenant obligations were then beginning to be systematically recorded: that may also have been when they began to be more systematically exacted. It was then, in Rodney Hilton's words, there was 'a feeling of immediate loss'.[6]

It is possible too that the language of feudalism itself acted as a brake on peasants' consciousness of themselves as a class. Earlier chapters have drawn on twelfth-century texts to show that the language of feudal tenure came to be part of the language of tenure at the peasant level also. 'Thinking feudally', in the terminology of 'tenure' and 'fief', seems initially to have allowed for no form of tenure specific to peasants: in feudal terms, a peasant farm was still land in 'fee simple', legally defined as 'an estate in land, held hereditarily for service'.[7] The principles of feudal tenure were enacted in the ceremonies of the honorial court, where lords granted tenants succession to land in return for 'relief', or took 'heriot' from the estate of the dead man, or gave a tenant permission to marry. When records of manorial courts become available, from the mid-thirteenth century, they record *villani* paying relief and heriot for their inheritances and land transfers in the same terms, and with a version of the same ceremony, as those of the honour court. Peasants may formerly have done so in the honour court alongside people of much greater wealth who were obliged to go through the same procedures. The work of Peter Coss has brought out how important it is to regard the concept of 'gentry', which would become such an effective bundle of cultural markers, as essentially a new creation of the thirteenth and fourteenth centuries.[8] Before that, as far as local society was concerned, many peasants in the eleventh and early twelfth centuries would have had no reason to regard themselves as members of an inferior class. It was only the thriving *ceorl* looking for political advancement who needed to have acquired the thegnly appurtenances of hall, kitchen, and bellhouse on his five hides: solid farmers outside the orbit of royal politics had no reason to do so. Rather, the reverse was true. The properties of many substantial Devon farmers, for instance, would have been very hard to distinguish from the neighbouring properties of thegns.[9] Domesday sokemen in East Anglia had *villani* 'under them'. Men like this who were employers of labour either in their own households or housed nearby were powerful in local society in their own right and beginning to be in a minority of local people who attended the hundred and shire courts. It is hard to imagine them making common cause with the lesser people of the countryside.

The Manor Court and Collective Action

Ironically, it may have been only when the manor became fully effective as an economic unit with the resumption of demesne farming late in the twelfth century that peasants would become capable of acting as a political community. In summoning their tenants from their own farms to work on their lord's land, landowners handed them a powerful and potentially subversive weapon.[10] Weekwork brought a new phenomenon onto the fields, large numbers of farmers working together under compulsion at precisely those times of year when their labour was most needed on their own land. Collective action for a lord could evoke the possibility of collective action on their own behalf. Weekwork, the harvest in particular, might bring peasants into a situation not so very far from that of industrial workers many centuries later: assembled in large numbers they became aware of the strength that lay in those numbers. The leaders of later peasant movements frequently turn out to have been prominent too in the organisation of the business of the manor and its court. That, after all, was where negotiations between lords and tenants took place and were recorded and it may have been that the manor court was where peasants would learn to organise and act collectively. In 1200 we are only on the eve of that era.[11]

It could well be that when peasants began to act collectively it was over boon-work, not weekwork. The 'boons' of haymaking and harvesting were called in, after all, at key points in the farming year when speed was of the essence and 'piling labour onto the land' could make the difference between the hay and corn being successfully brought in while the weather held, or serious loss. Consequently, those were the points at which the peasants' bargaining position was at its strongest.[12] Modern people, including many medieval historians, are inclined to regard all manual work as degrading. That is a handicap if we are to have any chance of understanding the early medieval rural world where there was considerable respect for the man behind the plough who 'feeds us all'. It is true that boon-works involved the same tasks as the weekwork owed by manorial tenants of the 'assized' customary tenancies: principally ploughing, haymaking, and harvesting. By the time that they come to be recorded as part of tenant obligations, as they were among those of the *geburas* in *Rectitudines singularum personarum*, it would be hard to argue against 'boons' having become to all intents and purposes compulsory. Free tenants owed them as well as *villani*. Yet, in terms of the moral economy, there was a profound difference between weekwork and boon-work, a difference which goes back to their origins. Reciprocity, considered earlier in this book as an important element in the moral economy, is embedded in the social meaning of boon-work. Even the persistence of the name was significant: boons were 'prayed for', not demanded. and for his part, just as he had in Wulfstan's time and long before, the lord was traditionally obliged to provide a meal. The work of Jean Birrell on the manorial custumals of the twelfth and thirteenth centuries has made it possible to hear a peasant point of view, in particular to appreciate the importance that peasants attached to the manner in which their work was rewarded. Their concern to be treated *honorifice*, 'honourably', at the boons evoked long-standing ideas of reciprocity and hospitality: Birrell observes that 'it was possible for the meals customarily provided to be presented as part of a reciprocal relationship, a just reward for services freely rendered.'[13] What food and drink were provided and how they were to be served were not only considered matters of great importance, they were also common knowledge, carefully recorded so that all the peasants of the neighbourhood knew their entitlements. Something of this care comes through from the comment by the author of *Rectitudines singularum personarum* that he had been at great pains to find out all he could about local variations of the customary 'feasts' he recorded, and he reminds us that they were 'local custom' as opposed to the 'rules of the estate'. Yet even on these occasions of solidarity, traditional notions of rank persisted. Harvest and haymaking could bring prosperous yeoman farmers, or the farm servants they sent in their stead, out to the harvest field to reap alongside peasants with smallholdings, but the social order was preserved in a 'hierarchy ... in the harvest field' in Birrell's term.[14] A yardlander set to supervise the harvest workers, sometimes 'with a rod', to make sure that the work was properly carried out by his fellow-tenants was perhaps the forerunner of the 'harvest lord' and 'lady' (both men) who negotiated with the landowner and organised the workers in nineteenth-century harvesting contracts.[15] It is at the boons we can most clearly see the persistence of a moral economy in which *geþyncðu*, due honour, mattered as much to later medieval peasants as it had to Wulfstan 'the Wolf'.

Legal Villeinage: Status

A belief in the honourable nature of boon-work was to become crucial in when the legal doctrine of villeinage was becoming clarified. Paul Hyams has brought out the essential difference between the twelfth and thirteenth centuries in this respect, using as evidence the practice in the courts and the legal doctrines expressed in two works, commonly referred to as 'Glanvill' and 'Bracton'.[16] We can add another dimension if we see legal developments as a response to what was happening in the world outside the courts. In the twelfth century, the legal view developed that villeinage was a matter of personal status: it was 'in the blood'. By the late twelfth century, slaves were becoming a thing of the past and Roman law concepts about slavery had become available to describe other kinds of people: this was the time at which Fitznigel's 'Dialogue of the Exchequer' uses the Roman law term *adscripticii* for 'those who are called *villani* for whom it is not allowed to depart from their condition if their lords object'. Glanvill's 'Treatise on the Laws and Customs of the Realm of England', also written in the late 1180s, similarly treats the condition of legal unfreedom as something essentially personal. The author uses the Latin equivalent of the *neifs* of *Leis Willelme:* villeins were *nativi a primitiva nativitate sua*, 'they are so called from their birth'. This was already the position around the year 1000 of the people documented by David Pelteret, who were 'born into' subjection on major inlands like the *geburas* described as '*inbyrde* to Hatfield' or Ely's *innati* carefully listed in the *Liber Eliensis*. Birth must always have mattered in establishing the unfree status of such people and is likely to have been common knowledge locally. The proof of villeinage in the common law through their 'blood', as set out in Glanvill, was much the same as was already practised: Ely's claim to two sisters went back to their great-grandparents.[17] Lords' entitlement to get back their runaway *neifs* had been expressed in *Leis Willelme* several decades before it was reinforced by the possibility of an action on status in the royal courts.[18] What the *Leis Willelme* author must have felt that Old English legal practice had sorely lacked was now coming into being: a body of law which defined 'neifs' as legally unfree. As later lawyers did, he too would perhaps have called it 'naifty'.

Legal Villeinage: Tenure

It was the work of thirteenth-century lawyers to expand the category of the legally unfree beyond the inland to include significant numbers of peasants at large. When they came to do so they fastened less on personal status and more on tenure and its obligations.[19] Boon-works came to be crucial in this situation. Peasants who appeared in court claimed as unfree by their lords admitted to owing boon-works but appear to have believed that owing *only* boon-works was in itself a mark of their free status.[20] Weekwork, by contrast, was closely associated with unfreedom. It may be that the form of words was more important to people at the time than we realise. Feudal 'incidents', the term given to their lords from tenants of fees, came to be seen as marks of freedom if they were perceived to be given voluntarily. The payment was the same, but was compatible with freedom if called *auxilium* or 'aid', but with unfreedom if baldly called 'tallage, literally a 'cut'. Rather as a farm labourer today will speak of 'helping out' one local farmer but 'working for' another, the distinction of boon-work was that it retained its connotations of being a favour done and rewarded.[21] Part of the explanation may have to do with the arbitrary nature of weekwork. While boon-work was highly specific – so many days to be worked, so many acres to be ploughed or reaped, so many people from the household to turn out, exactly what food was to be supplied – the unfree person, according to Bracton, is someone 'who doesn't know in the evening what work he will have to do in the morning' but 'is bound to do whatever he is bid'. Hyams, the authority on the legal doctrine on villeinage, considers that 'as a factual description of the villein's way of life this is of course nonsense'.[22] Maitland's discussion of the same passage was based on his knowledge of manorial custumals where labour obligations were very closely defined in terms of what constituted a 'day's work', exactly how far a tenant who owed carrying service was obliged to travel, what, if any, entitlements to food and drink an obligation implied, and so on. This seems much closer to what can be known about the actual conditions of weekwork. What Bracton tells us is that unfreedom lay in the fact that an individual tenant would not necessarily know which particular job the bailiff would put him on to the next day. This may have been a widely held opinion. It was clear to the dean of St. Paul's in 1181 that there was an important distinction between *qui colonorum libertate gauderent*, 'those who rejoice in freedom', and *qui gravarenter operibus*, 'those who are burdened with works'. The dean's account continues with 'These hold freely' where it gives a list of named people with very varied amounts of land for cash rents, but all of whom 'plough and reap at the lord's boons', *ad cibum eius*, with food provided by him. This apparently did not amount to their being 'burdened with works'.

The legal doctrine of villeinage, both as a condition of personal unfreedom and a form of unfree tenure, as Hyams shows, was not established at a stroke of a lawyer's pen but evolved in the course of judicial proceedings. By the late twelfth century, the actual business of going to law had been changing rapidly. The old local courts still met, but there was a new way of obtaining justice and that was through the 'royal' or public courts, where the common law, 'lawyers' law', was beginning to evolve. Language itself was becoming more divisive. Although people still read, wrote, and spoke Old English, the law had its own language, French, and 'the baronial classes', in Hyams' words, 'remembered their customs in French'.[23] Written records, not simply familiarity with tradition, were now essential or at least very desirable, to establish a claim. Peasants, most of whom were illiterate, were as aware of the importance of written record as were the nobility, many of whom were illiterate too: what mattered was knowledge about what the written record contained, not necessarily being able to read it. Michael Clanchy has characterised England after the Conquest as a distinctive period in the development of literate ways of thinking and doing business.[24] The concerns of the author of *Leis Willelme* over peasants having charters made, and produced in court, to secure their freedom come from early in the twelfth century and are evidence of individual actions by people who knew the value of documents in an era which was moving 'from memory to written record'. Now to go to law, it was no longer enough to bring a complaint to the attention of the hundred court to be decided by all the 'suitors' assembled there. Now a judge trained in the law would hold the court and rather than the oath-helpers who used to testify simply to a person's good reputation, judgement would be made by a panel of sworn men, 'jurors' who would decide the facts. In Maitland's words, the king's courts were 'turning judges into jurors'.[25] To start a case, one now needed to secure the correct kind of document: a writ. Nevertheless, the courts did not always find in favour of lords, and lords were not the only people who thought it worth taking a case to court. People could prove their freedom there as well as lose it.

New legal procedures to regain property that were brought in to speed up the business of settling the disputes and dispossessions that had occurred during the chaos of the civil war were intended for people who had lost land on a large scale, not for peasants with grievances against their lords. However, peasants were among the keenest of users of this new legal remedy: many sued their lords under novel disseisin and some did so successfully. Work by Janice Musson has established that a number of such cases brought before the itinerant justices were claims by individual peasants that their lords had effectively disseised them by infringing on their common pastures, appropriating grazing land, and barring their entitlement to cut turves.[26] This is exactly the kind of dispute over common rights which down the following centuries would involve direct action by communities. Our twelfth-century evidence, however, shows something rather different: legal action by individuals. What is striking is that they embarked on the legal process at all: to bring a plea would have needed the complainant knowing about, and obtaining, the correct kind of writ, the document needed to bring such a case. That cost money and needed a lawyer's advice, even at the level of the county court, but some peasants sued their lords in courts much higher up the judicial hierarchy: the royal courts sitting at Westminster. In a sense the legal doctrine of 'villeinage' was a by-product of this situation. Hyams has argued it is in drawing the line between those whom the king allowed access to his courts and those excluded, that the condition of personal unfreedom which became known as 'villeinage', and the tenure known as 'tenure in villeinage', began to be defined.[27]

When it came to what rights people had to their land, there was much less continuity than there had been about their status. In pre-Conquest England, the question hardly arose: rights in land were simply embedded. There is practically no Old English 'land law'. Bookland, land conveyed by charter, gave the recipient the power of alienation, it is true, and charters were valued evidence of ownership, but we do not know that owning bookland gave any securer title than owning 'old family land' gave the deep-rooted families of lords and warland farmers alike. After 1066, in order to legitimise the new social order, new land-lords, and a new king, rights in land became of the utmost importance and were entrenched through exemplification and performance. To have land was now to 'hold' it from someone else: the preceding chapters have attempted to show how important it had become for feudal tenants to be formally 'put in' to a fee and to swear fealty or do homage as part of the same transaction. Peasants were no different: they too had now to be 'put in' by landlords in a formal ceremony before inheriting their own land. The agreements and 'assizes', or 'settlements', arrived at between lords and their peasant tenants and given a historical justification as the 'custom of the manor', were exemplified in custumals drawn up and witnessed in the manor court. The written record established the basis for obligations which had shifted, in Stubbs' phrase, 'from status to contract'. Peasant who were able to participate in the new legal system as individuals, and do so successfully, are not likely to have felt the need for collective action.

Whatever was going on in the courts, it is likely that class-consciousness would develop much more rapidly among those who had benefitted least from social change. As we have seen, educated people in the twelfth and thirteenth centuries had no hesitation about presenting the Conquest as a watershed in social relationships. The imposition of a landowning and governing elite speaking a different language seems to have been absorbed at the level of the elite, where it appeared to Fitznigel that by his day a great deal of racial assimilation had since taken place. 'Nowadays, when English and Normans live close together and marry and give in marriage to each other, the nations are so mixed that it scarcely can be decided who is of English birth and who Norman'. He makes the distinction, however, that this applied solely to the upper ranks of society: '*de liberis loquor*, I speak of the free, excepting the *ascripticii qui villani dicuntur quibus non est liberum obstantibus dominis suis a sui status conditione discedere*, the *ascripticii* who are called *villani*, to whom it is not allowed, if their lords object, to depart from their condition'. Work on the relations between the two 'nations' by Hugh Thomas bears Fitznigel out.[28] He makes a useful distinction, which would resonate with students of later medieval rural society, between the mass of the rural population and 'the middling sort' comprising richer peasants, officials in wealthy households, and lords of small manors, all people who were likely to come into regular contact with French-speaking Normans. He draws attention among Norman immigrants to the 'Frenchmen', *francigenae* in Domesday, who 'would have rubbed shoulders with ordinary English peasants on a day-to-day basis'. Englishmen were lessees of manors and minor officials in both royal and seigneurial administrations, all positions which would have entailed frequent contacts with Norman landowners and office holders. For such people, participating in 'Anglo-Norman' culture, even on its fringes, may have been an attractive novelty and a means of advancement. But this is, with Fitznigel, to 'speak of the free'. He may well have been aware of the fact that from the perspective of the lower level of society, the situation already looked different. For some later medieval peasants, class and nationality were bound together: from their perspective, it was as a result of the Conquest that English people had lost their freedom and 'live in serfdom'. A fourteenth-century verse chronicle put it like this:

> 'Sithen he (William) and his haf had the lond in heritage,
> That the Inglis haf so lad that thei lyve in seruage,
> He sette the Inglis to be thralle,that was so fre......
> For alle this thraldom that now on Inglond es,
> thorgh Normanz it cam, bondage & destres'
> 'Fra Englisse blode Englande he refte

> Na maner soile with tham he lefte
> Duelle thai dale alls bondes and thralles
> And do alle that to thraldom falls.'[29]

Many other 'Inglis' people also looked to the past, but in a different way: their views will be the subject of the final chapter.

Notes

1 Powell, 'The three orders', 104. I am grateful to Paul Hyams for this reference.
2 Johnson, *Dialogue*, 41–2, my translation.
3 Bonnassie, *From Slavery to Feudalism*, 304–13.
4 Harvey, 'Domesday England' for the considerable amounts of cash which lords could have taken off initially from e.g. judicial profits.
5 Miller and Hatcher, *Medieval England*, 201–13. A florid invention of 'customary' renders which were commuted into cash payments may lie behind some of the customary rents listed in Neilson, s.v. 'Customary rents'.
6 Hilton, 'Freedom and villeinage', 14.
7 For a thorough analysis of a village in feudal terms, see Chibnall, *Sherington: Fiefs and Fields of a Buckinghamshire Village*.
8 Coss, *Origins of the English Gentry* and 'What's in a construct?', rightly correcting Faith, *English Peasantry*, 153 and chapter 6 more generally.
9 Faith, 'Cola's *tūn*', 78, and references there. The Thorns' notes in *Domesday Book. 9. Devon* are particularly informative in this respect.
10 This suggestion is the result of discussions with Jean Birrell.
11 Evans, 'Whose was the manor court?'.
12 Faith, '"Great Rumour"' (more accurately '"Great Tumult"'). Muller, 'The aims and organisation of a peasant revolt'.
13 Birrell, 'Peasants eating and drinking', 3. For bargaining over wage rates and the role of the 'harvest lord' in the nineteenth century: Morgan, 'The place of harvesters in nineteenth century village life'.
14 Birrell, 'Peasants eating and drinking', 15–16.
15 Hyams, *Kings, Lords and Peasants*, 194–7 at 194; Pollock and Maitland, *History of English Law*, i. 366–8.
16 Hyams, *Kings, Lords, and Peasants*, 119–22.
17 Pelteret, *Slavery*, 180–3.
18 Hyams, *Kings, Lords and Peasants*, 222–33.
19 Glanvill, *Treatise*, book v; Hyams, *Kings, Lords and Peasants*, 119–21.
20 Faith, *English Peasantry*, 259–60.
21 Tallage: Hyams, *Kings, Lords and Peasants*, 191–3.
22 Hyams, *Kings, Lords and Peasants*, 194 characterises this definition as having had a very limited application, being intended to provide a criterion for distinguishing between 'pure' villeinage and the 'privileged' villeinage of tenants who held manors which were 'ancient demesne', that is to say had been part of the *Terra Regis* in Domesday Book.
23 Hyams, 'Common law and the French connection', 91.

24 Clanchy, *From Memory to Written Record*, chapter 2.
25 Maitland, *Select Pleas*, 105.
26 Musson, 'Commoners'.
27 Hyams, *Kings, Lords and Peasants*, part III.
28 Thomas, *The English and the Normans*, chapter 11, quotation at p. 163.
29 Mofffat, 'Sin, conquest, servitude', quotation at p. 147.

16   Conclusion: Forward into the Past

English radical historians have always taken popular culture seriously in its own terms. Much of their work has brought out how often, in times of stress, rural protesters have looked back to better times in the past. E. P. Thompson's corn rioters were living through economic changes that were bringing in a new conceptual order based on reason and the dictates of the unfettered market and it was as a critique of this that they turned to an earlier moral economy exemplified in the Tudor market rules. Other historians have been quick to characterise such backward-looking reactions, common enough in English history, as naïve nostalgia. It does not seem to me to be any more scholarly to disbelieve what people in the past thought about their past than to believe it: our task is to understand it. That is what this book attempts to do. Its central concern is to understand how the appropriation of peasant labour by the elite was achieved, framing the problem in terms of the moral economy. Having begun by proposing that some essential elements of the moral economy of pre-Conquest England were rank, reciprocity, and reputation, I have not interpreted these as forming part of a 'legitimating theory' promoted by the elite to cloak their exploitation of others. Rather, I found that these values derived their strength from the fact that they were widely held across society and seemed best understood as the response of people to their circumstances. Of particular importance were their ideas about their own history. Whatever the actual scale of settlement had been, the belief of the people who became 'Anglo-Saxons' that they had come from overseas embedded 'our island story' in their ideas of who they were. In the settlement period many of their circumstances were those shared across post-Roman Europe. The earliest English law-codes assume much the same ranks in society as do other barbarian laws, albeit written down 'according to the custom of the Romans', and the context of the barbarian migrations had embedded rank in social relationships which set lords as military leaders over peasants as free warriors. Common too across Europe was the assumed existence of slaves. Reciprocity, understood not as equality but as the conviction that each action calls for its appropriate response, was embedded in poetry as well as written down as law, and was what made the peasant household a viable economic entity. Reciprocity is found underlying what appear at first to be some very inequitable situations. Thus, when the households of itinerant elites expected to be fed by the households of the countrysides they travelled through, they drew on the public obligations of the land itself and thus of the people who farmed it. That these people were free farmers, and that their public obligations were at the heart of their free condition, will turn out to explain a great deal of the 'moral economy' of Anglo-Saxon England. Reputation, and ideas of what made up a person's 'worth', not only made it possible for an increasingly lively commercial economy to develop but supported systems of 'local government' and dispute settlement which were apparently effective and some of which are still in existence. An informed commentator from the early eleventh century alerts us to the possibility that the old moral economy was then increasingly coming under threat from within. The impact of the Normans was on a different scale altogether. 'Feudal' theory, by defining social relationships in terms of 'tenure' was now much more influential than the old notions of rank and reciprocity, worth and reputation. What had been public assemblies became increasingly 'privatised' courts, either seigneurial or royal. What had been a largely free peasantry became drawn into the orbit of a new entity, the 'manor', and by the late twelfth century for many this meant an obligation to supply lords with labour.

The suggestion that the appropriation of peasant labour was greatly extended and regularised after 1066 is not an original one. Rather, it is a medieval one. It was the author of 'Bracton', not a modern historian, who first proposed that after the Conquest 'free men who held their holdings by free services or free customs ... when they were thrown out by more powerful people, on returning afterwards took the same holdings up again to hold in villeinage, doing work for them which was servile but set and specified.' When the peasants assembled in London in 1381 demanded 'an end to villeinage', villeinage was a legal condition which had only been created by lawyers in the previous century: there was nothing unrealistic about a fourteenth-century view that it was something that could be abolished. The authorities evidently thought so: the charters of manumission which the king had drawn up (and then revoked) were legal documents.[1]

While the appropriation of their labour was reason enough to demand 'an end to villeinage' in 1381, I think that we can find in early medieval England some further reasons why ordinary uneducated English people have so often and so persistently claimed to be free and hence better understand the terms in which they have done so. One is a long-standing acquaintance with, and veneration for, the law. The vernacular law codes, the earliest from the seventh century, have come down to us because they were carefully preserved over a very long period and, even when Roman law was becoming known, formed an important part of Anglo-Norman legal collections.[2] Another reason was the sheer amount of popular participation in running rural affairs. Historians sometimes describe the government of late-medieval England as 'self-government at the king's command'. In Anglo-Saxon England the reverse seems to have been nearer the truth: kings operated through structures and networks which had long been established to answer the needs of the rural economy. The institutions which come into our view in the written record as the hundred and the township were responses to the exigencies of peasant life, which demanded cooperation and collective action as effective ways of managing conflict. Peasants were accustomed to litigating and it was a shock to Norman legists, early in the twelfth century, to find them obtaining charters and taking their lords to court. They were alert to the possibilities offered by the new legal environment and were among the most eager users of the legal innovations of Henry II. It was precisely because they had shown themselves to be litigants that the legal definitions of villein status and tenure were developed. Not anarchy, but trust in long-established ways of seeking justice can now be shown to lie behind the demand made in the rising of 1381, according to the 'Anonimalle' chronicle, that 'there should be no law save the law of Winchester'. Long debated by historians, this part of their programme has now been elucidated by Juliet Barker, who has drawn attention to an Essex petition that 'no court shall be held in any vill apart from the leet of the Lord King annually and forever.' She comments on this: 'What the rebels specifically said they wanted to retain was the ancient royal system of criminal justice, founded on the annual view of frankpledge.'[3]

Recorded examples of English peasant resistance frequently show them claiming freedom as individuals, rather than as a political or religious condition.[4] Anglo-Saxon laws were framed much less in terms of general principles than of individuals' rights against, and compensation due from, one another and in the public courts an individual's reputation, 'worth', was the essential element in dispute settlement. Freedom was also envisaged in terms of the right, and obligation, to participate in public life. It was an important part of the pre-Conquest social order that, while highly privatised enclaves were exempt, most land owed public service. Peasant farmers who had land traditionally reckoned in 'hides', even fractions of hides, were farming land which meant that they were thereby members of the body politic, even if that dwindled over time to meaning little more than being liable to pay tax. Membership of hundreds, tithings, and townships did not simply entail communal agrarian responsibilities but the obligation of free men to participate in public life. One of these obligations was to fight. Army service was one of the three 'common burdens', the others being bridge work and work on fortifications incumbent of all warland and by implication those who had it. The extent to which peasants actually did army service has been raised in an earlier chapter: what mattered in envisioning freedom was their liability to do so. This liability, part of the old moral economy, could on occasion be called in aid even by rulers in the new post-Conquest regime. John Maddicott has drawn attention to the fact that England was exceptional in the degree of 'public participation' and this included participation in defence: Henry II's Assize of Arms resulted in an armed peasantry unique in medieval Europe. Opportunistic he may have been, but when John assembled his subjects in 1209 to swear loyalty by the Oath of Marlborough, he was calling on a long-established conception of the body politic. Maddicott sees this episode as invoking the 'great king-centred gatherings of the early post-Roman barbarian West, which emphasised the king's direct relationship with all free men'.[5] 'Our island story' had not lost its appeal.

Historians of later popular movements in England have noted the participants' respect for the official written record. This too has a deep history. Well before the Conquest, peasants had become used to the idea of bookland, land conveyed by charter, and their local knowledge of boundaries formed a vital component of these prestigious records. Early in the twelfth century *Leis Willelme* recorded what seemed to the writer the unlawful situation of ordinary people extracting written contracts from their lords. Juliet Barker writes of the concessions won, or thought to have been won, by the rebels in 1381: 'the rebels wanted the documentation in place so that they had their new-found freedoms enshrined in letters patent or charters. They were not destroying the past but securing their future, and they knew that it had to be done in writing.'[6] Peasant tenants of the church in the thirteenth and fourteenth centuries knew that documents were important in establishing the church's hold on land and people. They knew that there were charters that established that the land they farmed had once been the king's land and some thought that they had been freer then. The peasant tenants of major religious houses across southern England, who carried out a highly organised rising in 1377 in the belief that Domesday Book, by showing their land to be part of the king's 'ancient demesne' would prove them to be free people, hired lawyers and obtained official copies, or 'exemplifications', of Domesday entries to substantiate their case.[7] (Domesday did not do that for them, but neither did it, as has been argued, record their unfreedom: it is modern historians, not medieval rebels, who have thought that we can find unfree peasants in the *villani* of Domesday Book.) Being illiterate has never meant that ordinary people do not know the value of the written record.

Ideas about the past can delegitimise as well as legitimise. The second part of the book began with Archbishop Wulfstan looking back to a lost social order as a critique of his times. 'But now it has happened that since Edgar died, even as God willed, there are more robbers than righteous men; and it is a wretched thing that those who should be shepherds of the Christian people are robbers.'[8] I have proposed that the Norman Conquest brought profound social change, change which was so effective because it entailed not only a new form of social relations, those of feudal tenure, but also a new kind of moral economy, that of 'feudal thinking'. I do not think that people, even uneducated people, were unaware of these changes. As it had been for Wulfstan, their view of the past was for many people their *hwhilom wæs*, their 'once it was', by which to judge the present. That does not mean that it was an illusion. If peasants in the later middle ages felt that they had lost the freedom their predecessors enjoyed, many had good reasons for doing so.

Notes

1 Harvey, 'Draft letters patent of manumission'.
2 Faith, 'The "Great Rumour"'; Muller, 'The aims and organisation of a peasant revolt', 3, 10. Glastonbury had Badbury as the gift of King Eadred to Dunstan in the tenth century.
3 Barker, *England Arise*, 269.
4 This is the difference of emphasis between Hilton, *Bond Men Made Free* and Faith, '"Great Rumour"'.
5 Maddicott, 'Oath of Marlborough'.
6 Barker, *England Arise*, 391.
7 Faith, '"Great Rumour"'.
8 'Institutes of Polity', x: Rabin, *Political Writings*, 111–12.

Appendix   The Family Farm in Peasant Studies

Chayanov, *Theory of Peasant Economy*, although written in the context of agrarian policy in twentieth-century Russia, remains an influential model for the economy and dynamics of the family farm: Rösener, *Peasants*, chapter 10, on the peasant household economy in later medieval western Europe illustrates his influence. Duby, *Rural Economy and Country Life*, Herlihy, *Medieval Households*, Devroey, *Autour de Yoshiki Morimmoto. Les Structures* and *Puissants et Misérables*, and other works based on the Frankish *polyptyques* are thus all based on the family structure and working conditions of a particular stratum of families: those holding domainal or 'inland' tenancies subject to heavy labour services and other obligations. Their Anglo-Saxon equivalents are discussed Faith, *English Peasantry*, chapter 3. Devroey and Wilkins in *Autour de Yoshiko Morimoto* assemble essays proposing some alternative models beyond the territory of the *polyptyques*. Wickham, *Framing*, has set out the importance in early medieval Europe of the allodial peasant farm. Faith, 'Farms and families' gives an indication of the wide range of the population of peasant households in ninth-century Provence and discusses their inheritance strategies, for which, more broadly see Siddle, 'Inheritance strategies'. Hamerow, *Rural Settlements*, chapter 2 includes a consideration of the use of domestic space in peasant houses in early medieval England and Loveluck, *Northwest Europe in the Early Middle Ages* brings together the archaeology of peasant farmhouses across the region. Studies which relate houses and families to a rural economy very similar to that which is the background to the present book are much more common in the historiography of the Scandinavian countries: Bycock, *Viking Age Iceland*. Wickham has drawn attention to the similarities between the free peasantries of England, Scandinavia, and Brittany. The legal codes of Wales and Ireland are a much richer source of information about peasant life than those of the Anglo-Saxon kings. However, as much of the focus of the present book is on the society and culture that England 'after Rome' shared with much of northern Europe, it is from that society and culture that most of my material has been drawn.

Bibliography

Abels, R. P., *Lordship and Military Obligation in Anglo-Saxon England* (Berkeley: University of California Press, 1988)

Abrams, L., *Anglo-Saxon Glastonbury: Church and Endowment*. Studies in Anglo-Saxon History 8 (Woodbridge: The Boydell Press, 1996)

Adams, I. H., *Agrarian Landscape Terms: A Glossary for Historical Geography*. Special Publications Number Nine (London: Institute of British Geographers, 1976) Typescript

Algazi, G., 'Feigned reciprocities: lords, peasants. And the afterlife of late medieval social strategies'. In G. Algazi, V. Groebner and B. Jussen, eds. *Negotiating the Gift: Pre-Modern Figurations of Exchange* (Gottingen: Vandenhoek and Ruprecht, 2003), 95–125

Ammon, M., 'Piercing the *rithamscyld*: a new reading of Æthelbert 32', *Quaestio Insularis* 9 (2008), 34–51

Amt, E. and S. D. Church, *Dialogus de Scaccario: The Dialogue of the Exchequer* (Oxford: Oxford University Press, 2007)

AND: Anglo-Norman Dictionary online at www.anglo-norman.net/gate/

Arnold, C. J., *An Archaeology of the Early Anglo-Saxon Kingdoms*, 2nd ed. (London: Routledge, 1997)

Arnold-Forster, F., *Studies in Church Dedications or England's Patron Saints*, 3 vols. (London: Skeffington and Son, 1899)

Aston, M., M. Ecclestone, M. Forbes and T. Hall, 'Medieval farming in Winscombe parish in North Somerset', *Somerset Archaeology and Natural History* 155 (2012), 79–144

Aston, T. H., 'The ancestry of English feudalism', in R. Evans, ed., *Lordship and Learning: Studies in Memory of Trevor Aston* (Woodbridge: Boydell Press, 2004), 79–93

'The origins of the manor in England', *Transactions of the Royal Historical Society* 5th ser., 8 (1958), 59–83. Reprinted in T. H. Aston, P. R. Coss, Christopher Dyer, and Joan Thirsk, eds., *Social Relations and Ideas: Essays in Honour of R.H. Hilton* (Cambridge: Cambridge University Press, 1983), 1–25

Attenborough, F. L., *The Laws of the Earliest English Kings* (Cambridge: Cambridge University Press, 1922).

Bachrach, B. S., 'Writing Latin history for a lay audience c. 1000: Dudo of Saint Quentin at the Norman court', *Haskins Society Journal* 20 (2008), 58–77

Banham, D. and R. Faith, *Anglo-Saxon Farms and Farming* (Oxford: Oxford University Press, 2014)

Banham, D. A. R., *Food and Drink in Anglo-Saxon England* (Stroud: Tempus Publishing, 2004)

'The knowledge and use of food plants in Anglo-Saxon England' (Ph.D. diss., University of Cambridge, 1990)

Barker, J., *England Arise: The People, the King and the Great Revolt of 1381*, p.b. (London: Abacus, 2015)

Barnwell, P., 'Emperors, jurists and kings: law and custom in the late Roman and early medieval West', *Past & Present* 168.1(August 2000), 6–29

Barrow, G., *The Kingdom of the Scots: Government, Church and Society from the Eleventh to the Thirteenth Century* (London, Edward Arnold, 1972)

Bassett, S., 'In search of the origins of Anglo-Saxon kingdoms'. In S. Bassett, ed., *The Origins of Anglo-Saxon Kingdoms* (Leicester: Leicester University Press, 1989), 3–27

The Origins of Anglo-Saxon Kingdoms (Leicester: Leicester University Press, 1989)

Bates, D., *Normandy Before 1066* (New York: Longmans, 1982)

Bates, D., ed., *Regesta Regum Anglo-Normannorum: The Acta of William I (1066–1087)* (Oxford: Oxford University Press, 1998)

William the Conqueror, p.b. (New Haven, CT: Yale University Press, 2018)

Baxter, S., 'Archbishop Wulfstan and the administration of God's property'. In M. Townsend, ed., *Wulfstan, Archbishop of York: The Proceedings of the Second Alcuin Conference*. Studies in the Middle Ages (Turnhout, Belgium: Brepols, 2004), 101–205

The Earls of Mercia: Lordship and Power in Late Anglo-Saxon England (Oxford: Oxford University Press, 2007)

'Land tenure and royal patronage in the early English kingdom. A model and a case study', *Anglo-Norman Studies* 28 (2006), 19–46

'Lordship and justice: the judicial functions of soke and commendation revisited'. In S. Baxter, C. E. Karkov, J. Nelson and D. Pelteret, eds., *Early Medieval Studies in Memory of Patrick Wormald* (Farnham: Ashgate, 2001), 383–418

'The making of Domesday Book and the languages of lordship in conquered England'. In E. M. Tyler, ed. *Conceptualizing Multilingualism in England c. 800–1250* (Turnhout, Belgium: Brepols, 2011), 271–308

'The profits of royal lordship'. In S. Baxter, J. Crick., C. Lewis and F. Thorn, *Making Domesday: The Conqueror's Survey in Context* (Oxford: Oxford University Press, forthcoming)

'Title to property in the age of the Great Confiscation'. In Baxter, S., J. Crick., C. Lewis and F. Thorn, *Making Domesday: The Conqueror's Survey in Context* (Oxford: Oxford University Press, forthcoming)

Baxter, S. and J. Blair, 'Land tenure and royal patronage in the early English kingdoms: a model and a case study', *Anglo-Norman Studies* 28 (2006), 19–46

Baxter, S., J. Crick., C. Lewis and F. Thorn, *Making Domesday: The Conqueror's Survey in Context* (Oxford: Oxford University Press, forthcoming)

Becket, J. V., 'The peasant in England: a terminological confusion?', *Agricultural History Review* 32.2 (1984), 113–123

Birrell, J., 'Manorial custumals reconsidered', *Past & Present* 224 (August 2014), 3–37

'Peasants eating and drinking', *Agricultural History Review* 63.1 (2015), 1–18

Bisson, T. N., *Tormented Voices: Power, Crisis, and Humanity in Rural Catalonia 1140–1200* (Cambridge: Cambridge University Press, 1998)

Blackburn, M. A. S., ed., *Anglo-Saxon Monetary History: Essays in Memory of Michael Dolley* (Leicester: Leicester University Press, 1986)

ed., 'Coinage'. M. Lapidge, J. Blair, S. Keynes and D. Scragg, eds. *The Blackwell Encyclopædia of Anglo-Saxon England* (Oxford: Oxford: Blackwell, 1999), 113–17

ed., '"Productive" sites and the pattern of coin loss in England 600–1180'. In M. A. S. Blackburn, ed., *Anglo-Saxon Monetary History: Essays in Memory of Michael Dolley* (Leicester: Leicester University Press, 1986), 20–36

Blair, J., *Building Anglo-Saxon England* (Princeton and Oxford: Princeton University Press, 2018)

The Church in Anglo-Saxon Society (Oxford: Oxford University Press, 2005)

Bloch, M., *Feudal Society*, trans. L. A. Manyon (London: Routledge and Kegan Paul, 1961)

French Rural History: An Essay on Its Basic Characteristics, trans. J. Sondheimer (Berkeley: University of California Press, 1966)

'Personal liberty and servitude in the middle ages: contribution to a class study'. In W. R. Beer, ed. and trans., *Slavery and Serfdom in the Middle Ages: Selected Essays by Marc Bloch* (Berkeley: University of California Press, 1975), 33–91

Bonnassie, P., *From Slavery to Feudalism in South-Western Europe*, trans. J. Birrell (Cambridge: Cambridge University Press, 1991)

Bosworth, J. and T. N. Toller, *An Anglo-Saxon Dictionary* (Oxford, 1890), with T. N. Toller, and A. Campbell, *Supplement, based on the manuscript collections of Joseph Bosworth* (Oxford: Oxford University Press, 1921)

Bourne, J., 'Kingston: the place-name and its context'. In R. Jones and S. Semple, eds., *Sense of Place in Anglo-Saxon England* (Donington: Shaun Tyas, 2012), 260–83

Britnell, R. H., *The Commercialisation of English Society 1000–1500*, 2nd.ed. Manchester: Manchester University Press, 1996)

Brooks, N., *The Early History of the Church of Canterbury* (Leicester: Leicester University Press, 1984)

Brown, E. A., 'The tyranny of a construct: feudalism and historians of medieval Europe', *American Historical Review* 79.4 (October 1974), 1063–88

Burke, P., *Popular Culture in Early Modern Europe* (London: Temple Smith, 1978)

Butler, H. E., ed. and trans., *The Chronicle of Jocelin of Brakelond* (London and Edinburgh: Nelson, 1949)

Bycock, J., *Viking Age Iceland* (Harmondsworth: Penguin Books, 2001)

Cam, H. M., *The Hundred and the Hundred Rolls: An Outline of Local Government in Medieval England* (London: Merlin, 1963)

Liberties & Communities in Medieval England: Collected Studies in Local Administration and Topography (Cambridge: Cambridge University Press, 1944)

Campbell, J., 'Hundreds and leets: a survey with suggestions'. In C. Harper-Bill, ed., *Medieval East Anglia* (Woodbridge: Boydell and Brewer, 2005), 153–67

'The sale of land and the economics of power in early England: some problems and possibilities'. In J. Campbell, *The Anglo-Saxon State* (London: The Hambledon Press, 2000), 227–45

'Some agents and agencies of the Anglo-Saxon state'. In J. Campbell, *The Anglo-Saxon State* (London: The Hambledon Press, 2000), 201–25

'Some twelfth-century views of the Anglo-Saxon past'. In J. Campbell, *Essays in Anglo-Saxon History* (London: The Hambledon Press), 209–28

'Stubbs and the English state'. In J. Campbell, *The Anglo-Saxon State* (London: The Hambledon Press, 2000) 247–68

Cartularium Monasterii de Rameseia, ed. W. H. Hart and R. A. Lyons, *Rerum Britannicarum Medii Ævi Scriptores*, 2 vols. (London: Longmans and Co., 1886)

Catto, J., 'Andrew Horn: law and history in the fourteenth century'. In J. Catto, R. M. C. Davis, and J. M. Wallace-Hadrill, eds., *The Writing of History: Essays Presented to Richard William Southern* (Oxford: Clarendon Press, 1982), 367–91

Charles-Edwards, T. M., 'The distinction between land and moveable wealth in Anglo-Saxon England'. In P. H. Sawyer, ed., *English Medieval Settlement* (London: Edward Arnold, 1979), 97–104

'Early medieval kingships in the British Isles'. In S. Bassett, ed., *The Origins of Anglo-Saxon Kingdoms* (Leicester: Leicester University Press, 1989), 28–39

'Kinship, status and the origins of the hide', *Past & Present* 56 (1972), 3–33

'The making of nations in Britain and Ireland in the early middle ages'. In R. Evans, ed., *Lordship and Learning: Studies in Memory of Trevor Aston* (Woodbridge: Boydell Press, 2004), 11–37

Chayanov, A. V., *The Theory of Peasant Economy*, ed. D. Thorner, B. Kerblay and R. A. F. Smith, with a new introduction by Teodor Shanin (Madison: University of Wisconsin Press, 1986)

Chibnall, A. C., *Sherington: Fiefs and Fields of a Buckinghamshire Village* (Cambridge: Cambridge University Press, 1965)

Chibnall, M., *Anglo-Norman England 1066–1166*, p.b. (Oxford: Blackwell, 1987)

Chibnall, M., ed., *Charters and Custumals of the Abbey of Holy Trinity Caen*. British Academy Records of Social and Economic History, new series 5 (Oxford: Oxford University Press, 1982)

ed., *Select Documents of The English Lands of the Abbey of Bec*. Camden Third Series, vol. 5, 73 (London: Royal Historical Society, 1968)

Clanchy, M. T., *From Memory to Written Record: England 1066–1307*, 3rd ed. (Oxford: Wiley-Blackwell, 2013)

Clark, C., 'Domesday Book – a great red herring: thoughts on some late eleventh century orthographies'. In Peter Jackson, ed., *Words, Names and History: Selected Writings of Cecily Clark* (Cambridge: D.S. Brewer, 1996), 156–67

Clarke, C. A. M., *Writing Power in Anglo-Saxon England: Texts, Hierarchies, Economies* (Cambridge: D.S. Brewer, 2012)

Clarke, H. B., 'Condensing and abbreviating the data: Evesham C, Evesham M and the Breviate'. In D. Roffe and K. Keats-Rohan, eds., *Domesday Now:*

New Approaches to the Inquest and the Book, p.b. (Woodbridge: The Boydell Press, 2018), 247–62

Cole, A., 'Searching for early drove roads: *hryther, mersc-tūn and heord-wic*', *Journal of the English Place-Names Society* 47 (2015), 55–8

'The use of *netel* in place-names', *Journal of the English Place-Names Society* 35 (2003), 49–57

The use of ON *nata* in place-names', *Journal of the English Place-Names Society* 36 (2004), 51–3

Colgrave, B., and R. A. B. Mynors, eds., *Bede's Ecclesiastical History of the English People* (Oxford: Clarendon Press, 1969)

Coss, P., *The Aristocracy in England and Tuscany, 1000–1250*.

The Origins of the English Gentry (Cambridge: Cambridge University Press, 2003)

'What's in a construct? The gentry in Anglo-Saxon England'. In R. Evans, ed., *Lordship and Learning: Studies in Memory of Trevor Aston* (Woodbridge: Boydell, 2004), 95–107

Costen, M., *Anglo-Saxon Somerset* (Oxford: Oxbow, 2001)

Coven, A., '*Byrstas* and *bysmeras*: the Wounds of Sin'. In M. Townsend, ed., *Wulfstan, Archbishop of York: The Proceedings of the Second Alcuin Conference.* Studies in the Middle Ages (Turnhout, Belgium: Brepols, 2004), 396–411

Damian-Grant, P., *The New Historians of the Twelfth Century* (Woodbridge, Boydell, 1999)

Darby, H. C., *Domesday England* (Cambridge: Cambridge University Press, 1977)

Dark, K., *Civitas to Kingdom: British Political Continuity 300–800* (Leicester: Leicester University Press, 1994)

Davis, J., *Medieval Market Morality: Life, Law and Ethics in the English Market-place, 1200–1500* (Cambridge: Cambridge University Press, 2012)

Davies, W., 'Sale price and valuation in Galicia, Castile and Leon in the tenth century', *Early Medieval Europe* 11 (2002), 149–74

Davies, W. and P. Fouracre, eds., *The Settlement of Disputes in Early Medieval Europe* (Cambridge: Cambridge University Press, 1986)

Devroey, J.-P., *Études sur le Grand Domaine Carolingien* (Aldershot: Variorum Reprints, 1993)

Puissants et Misérables: Système Social et Monde Paysan dans l'Europe des Francs (VIᵉ-IXᵉ siècles) (Brussels: Académie Royale de Belgique, Classe des Lettres, 2006)

Devroey, J.-P., and A. Wilkin, eds., *Autour de Yoshiki Morimoto. Les Structures Agricoles en dehors du Monde Carolingien: Formes et genèse* (Brussels: Timperman, 2012)

DMLBS: Dictionary of Medieval Latin from British Sources online at https://logeion.uchicago.edu/lexidium

Dodgshon, R., *From Chiefs to Landlords: Social and Economic Change in the Western Highlands c. 1493–1820* (Edinburgh University Press,1998)

Domesday Book. 26. Cheshire including Lancashire, Cumbria and North Wales, ed. P. Morgan, A. Rumble, and J. Morris (Chichester: Phillimore, 1978)

Domesday Book. 9. Devon, ed. C. and F. Thorn from a draft translation prepared by C. Thorn, A. O'Driscoll, and J. Morris. 2 vols. (Chichester: Phillimore, 1985)

Domesday Book. 31. Lincolnshire, ed. P. Morgon, C. Thorn and S. West. (Chichester: Phillimore, 1986)

Domesday Book. 11. Middlesex, ed. S. Wood and J. Morris (Chichester: Phillimore, 1986)

Domesday Book. 8 Somerset, ed. Frank Thorn from a draft translation prepared by Caroline Thorn and J. Morris (Chichester: Phillimore, 1975)

Domesday Book. Studies (London: Alecto Historical Editions, 1987)

Domesday Book. 34. Suffolk, ed. A. Rumble from a draft translation by Marian Hepplestone and J. Morris (Chichester: Phillimore, 1986)

Domesday Book: 24. Staffordshire, ed. A. Hawkins, A. Rumble, and J. Morris (Chichester: Phillimore, 1976)

Douglas, D. C. and G. W. Greenaway, eds., *English Historical Documents ii. 1042–1189* (London: Eyre and Spottiswood, 1953)

Duby, G., *Rural Economy and Country Life in the Medieval West*, trans. Cynthia Postan (London: Edward Arnold (Publishers) Ltd. 1968)

Dumville, D., 'Kingship, genealogies, and regnal lists'. In P. H. Sawyer and I. N. Wood, eds., *Early Medieval Kingship* (Leeds: School of History, University of Leeds, 1977), 72–104

Dyer, C., *Making a Living in the Middle Ages: The People of Britain 850–1520* (New Haven, CT.: Yale University Press, 2002)

Eagles, B., '"Small shires" and *regiones* in Hampshire and the formation of the shires of eastern Wessex', *Anglo-Saxon Studies in Archaeology and History* 19 (2015), 122–52

The Ecclesiastical History of Orderic Vitalis. Volume II. Books III and IV, ed. and trans. with introduction and notes by Marjorie Chibnall (Oxford: Clarendon Press, 1969)

Evans, R., 'Whose was the manor court?'. In R. Evans, ed., *Lordship and Learning: Studies in Memory of Trevor Aston* (Woodbridge: Boydell, 2004), 155–68

Faith, R., 'Cola's *tūn*: rural social structure in late Anglo-Saxon Devon'. In R. Evans, ed., *Lordship and Learning: Studies in Memory of Trevor Aston* (Woodbridge: Boydell, 2004), 63–78

'Demesne resources and labour rent on the manors of St Paul's Cathedral 1066–1222, *Economic History Review* 47 (1994), 657–78

The English Peasantry and the Growth of Lordship (Leicester: Leicester University Press, 1997)

'Farms and families in ninth-century Provence', *Early Medieval Europe* 18.2 (May 2010), 175–201

'The "Great Rumour" of 1377 and peasant ideology'. In R. H. Hilton and T. H. Aston, eds., *The English Rising of 1381* (Cambridge: Cambridge University Press, 1984), 43–73

'Peasant families and inheritance customs in medieval England', *Agricultural History Review* xiv, part ii (1966), 77–95

'Some Devon farms before the Norman Conquest'. In S. Turner and B. Sylvester, eds., *Life in Medieval Landscapes. People and Places in the Middle Ages. Papers in Memory of H.S.A. Fox* (Oxford: Windgather, 2012), 73–88

'Tidenham, Gloucestershire, and the history of the manor in England', *Landscape History* 16 (1994), 39–51

Fauroux, M. and L. Musset, *Receuil des Actes des Ducs de Normandie de 911 à 1066: complète d'un index rerum*, Mémoires de la Société des Antiquaires de Normandie, vol. 36 (Caen 1961)

Finberg, H. P. R., 'The Domesday plough-team', *English Historical Review* 66 (1951), 67–71

Finn, F., *The Domesday Inquest and the Making of Domesday Book* (London: Longmans, 1960)

  Welldon, Domesday Studies: The Eastern Counties (London: Longmans,1967)

Fleming, R., *Domesday Book and the Law: Society and Legal Custom in Early Medieval England* (Cambridge: Cambridge University Press, 1998)

  'Oral testimony and the Domesday Inquest', *Anglo-Norman Studies* 17 (1995), 101–2)

Forrest, I., *Trustworthy Men: How Inequality and Faith Made the Medieval Church* (Princeton, N.J.: Princeton University Press, 2018)

Fowler, P. *Farming in the First Millennium A.D.: British Agriculture Between Julius Caesar and William the Conqueror* (Cambridge: Cambridge University Press, 2002)

Fox, H. S. A., 'Exploitation of the landless by lords and tenants in early medieval England'. In Z. Razi and R. Smith, eds., *Medieval Society and the Manor Court* (Oxford: Clarendon Press, 1996), 518–68

Frantzen, A. J., *Food, Eating and Identity in Early Medieval England* (Woodbridge: Boydell Press, 2014)

Freedman, P., *The Origins of Peasant Servitude in Medieval Catalonia* (Cambridge: Cambridge University Press, 1991)

Gardiner, M., 'The origins and persistence of manorial buildings in England'. In M. Gardiner and S. Rippon, eds., *Medieval Landscapes* (Macclesfield: Windgather, 2007), 170–82

Garmonsway, G. N., ed., *Ælfric's Colloquy*, rev. ed. (Exeter: University of Exeter Press, 1991)

Garnett, G., *A Broken Chain: The Norman Conquest in English History* (Oxford: Oxford University Press, forthcoming 2020)

  Conquered England: Kingship, Succession and Tenure 1066–1166 (Oxford: Oxford University Press, 2007)

Gelling, M., *Signposts to the Past: Place-Names and the History of England* (Chichester: Phillimore, 1978)

Gelling, M., and A. Cole, *The Landscape of Place-Names* (Stamford: Shaun Tyas, 2000)

Gerriets, M., 'Money in early Christian Ireland according to the Irish Laws', *Comparative Studies in Society and History* 27 (The Hague: Mouton & Co., Cambridge: Cambridge University Press, 1985), 323–9

Glanvill. *Tractatus de legibus et consuetudinibus regni angliae qui Glanvilla vocatur*, ed. G. D. G. Hall (London and Edinburgh: Nelson, 1965)

Goebel, J., Jr., *Felony and Misdemeanor: A Study in the History of Criminal Law* (Philadelphia: University of Pennsylvania Press 1976)

Goetz, H. W., 'Social and military institutions'. In R. McKitterick, ed., *The New Cambridge Medieval History II c.700–c.900* (Cambridge: Cambridge University Press,1995), 451–80

Grierson, P. and M. Blackburn, *Medieval European Coinage: With a Catalogue of Coins in the Fitzwilliam Museum, Cambridge*. Volume 1. *The Early Middle Ages (5th–10th Centuries)* (Cambridge: Cambridge University Press, 1986)

Gurevich, A., *The Anglo-Saxon Chronicle*, p.b., trans. and ed. M. J. Swanton (London: Dent, 1997)

Medieval Popular Culture: Problems of Belief and Perception, trans. J. M. Bak and P. A. Hollingsworth (Cambridge: Cambridge University Press, 1988)

Hale, W., *The Domesday of St Paul's of the Year MCCXXII or Registrum de visitatione maneriorum per Robertum Decanum*, Camden Society 69 (London: 1958)

Hall, A., 'The instability of place-names in Anglo-Saxon England and early medieval Wales, and the loss of Roman toponymy'. In R. Jones and S. Semple, eds., *Sense of Place in Anglo-Saxon England* (Donington: Shaun Tyas, 2012), 101–29

Halliwell, J. O., *A Dictionary of Archaic and Provincial Words, Obsolete Phrases and Archaic Customs*, 2. vols. (London: John Russell Smith,1847)

Hamer, R. F. S., *A Choice of Anglo-Saxon Verse Selected and with a Parallel Verse Translation* (London: Faber,1970)

Hamerow, H., *Early Medieval Settlements: An Archaeology of Rural Communities in North-West Europe 400–900* (Oxford: Oxford University Press, 2002)

Rural Settlements and Society in Anglo-Saxon England (Oxford: Oxford University Press, 2012)

Hamerow, H., D. Hinton and S. Crawford, eds., *The Oxford Handbook of Anglo-Saxon Archaeology* (Oxford: Oxford University Press, 1999)

Härke, H., '"Warrior graves": the background of the Anglo-Saxon burial rite', *Past & Present* 126 (1990), 22–43

Hart, C. R., *The Early Charters of Northern England and the North Midlands* (Leicester: Leicester University Press, 1975)

Harvey, B. F., 'Draft letters patent of manumission and pardon for the men of Somerset', *English Historical Review* 80 (1965), 89–91

'The life of the manor'. In A. Williams, ed., *Domesday Book Studies*, 9 (London: Alecto Historical Editions, 1987), 39–41

Westminster Abbey and Its Estates in the Middle Ages (Oxford: Clarendon Press, 1977)

Harvey, P. D. A., *Manorial Records. British Records Association: Archives and the User*, no. 5 (London: British Records Association, 1984)

'The manorial reeve in twelfth-century England'. In R. Evans, ed., *Lordship and Learning: Studies in Memory of Trevor Aston* (Woodbridge: Boydell, 2004), 125–138

Harvey, P. D. A., ed., *The Peasant Land Market in Medieval England* (Oxford: Clarendon Press, 1984)

ed., '*Rectitudines singularum personarum* and *Gerefa*', *English Historical Review* 426 (January 1993), 1–22

Harvey, S. P. J., 'Anglo-Norman governance', *Transactions of the Royal Historical Society* 5th series, 25 (1975)

Domesday: Book of Judgement (Oxford: Oxford University Press, 2014)

'Domesday England'. In H. E. Hallam, ed., *The Agrarian History of England and Wales*. Vol. II. *AD 1042–1350* (Cambridge: Cambridge University Press, 1988), 1–136

'Evidence for settlement study: Domesday Book'. In P. H. Sawyer, ed., *Medieval Settlement Continuity and Change* (London: Edward Arnold, 1976)

'The extent and profitability of demesne agriculture in England in the later eleventh century'. In T. H. Aston, P. R. Coss, Christopher Dyer and Joan Thirsk, eds., *Social Relations and Ideas: Essays in Honour of Rodney Hilton* (Cambridge: Cambridge University Press, 1983), 45–72

Haskins, C. H., *Norman Institutions* (Cambridge, MA.: Harvard University Press, 1918)

Hatcher, J., 'English villeinage and serfdom: towards a reassessment', *Past & Present* 90.1 (February 1981), 3–39

Henry de Bracton, De legibus et consuetudinibus angliae, ed. G. E. Woodbine, reissued with translation by S. E. Thorne, 4 vols. (Cambridge MA.: Harvard University Press, 1968–77)

Herlihy, D., *Medieval Households* (Cambridge, MA.: Harvard University Press, 1985)

Hey, G., *Yarnton: Saxon and Medieval Settlement and Landscape:Results of Excavations 1990–96*. Oxford Archaeology Thames Valley Landscapes Monograph 20 (Oxford: Oxford Institute of Archaeology for Oxford Archaeology, 2004)

Hills, C., *Origins of the English* (London: Duckworth, 2003)

Hilton, R. H., *Bond Men Made Free: Medieval Peasant Movements and the English Rising of 1381* (London: Methuen, 1973)

'Freedom and villeinage in England', *Past & Present* 31 (July 1965), 3–19

Hilton, R. H., ed., *The Stoneleigh Leger Book. Publications of the Dugdale Society*, 24 (1966)

Hines, J., 'Social structures and social change in seventh-century England: the law codes and complementary sources', *Historical Research* 86 (2103), 223, 394–407

Hinton, D., 'Coins and commercial centres in Anglo-Saxon England'. In M. Blackburn, ed., *Anglo-Saxon Monetary History: Essays in Memory of Michael Dolley* (Leicester: Leicester University Press, 1986), 11–26

Historia Ecclesie Abbendonensis: The History of the Church of Abingdon. Vol. II. ed. and trans. John Hudson (Oxford: Clarendon Press, 2002)

Holt, J. C., *Colonial England* (London: Hambledon Press 1997)

'1086'. In J. C. Holt, ed., *Domesday Studies: Novocentenary Coference, Royal Historical Society and Institute of British Geographers, Winchester 1986* (Woodbridge: Boydell Press, 1987), 41–64

Homans, G. C., *English Villagers of the Thirteenth Century* (Cambridge, MA.: Harvard University Press, 1941)

'The rural sociology of medieval England', *Past & Present* 4 (1953), 32–43

Hone, N. J. and J. S. Green, eds., *A Mannor and Court Baron (Harleian m.s. 6714)*, (London: The Manorial Society, 1909)

Hooke, D., 'Place-name hierarchies and interpretations in parts of Mercia'. In O. J. Padel and D. N. Parsons, eds., *A Commodity of Good Names: Essays in Honour of Margaret Gelling* (Donnington: Shaun Tyas, 2008), 180–95

Howe, N., *Migration and Mythmaking in Anglo-Saxon England* (Notre Dame, Ind.: University of Notre Dame, 2001)

Howkins, A., *Reshaping Rural England: A Social History 1850–1925* (London: Routledge, 1991)

Hudson, J., 'Administration, family and perceptions of the past in late twelfth-century England: Richard FitzNigel and the Dialogue of the Exchequer'. In P. Magdalino, ed., *The Perception of the Past in Twelfth Century Europe* (London, Hambledon Press, 1992), 75–98

'Anglo-Saxon land law and the origins of property'. In G. Garnett and J. Hudson, eds., *Law and Government in Medieval England and Normandy: Essays in Honour of Sir James Holt* (Cambridge: Cambridge University Press, 1994), 198–222

The Formation of the English Common Law: Law and Society in England from the Norman Conquest to Magna Carta, pb. (London: Longman, 1996)

'Imposing feudalism on Anglo-Saxon England: Norman and Angevin presentation of pre-Conquest lordship and landholding'. In S. Bagge, M. H. Gelting and T. Lindkvist, eds., *Feudalism: New Landscapes of Debate* (Turnhout, Belgium: Brepols, 2011), 115–34,

Hyams, P. R., 'The common law and the French connection', *Anglo-Norman Studies* (1982), 77–92

Kings, Lords and Peasants in Medieval England: The Common Law of Villeinage in the Twelfth and Thirteenth Centuries (Oxford: Oxford University Press, 1980)

'Notes on the transformation of the fief into the common law tenure in fee'. In S. Jenks, J. Rose and C. Whittick, eds., *Laws. Lawyers, and Texts: Studies in Medieval Legal History in Honour of Paul Brand* (Leiden: Brill 2012), 23–49

'Warranty and good lordship in twelfth century England', *Law and History Review* 5 (1987), 437–503

Ingulf's Chronicle of the Abbey of Croyland: With the Continuations by Peter of Blois and Anonymous Writers, ed. H. T. Riley (London: Rolls Series, 1854)

Jenkyns, J., 'Charter bounds'. In M. J. Lapidge, J. Blair, S. Keynes and D. Scragg, eds., *The Blackwell Encyclopaedia of Anglo-Saxon England* (Oxford: Blackwell, 1999)

Johnson, C., *The Course of the Exchequer by Richard Son of Nigel translated from the Latin with introduction and notes by Charles Johnson as Dialogus de Scaccario* (London: Nelson, 1950)

Jolliffe, J. E. A., 'Alod and fee', *Cambridge Historical Journal* 5.3 (1937), 225–34

Pre-Feudal England: The Jutes (Oxford: Oxford University Press and London: Frank Cass 1933)

Kapelle, W. E., *The Norman Conquest of the North: The Region and its Transformation, 1000–1135* (London: Croom Helm,1979)

Karn, N., '*Quadripartitus, Leges Henrici Primi* and the scholarship of English law in the early twelfth century', *Anglo-Norman Studies* 37 (2014), 149–60

Kelly, F., *Early Irish Farming* (Dublin: School of Celtic Studies, Dublin Institute of Advanced Studies, 2000)

Kelly, S. E., ed., *Charters of Peterborough Abbey*. Anglo-Saxon Charters 14 (British Academy and Oxford: Oxford University Press, 2009)

ed., *Charters of St Paul's, London*. Anglo-Saxon Charters 10 (British Academy and Oxford: Oxford University Press, 2004)

Keynes, S., 'An Abbot, an Archbishop and the Danish Raids of 1006–1007 and 1009–1012', *Anglo-Saxon England* 36 (2007), 151–220

'*heregeld*'. In M. Lapidge, J. Blair, S. Keynes and D. Scragg, eds., *The Blackwell Encyclopaedia of Anglo-Saxon England* (Oxford: Blackwell, 1999)

Keynes, S. and M. Lapidge, eds. and trans., *Alfred the Great: Asser's Life of King Alfred and Other Contemporary Sources* (Harmondsworth: Penguin Books, 1983)

Kilger, C., 'Wholeness and holiness: counting, weighing and valuing silver in the early Viking period and the Kauping Excavation Project, University of Oslo'. In D. Skre and J. Hines, eds., *Means of Exchange: Dealing with Silver in the Viking Age* (Aarhus: Aarhus University Press, 2007), 253–9

King, V., 'St Oswald's tenants'. In N. Brooks and C. Cubitt, eds., *St Oswald of Worcester: Life and Influence* (Leicester: Leicester University Press, 1996), 100–16

Lambert, T. B., *Law and Order in Anglo-Saxon England* (Oxford: Oxford University Press, 2017)

'Theft, homicide and crime in late Anglo-Saxon law', *Past & Present* 214 (February 2012), 3–43

Lane, B., 'Westbury-sub-Mendip, Somerset – an irregular agglomerated polyfocal settlement?' *Medieval Settlement Research* 32 (2017), 21–26

Langdon, J., *Horses, Oxen and Technological Innovation: The Use of Draught Animals in English Farming from 1066–1500* (Cambridge: Cambridge University Press, 1986)

Lapidge, M., J. Blair, S. Keynes and D. Scragg, eds., *The Blackwell Encyclopaedia of Anglo-Saxon England* (Oxford: Blackwell, 1999)

Lavelle, R., 'Royal estates in Anglo-Saxon Wessex' (Ph.D. diss., University of Winchester, 2001)

Laws of the Alamans and Bavarians, trans. with an introduction by T. J. Rivers (Philadelphia: University of Pennsylvania Press, 1977)

Le Goff, J., *Time, Work and Culture in the Middle Ages*, trans. Arthur Goldhammer (Chicago: Chicago University Press, 1980)

Le Patourel, J., *The Norman Empire* (Oxford: Clarendon Press, 1976)

Leges Henrici Primi, ed. with translation and commentary by L. J. Downer (Oxford: Clarendon Press, 1972)

Lennard, R. V., 'The composition of the Domesday *caruca*', *English Historical Review* 81 (1966), 770–5

'The economic position of the bordars and cottars of Domesday Book', *Economic Journal* 61 (1951), 342–71

Rural England 1086–1135: A Study of Agrarian Conditions (Oxford: Clarendon Press, 1959)

Letts, J. B., *Smoke Blackened Thatch: A Unique Source of Late Medieval Plant Remains from Southern England* (London and Reading: Ancient Monuments Laboratory, English Heritage and The Rural History Centre, University of Reading, 1999)

Lewis, C. P., 'The invention of the manor in eleventh-century England', *Anglo-Norman Studies* 34 (2012), 123–150

Liber Eliensis: A History of the Isle of Ely from the Seventh Century to the Twelfth Compiled by a Monk of Ely in the Twelfth Century, trans. J. Fairweather (Woodbridge: Boydell Press, 2002)

Liber Eliensis, ed. E. O. Blake. Camden Third Series xcvii (London: Royal Historical Society 1962)

Liebermann, F., *Die Gesetze der Angelsachsen*, 3 vols. (Halle: M. Niemeyer, 1903–1916)

Loveluck, C. P., *Northwest Europe in the Early Middle Ages c.600–1150: A Comparative Archaeology* (Cambridge: Cambridge University Press, 2013)

Loyn, H. R., *Anglo-Saxon England and the Norman Conquest*, 2nd ed. (London: Longmans ,1982)

The Governance of Anglo-Saxon England 500–1087 (London: E. Arnold, 1984)

'The term ealdorman in the translations prepared at the time of King Alfred', *English Historical Review* 68 (1953), 513–25

Maddicott, J., 'The Oath of Marlborough 1209: fear, government and popular allegiance in the reign of King John', *English Historical Review* 121.1 (April 2011), 280–318

Maitland, F. W., *Domesday Book and Beyond: Three Essays in the Early History of England*, rev. ed., p.b. (London: Collins, 1960)

Select Pleas in Manorial and Other Seignorial Courts. Vol. 1. *The Reigns of Henry III and Edward I*. Publications of the Selden Society 2 (1889)

Matthew, D., *The Norman Monasteries and Their English Possessions* (Oxford: Oxford University Press, 1962)

McKerracher, M., *Farming Transformed in Anglo-Saxon England: Agriculture in the Long Eighth Century* (Bollington: Windgather Press, 2018)

Metcalf, M., 'Variations in the composition of the currency at different places in England'. In T. Pestell and K. Ulmschneider, eds., *Markets in Early Medieval Europe: Trading and 'Productive' Sites, 650–850* (Macclesfield: Windgather, 2003), 37–47

Miller, E., *The Abbey and Bishopric of Ely: The Social History of an Ecclesiastical Estate from the Tenth to the Early Fourteenth Century* (Cambridge: Cambridge University Press, 1951)

Miller, E. and J. Hatcher, *Medieval England: Rural Society and Economic Change 1086–1348* (London: Longman,1978)

Milsom, S. F. C., *The Legal Framework of English Feudalism* (Cambridge: Cambridge University Press, 1976)

The Mirror of Justices, ed. W. J. Whittaker. Selden Society 7 (1893)

Mitchell, B., *An Invitation to Old English & Anglo-Saxon England* (Oxford: Blackwell, 1995)

Moffat, D., 'Sin, conquest, servitude: English self-image in the chronicles of the early fourteenth century'. In A. J. Frantzen and D. Moffats, eds., *The Work of Work: Servitude, Slavery and Labor in Medieval England* (Glasgow: Cruithne Press, 1994), 146–68

Molyneux, G., *The Formation of the English Kingdom in the Tenth Century* (Oxford: Oxford University Press, 2015)

Morgan, D. H., 'The place of harvesters in nineteenth-century village life'. In R. Samuel, ed., *Village Life and Labour*. History Workshop Series (London and Boston: Routledge & Kegan Paul, 1975), 27–72

Morimoto, Y., 'Trois notes sur la critique textuelle du polyptyque de Prum'. In Y. Morimoto, *Études sur l'economie rurale du Haut Moyen Age* (Brussels: De Boeck et Larcier, 2008), 213–51

Morris, W. A., *The Frankpledge System* (New York: Longmans, Green & Co., 1910)

Muller, M., 'The aims and organisation of a peasant revolt in early fourteenth-century Wiltshire', *Rural History* 14 (April 2003), 1–20

Musset, L., 'Les domaines de l'époque franc et les destinées du régime domainial du IXe au XIe siècle', *Bulletin de la société des antiquaires de Normandie* 49 (1946 for 1942–5), 7–97

'La tenure en bordage: aspects normands et mançeaux', *Revue Historique de Droit Français et Étranger*, 4th series 28 (1950), 140

Musson, J., 'Commoners and the Assize of Novel Disseisin 1194–1222' (Ph.D. thesis, University of Nottingham, 2016)

Naismith, R., 'The Ely memoranda and the economy of the late Anglo-Saxon fenland', *Anglo-Saxon England* 45.12 (2016), 333–77

Money and Power in Anglo-Saxon England: the Southern English Kingdoms, 757–865 (Cambridge: Cambridge University Press, 2012)

'Payments for land and privilege in Anglo-Saxon England', *Anglo-Saxon England* 41 (2012), 277–342

'The social significance of monetization in the early middle ages' *Past & Present* 223 (May 2014), 3–39

Nightingale, P., 'The evolution of weight standards and the creation of new monetary and commercial links in northern Europe from the tenth to the twelfth century', *Economic History Review* 38 (May 1985), 192–209

Neilson, N., *Customary Rents*. Oxford Studies in Social and Legal History, ed. P. Vinogradoff (Oxford: Clarendon Press, 1910)

Newby, H., *The Deferential Worker: A Study of Farm Workers in East Anglia* (Harmondsworth: Penguin Education, 1979)

Northamptonshire Assize Rolls 1202–1203, ed. D. M. Stenton. Northamptonshire Record Society Publications 5 (1930)

O'Brien, B. R., *God's Peace and King's Peace: The Laws of Edward the Confessor* (Philadelphia: University of Pennsylvania Press, 1999)

Oliver, L., *The Beginnings of English Law* (Toronto: University of Toronto Press, 2002)

Oosthuizen, S., *The Anglo-Saxon Fenland* (Bollington: Windgather Press, 2017)

Orchard, A., *The Poetic Art of Aldhelm* (Cambridge: Cambridge University Press, 1994)

The Order of Keeping a Court Leet and Court Baron. Manorial Society Publication 8 (1914)

Otaka, Y., 'Sur la langue des *Leis Willelme*', in I. Short, ed., *Anglo-Norman Anniversary Essays*. Anglo-Norman Text Society Occasional Publications 53 (1993), 293–308

Palmer, B., 'The hinterlands of three southern English emporia: some common themes'. In T. Pestell and K. Ulmschneider, eds., *Markets in Early Medieval*

Europe: Trading and 'Productive' Sites, 650–850 (Macclesfield: Windgather, 2003), 48–60

Palmer, J. N. N., 'The Domesday manor'. In J. C. Holt, ed., *Domesday Studies: Novocentenary Coference, Royal Historical Society and Institute of British Geographers, Winchester 1986* (Woodbridge: Boydell Press, 1987) 139–53

Pelteret, D. A. E., *Catalogue of English Post-Conquest Vernacular Documents* (Woodbridge: Boydell Press, 1990)

Slavery in Early Medieval England: From the Reign of Alfred Until the Twelfth Century (Woodbridge: Boydell Press, 1995)

'Two Old English lists of serfs', *Medieval Studies* 48 (1986), 470–513

Pestell, T. and K. Ulmschneider, eds., *Markets in Early Medieval Europe: Trading and 'Productive' Sites, 650–850* (Macclesfield: Windgather, 2003)

The Peterborough Chronicle 1070–1154, ed. Cecily Clark, 2nd. ed. (Oxford: Clarendon Press, 1976)

Plummer, C., *Venerabilis Baedae Opera Historica* (Oxford: Clarendon Press, 1896)

Pollock, F. and F. W. Maitland, *The History of English Law*, 2 vols. (Cambridge: Cambridge University Press, 1968)

Postan, M. M., 'The Famulus: the estate worker in the twelfth and thirteenth centuries', *Economic History Review* Suppl. 2 (1954)

Powell, T., 'The three orders in Anglo-Saxon England', *Anglo-Saxon England* 23 (1994), 103–32

Power, E., *Medieval People* (London: Methuen, 1986)

Pratt, D., 'Demesne exemptions from royal taxation in Anglo-Saxon and Anglo-Norman England', *English Historical Review* 128.530 (Feb. 2013), 1–33

Purkiss, R., 'Early royal rights in the Liberty of St Edmund', *Anglo-Norman Studies* 41 (2019), 155–73

Raban, S., *A Second Domesday? The Hundred Rolls of 1279–1280* (Oxford: Oxford University Press, 2004)

Rabin, A., ed. and trans., *The Political Writings of Archbishop Wulfstan of York* (Manchester: Manchester University Press, 2015)

Raftis, J. Ambrose, *The Estates of Ramsey Abbey: A Study in Economic Growth and Orgaization*. Studies and Texts 3 (Toronto: Pontifical Institute of Medieval Studies, 1957)

Razi, Z. and R. Smith, eds., *Medieval Society and the Manor Court* (Oxford: Clarendon Press, 1996)

'The origins of the English manorial court rolls as a written record: a puzzle', in Z. Razi and R. Smith, eds., *Medieval Society and the Manor Court* (Oxford: Clarendon Press, 1996), 36–68

Rebanks, J., *The Shepherd's Life: A Tale of the Lake District* (London: Allen Lane, 2015)

Reed, M., 'The peasantry of nineteenth century England: a neglected class?' *History Workshop Journal* 18 (Autumn 1984), 53–76

Reynolds, S., 'Bookland, folkland and fiefs', *Anglo-Norman Studies* 14 (1992), 211–27

Fiefs and Vassals: The Medieval Evidence Re-interpreted (Oxford: Oxford University Press, 1994)

Kingdoms and Communities in Western Europe 900–1300 (Oxford: Oxford University Press, 1984)

'Tenure and property in medieval England', *Historical Research* 88 (2015), 563–76

Richardson, H. G. and G. O. Sayles, *Law and Legislation from Æthelbert to Magna Carta* (Edinburgh: Edinburgh University Press, 1966)

Rio, A., *Slavery after Rome 500–1100* (Oxford: Oxford University Press, 2017)

Roach, L., 'Public rites and public wrongs: ritual aspects of diplomas in tenth- and eleventh-century England', *Early Medieval Europe* 19 (2011), 182–203

Robertson, A. J., ed., *Anglo-Saxon Charters*, 2nd ed. (Cambridge: Cambridge University Press, 1956)

    ed., *The Laws of the Kings of England from Edmund to Henry I* (Cambridge: Cambridge University Press, 1925)

Roffe, D., *Decoding Domesday* (Woodbridge: Boydell Press, 2007)

Introduction. *Domesday Book: Lincolnshire* (London: Alecto Historical Editions, 1992)

Rösener, W., *Peasants in the Middle Ages*, trans. with a foreword and glossary by Alexander Stützer (Cambridge: Polity, 1992)

Runciman, W. G., 'Accelerating social mobility: the case of Anglo-Saxon England', *Past & Present* 104 (1984), 3–30

Salter, H. E., *The Eynsham Cartulary* (Oxford Historical Society, 1907–8)

Sargent, S. D., 'An examination of the Laws of William the Conqueror' (M.St. thesis no. 1911, University of Massachusetts, February 2014)

Sarris, P., *Empires of Faith: The Fall of Rome to the Rise of Islam, 500–700* (Oxford: Oxford University Press, 2011)

Sawyer, P. H., *Anglo-Saxon Charters: An Annotated List and Bibliography*, (London: Royal Historical Society, 1968)

Schofield, P. R., 'Land, family and inheritance in a later medieval community: Birdbrook, 1293–1412' (D. Phil. thesis, University of Oxford, 1992)

    'The late medieval view of frankpledge and the tithing system: an Essex case study'. In Z. Razi and R. Smith, eds., *Medieval Society and the Manor Court* (Oxford: Clarendon Press, 1996), 408–49

    Peasants and Historians: Debating the Medieval English Peasantry (Manchester: Manchester University Press, 2016)

Scott, J., *The Moral Economy of the Peasant: Resistance and Rebellion in Southeast Asia* (New Haven, CT.: Yale University Press, 1976)

Siddle, D., 'Inheritance strategies and lineage development in peasant society' *Continuity and Change* 1.3 (1986), 333–61

Smith, A., *An Inquiry into the Nature and Causes of the Wealth of Nations*, p.b. (Oxford: Oxford University Press, 1993)

Smith, J. M. H., *Europe after Rome* (Oxford: Oxford University Press, 2005)

Southern, R., 'Ranulf Flambard and early Anglo-Norman administration' *Transactions of the Royal Historical Society* 4th series, 16 (1933), 95–128

Spufford, P., *Money and Its Use in Medieval Europe* (Cambridge: Cambridge University Press, 1988)

Stacy, N., *Survey of the Estates of Glastonbury Abbey 1135–1201* (Oxford: Oxford University Press, 2001)

Stafford, P., 'The farm of one night and the organisation of King Edward's estates in Domesday Book', *English Historical Review* 33 (1980), 491–52
Stanley, E. G., 'The *familia* in Anglo-Saxon society: "household", rather than "family, home life" as understood', *Anglia* 126 (2008), 37–64
Stenton, D. M., *English Justice between the Norman Conquest and the Great Charter 1066–1215* (London: George Allen and Unwin, 1965)
Stenton, F. M., *Anglo-Saxon England*, 3rd ed. (Oxford: Clarendon Press, 1971)
Stevenson, W. H., 'A contemporary description of the Domesday Survey', *Economic History Review* 22 (1907), 72–84
Stone, I., 'Connections and collaborations between centres of historical writing in thirteenth-century London and Southwark', *Medieval Studies* 79 (2017), 205–47
Stoodley, N., 'Childhood to old age'. In H. Hamerow, D. Hinton and S. Crawford, eds., *The Oxford Handbook of Anglo-Saxon Archaeology* (Oxford: Oxford University Press, 2011, 641–66
Swanton, M., *Beowulf* (Manchester: Manchester University Press, 1978)
Tabuteau, E. Z., *Transfers of Property in Eleventh-Century Norman Law* (Chapel Hill: University of North Carolina Press, 1988)
Taylor, A., 'Homage in the Latin chronicles of eleventh- and twelfth-century Normandy'. In D. Bates, E. D'Angelo and E. van Houts, eds., *Peoples, Texts, Artefacts: Cultural Transmission in the Medieval Norman Worlds* (London: Institute of Historical Research, 2017), 241–63
Thacker, A., 'Some terms for noblemen in Anglo-Saxon England', *Anglo-Saxon Studies in Archaeology and History* 2 (1981), 201–36
Thomas, H. M., *The English and the Normans: Ethnic Hostility, Assimilation, and Identity 1066–1220* (Oxford: Oxford University Press, 2003)
Thompson, E. P., 'The moral economy of the English crowd in the eighteenth century', *Past & Present* 50 (February 1971), 76–136, reprinted in E. P. Thompson, *Customs in Common* (London: Penguin Books, 1993), 185–258
Thorn, F., '*Non Pascua sed pastura*: the changing choice of terms in Domesday Book'. In D. Roffe and K. Keats-Rohan, eds., *Domesday Now: New Approaches to the Inquest and the Book*, p.b. (Woodbridge: The Boydell Press, 2018), 109–36
Tsurashima, H., *Boldon Book: Northumberland and Durham*, ed. D. Austin (Chichester: Phillimore 1982)
'Domesday interpreters' *Anglo-Noman Studies* 18 (1995), 201–22
Verhulst, A., 'Étude comparative du régime dominiale à l'est et à l'ouest du Rhin à l'époque carolingien'. In A. Verhulst, *Rural and Urban Aspects of Early Medieval North-West Europe* (Aldershot: Variorum, 1992), 87–101
Vinogradoff, P., *English Society in the Eleventh Century* (Oxford: Clarendon Press, 1908)
Wareham, A. C., 'Fiscal policies and the institution of a tax state in Anglo-Saxon England in a Comparative Context', *Economic History Review* 65.3 (August 2012), 910–31
Welch, M., 'The mid-Saxon "final phase"', in H. Hamerow, D. Hinton and S. Crawford, eds., *Oxford Handbook of Anglo-Saxon Archaeology* (Oxford: Oxford University Press, 2011) 266–87

Whitelock, D., *The Beginnings of English Society (The Anglo-Saxon Period)* (Harmondsworth: Penguin Books, 1954)

English Historical Documents. Vol. I. *c. 500–1042* (London: Eyre and Spottiswoode, 1955)

Sermo Lupi ad Anglos, 2nd ed. (London: Methuen, 1952)

Whitelock, D., M. Brett and C. N. L. Brooke, *Councils and Synods with Other Documents Related to the English Church.* Vol. I. *A.D. 871–1204.* Part I. *871–1066* (Oxford: Clarendon Press, 1981)

Wickham, C., *Framing the Early Middle Ages: Europe and the Mediterranean, 400–800* (Oxford: Oxford University Press, 2005)

'The other transition: from the ancient world to feudalism', *Past & Present* 103.3 (May 1984), 3–36

'Rural societies in Carolingian Europe', in R. Mc Kitterick, ed., *The New Cambridge Medieval History.* Volume II. *c. 700–c. 900* (Cambridge: Cambridge University Press, 1995), 510–37

William of Malmesbury, Chronicle of the Kings of England from the Earliest Period to the Reign of King Stephen, ed. and trans. J. A. Giles (London: Henry G. Bohn, 1847)

Williams, A., '"A bell-house and a *burhgeat*: lordly residences in England before the Norman Conquest'. In C. Harper-Bill and R. Harvey, eds., *The Ideals and Practice of Medieval Knighthood* (Woodbridge: Boydell Press, 1986), 221–40

Williams, A., *The English and the Norman Conquest* (Woodbridge: Boydell Press, 1995)

'How land was held before and after the Conquest'. In *Domesday Book. Studies* (London: Alecto Historical Editions, 1987), 37–8

'Hunting the Snark and finding the Boojum: the tenurial revolution revisited'. In D. Roffe and K. Keats-Rohan, eds., *Domesday Now: New Approaches to the Inquest and the Book* (Woodbridge: Boydell Press, 2018) 155–68

'Land tenure'. In M. Lapidge, J. Blair, S. Keynes and D. Scragg, eds., *The Blackwell Encyclopaedia of Anglo-Saxon England* (Oxford: Blackwell, 1999),

Williams, G., 'The circulation and function of coinage in conversion-period England'. In B. Cook and G. Williams, eds., *Coinage and History in the North Sea World: Essays in Honour of Marion Archibald* (Leiden: Brill, 2006), 145–92

Williamson, T., *Environment, Society and Landscape in Early Medieval England: Time, and Topography* (Woodbridge: Boydell Press, 2013)

Shaping Medieval Landscapes: Settlement, Society, Environment (Macclesfield: Windgather Press, 2003)

Winchester, A., *Discovering Parish Boundaries* (Princes Risborough: Shire, 2000)

Wormald, P., 'Archbishop Wulfstan and the holiness of society'. In D. Pelteret, ed., *Anglo-Saxon History. Basic Readings* (New York: Garland, 2000), 225–51

'Charters, law and the settlement of disputes in Anglo-Saxon England'. In W. Davies and P. Fouracre, eds., *The Settlement of Disputes in Early Medieval Europe* (Cambridge: Cambridge University Press, 1986), 149–68

The First Code of English Law (Canterbury: Canterbury Commemoration Society 2005)

Legal Culture in the Early Medieval West. Law as Text, Image and Experience (London: Hambledon Press, 1999)

The Making of English Law: King Alfred to the Twelfth Century. Vol. I. *Legislation and Its Limits* (Oxford: Blackwell, 1999)

'Oswaldslow: an immunity?'. In N. Brooks and C. Cubitt, eds., *St Oswald of Worcester: Life and Influence* (Leicester: Leicester University Press, 1996), 117–28

Wright, C. E., *The Cultivation of Saga in Anglo-Saxon England* (Edinburgh: Oliver and Boyd, 1939)

Index